HIDDEN HIGHWAYS
NORTHERN CALIFORNIA

HIDDEN HIGHWAYS
NORTHERN CALIFORNIA

SECOND EDITION

Richard Harris and Ray Riegert

Ulysses Press

Published by:
ULYSSES PRESS
P.O. Box 3440
Berkeley, CA 94703
www.ulyssespress.com

ISBN 1-56975-346-6
ISSN 1531-5789

Printed in Canada by Transcontinental Printing

10 9 8 7 6 5 4 3

FRONT COVER PHOTOGRAPHY: Mary Liz Austin (Morning fog on meadow
with bigleaf lupine and Oregon white oaks in northern California)
DESIGN: Sarah Levin, Leslie Henriques, Bryce Willett
EDITORIAL AND PRODUCTION: Kate Allen, Lily Chou, Claire Chun,
    Marin Van Young
INDEX: Sayre Van Young

Distributed in the United States by Publishers Group West
and in Canada by Raincoast Books

All maps copyright © 2001 CSAA. All rights reserved.
Used with permission. www.aaa.com

HIDDEN is a federally registered trademark of BookPack, Inc.

Ulysses Press 🕮 is a federally registered trademark of BookPack, Inc.

The authors and publisher have made every effort to ensure the
accuracy of information contained in *Hidden Highways Northern
California*, but can accept no liability for any loss, injury, or incon-
venience sustained by any traveler as a result of information or
advice contained in this guide.

Some photographs and illustrations were used by permission and
are the property of the original copyright owners. See photo credits
on page 303.

CONTENTS

MAPS

OUTDOOR ADVENTURE SYMBOLS

The following symbols accompany national, state and regional park listings,
as well as beach descriptions throughout the text.

▲	Camping			Surfing
	Hiking			Waterskiing
	Biking			Windsurfing
	Horseback Riding			Canoeing or Kayaking
	Downhill Skiing			Boating
	Cross-country Skiing			Boat Ramps
	Swimming			Fishing
	Snorkeling or Scuba Diving			

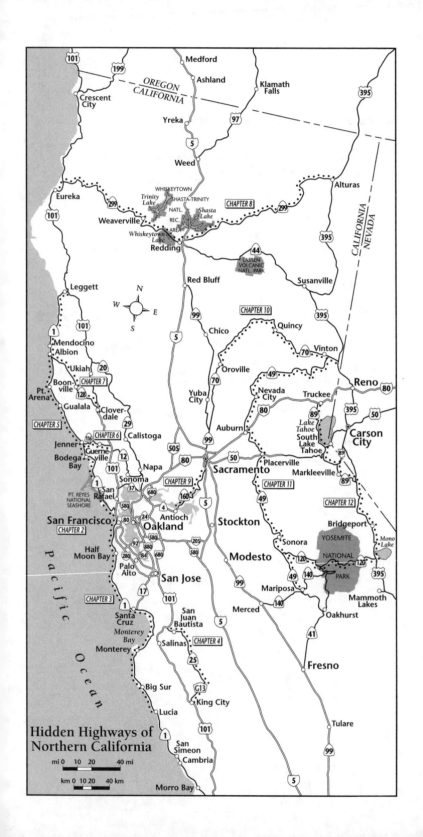

Hidden Highways of
Northern California

mi 0 10 20   40 mi

km 0 10 20   40 km

1 HITTING THE HIGHWAY

America's romance with the open road got its start in 1915, the year construction began on the Lincoln Highway. It was to be the first paved automobile road linking the Atlantic and the Pacific. From its starting point in the nation's capital it followed the classic routes of western migration—the Cumberland Trail, the Oregon–California Trail, and the Central Pacific Transcontinental Railroad—for 3000 miles to arrive at last in San Francisco.

When it was completed in 1923, motoring clubs wasted no time in organizing caravans to explore the Lincoln Highway. One of the first such expeditions was a highly publicized Ford

Model T trip whose participants included Henry Ford himself, as well as Thomas Edison, Harvey Firestone, John Borroughs, and President Warren G. Harding. Instantly cross-country road trips became the ultimate adventure of the era, the stuff of which legends were made—and anyone who owned one of the 15 million automobiles then on the road could give it a try.

Times have changed. Today, the old Lincoln Highway has become Interstate 80, one of the busiest roadways in America. As Americans know all too well, the magic of wide open spaces has long since given way to a maze of freeway signs, exit-only lanes and toll bridges that provide outstanding views of the tail lights directly in front of you. It's all too easy to go through life without experiencing the sheer joy of being the only driver in sight on a long stretch of empty highway.

Fortunately, Northern California can still boast more than its share of "hidden highways"—those picturesque stretches of two-lane blacktop that are used mainly by locals and curious motorists with plenty of time for sightseeing. Scenic routes take longer, and most of the routes in this book remain relatively traffic-free because interstate highways and other major freeways offer much faster alternatives. Since their use is primarily recreational, these hidden highways are busiest on weekends and nearly empty during the week.

Except for San Francisco's 49-Mile Drive, all routes included in *Hidden Highways of Northern California* are paved U.S. or state highways. All can be driven in a standard passenger car, though large motorhomes and travel trailers may have difficulty with the steep grades and tight curves on some stretches of road through the coastal mountains and the Gold Country. The routes described in this book are suitable for one-, two-, or three-day excursions from the Bay Area. In many cases they connect with one or more other hidden highways, making extended tours of a week or so possible.

Travelers today possess an awareness and imagination lacking in their outlandish predecessors. Vacations were once escapes from routine. People charted two weeks a year as an island-in-time where they changed from wool suits to bathing suits. In desperate attempts to forget office hours and car payments, they gravitated to overcrowded tourist areas where life proved as frenzied as back home.

Now travel is becoming a personal art form, and in California, the automobile becomes its paintbrush and the highway its canvas. A destination no longer serves simply as a place to relax: it's also a point of encounter, where experience runs feverish and reality unravels. It's a state of mind, a willingness not only to accept but seek out the uncommon and unique. This book is written for those taking up the challenge of this freewheeling style. It's intended not for tourists but travelers—people who are equally at ease on a city boulevard, a small-town main street from the Gold Rush era, a cool trail among the redwoods where only an occasional stray beam of sunshine penetrates the forest canopy, or a secluded strand of beach where the only footprints are their own.

The tourism industry has a knack for transforming everyday life into a spectacle and making tourists feel like visitors to a huge, outdoor human zoo. The result is a kind of Heisenberg-uncertainty-principle-of-tourism, whereby the mere presence of outsiders changes the human landscape forever. Local residents become actors, historic places are transformed into theme parks, and visitors see something that more nearly

reflects themselves than the indigenous culture. Like Heisenberg's dilemma, the phenomenon is unavoidable. But given the sensitivity and circumspection contemporary travelers are demonstrating, it is possible to gaze into America's cultural kaleidoscope without greatly disturbing the glass pieces.

In the following pages, as in all Ulysses Press Hidden guides, we approach Northern California quietly and intimately, taking you beyond the surface and into the heart of the place. Though we point out the standard sightseeing highlights along the routes we describe, equal billing goes to the communities and landscapes that define the character and texture of a place. We tell you about environmental controversies, odd historical incidents, and legendary local characters. We invite you to experience each place as something larger and richer than the sum of its tourist attractions. While this fresh style of travel appeals to people ranging in age from sprout to senior citizen, it has been taking shape for only a few decades. Better informed, more sensitive and adventurous, we travel for education as much as enjoyment. Rather than proclaiming answers, we ask questions. Cyberspace, with the Bay Area as its epicenter, overlays the region with a whole new dimension of existence, and the kaleidoscope of cultures, philosophies, and dreams invites us to reach out and touch the ephemeral spirit of place.

More than anywhere in the country, Northern California is a place for creative travelers. It's a multicultural extravaganza as well as a region of exceptional natural beauty. Continents have drifted into San Francisco Bay in ways geologists will never explain. Asia overlaps the entire state, Mexico is shifting north, and tides are carrying the rest of the world closer. Chinese are moving into Italian neighborhoods, French vintners have invaded the Wine Country, and Scandinavians are discovering the snows of the High Sierra.

Northern California is a destination best suited to a particular pattern of exploration. It's a place where experience and adventure form a pattern of overlapping layers that the new traveler, like an ar-

chaeologist, will personally uncover. All you need is a full tank of gas, a clean windshield, an open spirit, and unquenchable curiosity. Oh, and maybe a cassette tape of that old San Francisco band, Steppenwolf, howling "Born to Be Wild" . . . .

WHERE TO GO

*T*he grand tour of Northern California's secret scenic routes begins with San Francisco's 49-Mile Drive, taking you on a zigzag tour of famous sights like Chinatown, North Beach, and Fisherman's Wharf before leading you off to the city's "backcountry" to discover the windswept heights of Twin Peaks, some of San Francisco's highest hills, and the wide strand of Pacific beach that extends along the western shore. It provides an ideal city overview for newcomers and out-of-town guests. But don't try it without a navigator.

Route 1 South takes you from San Francisco down the Pacific coast on a diverse journey that passes through Santa Cruz with its classic amusement park and surfing scene, then to Monterey's marvelous historic district and the Carmel haunts of the super rich before heading

for Big Sur, an area so wild that it was inaccessible by road well into
the 20th century. Here the highway itself is one of the main sightseeing
highlights, one of the greatest engineering achievements in the history
of road building.

While discovering what lies south of San Francisco, why not check
out Route 25, a little-used detour that follows the San Andreas Rift
down a narrow valley so empty it's eerie? The high point of the trip
is a visit to Pinnacles National Monument, a wonderland of rock spires,
creeks, and caves that is one of the least-known national park units
in California.

Route 1 North takes you along what must certainly be the most
magical part of the California coast. Nearly 200 miles long, this route
can't easily be driven in a day—but who would want to speed past the
scenic pleasures that lie along this highway? Tidepools, lighthouses,
sea cliffs, pocket beaches, small villages where oyster farming is
the main industry and others whose economies hinge on bed and
breakfasts and art galleries—all are part of this world where, with
few exceptions, the major towns have only a few hundred residents.

Two highways over the coastal mountains provide shortcuts that
bring every part of Route 1 North within convenient weekend-trip
distance. Each of them provides a passageway through another unique
area that is fascinating in its own right. Route 116 leaves fast, busy
Route 101 near the applesauce empire of Sebastopol, where botanist
Luther Burbank cultivated his experimental fruit orchards, and
meanders through lofty redwood forests, past champagne cellars
and through what may be California's most self-consciously diverse
resort community, before reaching the Sonoma coast at Jenner.

Route 128 exits the freeway just a few miles farther north and
follows a more northerly course to reach the coast near Mendocino.
Along the way it takes you through the eccentric little fruit-growing
and beer-brewing community of Boonville, famed for its unique
"lingo," and neighboring Philo, center of the legendary Anderson
Valley wine country, before entering a magnificent redwood forest.

If you want to extend your trip beyond the north end of Route 1,
continue up the coast to Eureka and catch Route 299 across the northern reaches of the state. You'll follow the Trinity River through Bigfoot

country, past premier whitewater rafting areas and historic ghost towns, before reaching Whiskeytown-Shasta-Trinity National Recreation Area with its boundless fishing, boating, and hiking possibilities. Continuing eastward brings you to the volcanic landscape that forms the southern tip of the Cascade Range—and eventually, within view of the Nevada state line—revealing just how far out in the middle of nowhere you can drive and still be in California.

Looking eastward from the Bay Area, the first in a series of interconnected hidden highways is Route 160, which crosses the watery bottomland of the California Delta along the tops of levees that keep the Sacramento River in its course. Though not a long drive, this route takes you through an area so unusual you won't believe you're still in California—a land of windsurfing, pear orchards, historic Chinese villages, and gourmet crawdads. At the end of the road is Sacramento, the state capital.

From Sacramento, Route 70 heads north through Oroville and into the northernmost reaches of the Sierra Nevada, making its way up the spectacular Feather River Canyon. As dramatic as the natural beauty of the area are the human accomplishments—the railroad, the highway, and the hydroelectric dams—that symbolized the "conquest" of this

rugged country in decades past. Beyond, the wide land remains uncon-
quered even now.

The end of Route 70 also marks the start of Route 49, the highway
that links historic Gold Rush boom towns through the foothills on the
western slope of the Sierra Nevada. Once these 19th-century towns
may have looked alike, but today many of
them have evolved distinctive characters
through differing approaches to
historic preservation and tourist
development. This is the longest
route in *Hidden Highways of Northern California*, and it need not be
explored all at once. Several routes
from the Bay Area make it easy to explore the Gold Country in separate segments.

The south end of the Gold Country route brings you close to
the entrance of Yosemite National Park. Although the park is one of
Northern California's top tourist destinations, most visitors pack into
the well-developed valley around Yosemite Village. We'll show you
another side of Yosemite, following Route 120, the Tioga Pass Road,
over the crest of the Sierra to the eastern slope. At the mouth of the
canyon below the park's east entrance, the highway joins Route 395 for
a beautiful drive that takes in the strange stone formations of Mono Lake
and the carefully preserved old ghost town of Bodie before hooking up
with Route 89, which follows the shore of Lake Tahoe and leaves you
at the on-ramp to Interstate 80, just a few hours from the Bay Area.

WHEN TO GO

*S*pring and particularly autumn are the ideal times to visit just
about any part of Northern California. Generally, the region has
three different climatic zones—the coast, the broad central valley, and
the alpine Sierra Nevada.

San Francisco and the rest of the Pacific shore enjoy mild temperatures year-round, since the coastal fog creates a natural form of air

conditioning and insulation. The mercury rarely drops below 40° or rises above 70°, with September and October being the hottest months, and December and January the coolest. During the winter, the rainy season brings overcast days and frequent showers, and mudslides can occasionally close coastal highways. Summer is San Francisco's peak tourist season, when large crowds can present problems. It's also a period of frequent fog; especially in the morning and evening, fog banks from offshore blanket the city and head inland through the Golden Gate. On Route 1 and other coastal highways, whiteout fog banks can roll in quickly, making driving hazardous or impossible.

The seasons vary much more in the interior valleys, creating a second climatic zone. In the California Delta and the Gold Country, summer temperatures often top 90°. There's less humidity, winters are cooler, and the higher elevations receive occasional snowfall. Like the coast, this piedmont region experiences most of its rain during winter months.

The Sierra Nevada and Cascade Ranges experience Northern California's most dramatic weather. During summer, the days are warm, the nights cool. Spring and autumn bring crisp temperatures and colorful foliage changes (which the coastline, with its unvarying seasons, rarely undergoes). Then in winter, the thermometer plummets and snow falls so heavily as to make these mountain ranges spectacular ski areas. Tire chains are essential equipment in the mountains during the late fall, winter, and early spring. When snow starts to fall, the highway patrol will not let you drive without chains. Most winter sports areas in the Sierra have roadside "Sno-Park" signs; these mean you need a special parking permit, sold at cross-country ski and snowmobile rental places. Virtually all winter recreation in the Sierra Nevada is on the west side of the mountains and around Lake Tahoe. Except for Interstate 80, all other highways over the Sierra are closed in winter.

SECRETS OF SUCCESSFUL PACKING

There are two important guidelines when deciding what to take on a trip. The first is as true for San Francisco and Northern California as anywhere in the world—pack light. Dress styles here are relatively informal and laundromats or dry cleaners are ubiquitous. The airlines allow two suitcases and a carry-on bag; try to take one suitcase and perhaps a small accessory case.

The second rule is to prepare for cool weather, even if the closest you'll come to the mountains is the top of Nob Hill. "The coldest winter I ever spent," Mark Twain remarked, "was a summer in San Francisco." While the city's climate is temperate, temperatures sometimes descend below 50°. Even that might not seem chilly until the fog rolls in and the ocean breeze picks up. A warm sweater and jacket

are absolute necessities. Pack shorts for the summer or autumn. You'll encounter similar weather conditions in all coastal areas of Northern California, where the Pacific Ocean moderates the climate. If you plan to tour inland, though, it's a different story. The Wine Country, the Delta, and the Gold Country can be very hot during the summer, and you'll want the lightest, coolest clothing possible.

Yosemite and other parts of the Sierras have deep snow and subfreezing temperatures for most of the winter, so a parka, hat, gloves, and warm boots are in order. Even in early fall and late spring, campers will discover that the thermometer quickly plunges below freezing as the sun goes down. The best plan, whenever you're planning a trip around the interior of California, is to dress in layers and be prepared for anything.

WHERE TO SLEEP

In most towns along these hidden highway routes, one or two lodgings stand out as unique. Sidebars in this book will let you know about sleeping under the redwoods in Big Sur, or an inn within earshot of San Francisco's Opera House, a houseboat on beautiful

Shasta Lake, and the historic Gold Country hotel where President Grant and Mark Twain stayed. Each offers a unique experience; try the one that appeals to you.

Even at the most "hidden" of our recommendations, you'll want to reserve your room well in advance, particularly in summer, when facilities fill up quickly. The price category at the end of each lodging listing is for the high season; rates may decrease in low season.

- *Budget* hotels are generally less than $60 per night for two people; the rooms are clean and comfortable but lack luxury.
- *Moderate* hotels run $60 to $120 and provide larger rooms, plusher furniture, and more attractive surroundings.
- *Deluxe* accommodations charge between $120 and $175 for a homey bed and breakfast or a double in a hotel or resort.
- *Ultra-deluxe* lodgings, the finest the region has to offer, come with all the amenities—and a price tag above $175 a night (sometimes *way* above . . .).

For a broader survey of extraordinary lodging options in all price ranges, read *Hidden San Francisco & Northern California* by Ray Riegert (Berkeley: Ulysses Press, 10th ed. 2002).

EATING ON THE ROAD

*T*he Bay Area (as any Northern Californian will tell you at any opportunity) is the epicenter of the culinary arts in the Western Hemisphere—and restaurant trends spread quickly to every small town from the North Coast to the Gold Country. In fact, it may seem as if Northern California has more restaurants than people. There may still be one or two towns along California's hidden highways where the most exotic item on the menu is a BLT with fries, but they're few and far between. Sidebars in this book will let you know where you can dine along Route 1 with a view of a sea lion colony, feast on crawfish on the Delta, or savor Cantonese food in the Gold Country at California's oldest restaurant. Each offers a unique experience; try the

one that appeals to you. Reservations are a good idea on weekends everywhere and every day in San Francisco.

The restaurants are categorized as budget, moderate, deluxe, or ultra-deluxe in price.

- *Budget* restaurants offer dinner entrées priced at $9 or less. The ambience is informal café-style and the crowd is often a local one.
- *Moderate* restaurants range between $9 and $18 at dinner and offer pleasant surroundings, a more varied menu, and a slower pace.
- *Deluxe* establishments tab their entrées above $18, featuring sophisticated cuisines, plush decor, and more personalized service.
- *Ultra-deluxe* dining rooms, where $25 will only get you started, are gourmet gathering places where the cooking (hopefully) is a fine art form and service is a way of life.

For a broader survey of top dining options in all price ranges, read *Hidden San Francisco & Northern California* by Ray Riegert (Berkeley: Ulysses Press, 10th ed. 2002).

PITCH YOUR TENT (OR PARK YOUR RIG)

California has more than 260 state parks and recreation areas with camping facilities for tents and recreational vehicles (though few of them offer electrical hookups). We've included basic information on state park campgrounds along the hidden highway routes in this book. For a complete listing of all state-run campgrounds, send $5 for the *Guide to California State Parks* to the California Department of Parks and Recreation. ~ P.O. Box 942896, Sacramento, CA 94296; 916-653-6995. Reservations for most campgrounds can be made by calling

800-444-7275; www.reserveamerica.com. Be sure
to check out their website: www.parks.ca.gov.

This book also lets you know about areas
where you'll find national forest campgrounds, though the individual
campgrounds are not described. They are
generally more primitive than state park
campgrounds and do not have hookups. A fee is
charged at these facilities and the maximum length
of stay varies from park to park. For maps and information, contact the
U.S. Forest Service. ~ 1323 Club Drive, Vallejo, CA 94592; 707-562-
8737, fax 707-562-9045; www.r5.fs.fed.us. While campsites at some of
the more popular areas can be reserved in advance through National
Forest Recreation Reservations (800-280-2267), most national forest
campgrounds operate on a first-come, first-serve basis.

In addition to state and national campgrounds, Northern California
offers numerous municipal, county, and private facilities.

TRAVELING WITH CHILDREN

Visiting Northern California with kids can be a real adventure,
and if properly planned, a truly enjoyable one. To ensure that
your trip will feature the joy, rather than the strain, of parenthood,
remember a few important guidelines.

Children under age 5 or under 40 pounds must be in approved
child restraints while riding in cars/vans. The back seat is safest.

Use a travel agent to help with flight arrangements; they can reserve
spacious bulkhead seats. Also plan to bring everything you need
on board—diapers, food, toys, and extra clothes for kids and parents
alike. If the trip to Northern California involves a long journey, plan
to relax and do very little during the first few days.

Always allow extra time for getting places. Book reservations well
in advance and make sure the hotel has the extra crib, cot, or bed you
require. It's smart to ask for a room at the end of the hall to cut down

on noise. Also keep in mind that many bed-and-breakfast inns do not allow children.

Most towns have stores that carry diapers, food, and other essentials; in cities and larger towns, convenience stores are often open all night (check the Yellow Pages for addresses). In San Francisco, Cala Foods has several large groceries, including locations at 690 Stanyan Street, 4201 18th Street, and South Van Ness Avenue and Hyde Street, which are open 24 hours a day.

Hotels often provide access to babysitters or you can check the Yellow Pages for state licensed and bonded babysitting agencies.

A first-aid kit is always a good idea. Also, check with your pediatrician for special medicines and dosages for colds and diarrhea.

Finding activities to interest children in Northern California could not be easier. Especially helpful in deciding on the day's outing are *Places to Go with Children in Northern California* (Chronicle Books) and the "Datebook" of the Sunday *San Francisco Chronicle*.

SENIOR TRAVELERS

Northern California is an ideal spot for older vacationers. The mild climate makes traveling in the off-season possible, helping to cut down on expenses. Many museums, theaters, restaurants, and hotels offer discounts to seniors (requiring a driver's license, Medicare card, or other age-identifying card). Be sure to ask your travel agent when booking reservations.

The **American Association of Retired Persons**, or AARP, offers members travel discounts and provides escorted tours. ~ 601 E Street NW, Washington DC 20049; 800-424-3410; www.aarp.org, e-mail member@aarp.org.

Be extra careful about health matters. Bring any medications you use, along with the prescriptions. Consider carrying a medical record with you—including your current medical status and medical history, as well as your doctor's name, phone number, and address. Also be sure to confirm that your insurance covers you away from home.

INFORMATION FOR DISABLED TRAVELERS

*C*alifornia stands at the forefront of social reform for persons with disabilities. During the past decade, the state has responded to the needs of the blind, wheelchair-bound, and others with a series of progressive legislative measures.

The **Department of Motor Vehicles** provides special parking permits for the disabled. Many local bus lines and other public transit facilities are wheelchair accessible. ~ 1377 Fell Street, San Francisco; 800-777-0133; www.dmv.ca.gov.

There are also agencies in Northern California assisting travelers with disabilities. For tips and information about the San Francisco Bay Area, contact the **Center for Independent Living**, a self-help group that has led the way in reforming access laws in California. ~ 2539 Telegraph Avenue, Berkeley; 510-841-4776, fax 510-841-6168; www.cilberkeley.org.

There are many organizations offering general information. Among these are:

- The **Society for Accessible Travel & Hospitality** (SATH). ~ 347 5th Avenue, #610, New York, NY 10016; 212-447-7284, fax 212-725-8253; www.sath.org, e-mail sathtravel@aol.com.
- The **MossRehab**. ~ 5501 Old York Road, Philadelphia, PA 19141; 215-456-5501; www.mossresourcenet.org.
- **Mobility International USA**. ~ P.O. Box 10767, Eugene, OR 97440; 541-343-1284, fax 541-343-6812; www.miusa.org, e-mail info@miusa.org.
- **Travelin' Talk**, a network of people and organizations, also provides assistance. ~ P.O. Box 1796, Wheat Ridge, CO 80034; 303-232-2979; www.travelintalk.net, e-mail info@travelintalk.net.
- **Access-Able Travel Service** has worldwide information online. ~ www.access-able.com.

Or consult the comprehensive guidebook, *Access to the World—A Travel Guide for the Handicapped*, by Louise Weiss (Holt, Rinehart & Winston).

Many hotels and motels feature facilities for those in wheelchairs. Be sure to check in advance when making room reservations.

TRAVELING WITH PETS

A dog, or sometimes even a cat, can make a wonderful travel companion if he or she has learned to enjoy riding in your car. Be aware, however, that national parks and monuments, as well as most California state parks, prohibit pets on backcountry trails in order to protect wildlife, so focus your hiking plans on national forest areas, where dogs are welcome on hiking trails. Many places—not only cities but also rural areas such as the Sonoma coast, are very strict about enforcing leash laws.

Many bed-and-breakfast inns and a growing number of standard motels will not accept pets, and those that do may require an additional damage deposit. Phone ahead to find out. Campgrounds at California state parks charge extra for pets.

In California it is illegal to carry a dog in the open bed of a pickup truck. And of course, never leave a pet unattended in a vehicle, even with the windows partly open. Besides placing your pet at risk, leaving him or her alone in the car in hot weather, cold weather, or anytime without water can result in a criminal charge of animal abuse under California law.

2 THE 49-MILE DRIVE

Circumnavigating San Francisco

San Francisco's 49-Mile Drive came into being in 1938 in preparation for the Golden Gate International Exposition. The eight-month-long event celebrated the recent openings of both the Golden Gate Bridge and the Bay Bridge. It also marked the emergence of San Francisco as a world-class tourist destination. Each of the more than ten million visitors flocked to the exposition on Treasure Island—the manmade island at the middle of the Bay Bridge—and received a map of 49-Mile Drive, which featured elaborate illustrations of the city's major landmarks and sightseeing attractions. (Today these original maps are prized as collectors' items; you can see one on display

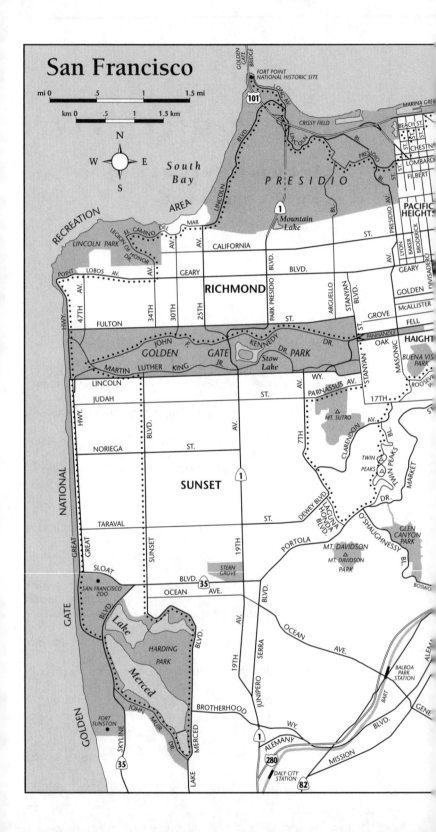

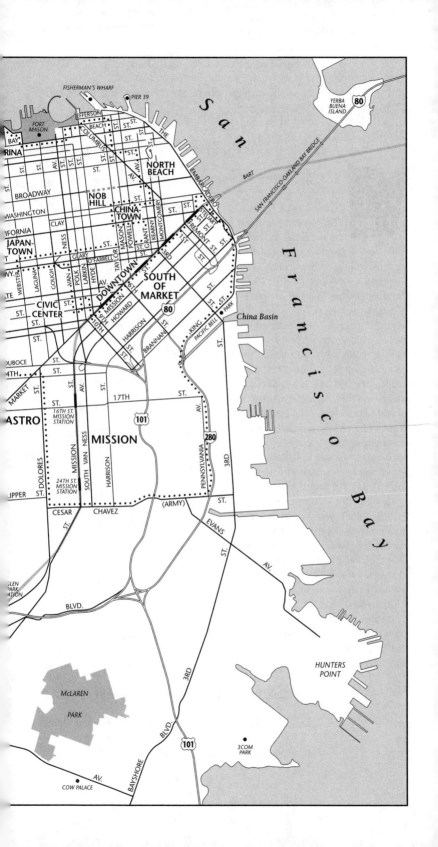

in San Francisco's City Hall, located in the Civic Center complex where the driving tour route officially begins.)

Much has changed in San Francisco since 1938. Yet 49-Mile Drive (with some rerouting over the years) still offers a quick introduction to this vibrant, progressive city. From the Civic Center it guides you through the heart of downtown, then Japantown, Chinatown, and North Beach before reaching the waterfront and following it from Fisherman's Wharf to the Marina.

Today, the most "hidden" thing in the downtown area is parking, so driving and sidewalk sightseeing no longer mix very well. In addition, so many points of interest have proliferated along the route that there's not enough time to see them all in the same day. The best strategy is to take 49-Mile Drive (or at least the last 40 miles of it) for an overview of

Okay, let's be honest. Driving your car around downtown San Francisco ranks among the most stressful activities Northern California has to offer visitors. The first nine miles of the city's 49-Mile Drive require two hours to complete—just slightly faster than walking speed. Instead, why not bypass the city center on your driving tour? Follow Route 101 (Van Ness Avenue) north all the way across the city, continuing straight to Bay Street instead of following 101 as it turns onto Lombard Street, and join the official 49-Mile Drive at Fort Mason. Follow the seagull signs for a great tour of San Francisco's backcountry, including the Presidio, Ocean Beach, Lake Merritt, Golden Gate Park, Twin Peaks, and Mission Dolores before returning to Route 101 near the Civic Center. On another day, visit the central San Francisco sights you skipped by leaving your car at one of the East Bay BART stations, where parking is free for passengers. Ride the train into the city, getting off at the Powell Street station. This leaves you within easy walking distance of the Civic Center, Union Square, Japantown, Chinatown, and Yerba Buena Park—and right next to the Hyde–Powell Cable Car terminal, which takes you to the Fisherman's Wharf area.

what the city has to offer. If you wish to stop along the way, choose the Presidio, Golden Gate National Recreation Area, and Golden Gate Park: these areas have ample parking on weekdays and are harder to reach on foot or by public transportation than the sights downtown. Later, leave your car behind and return to specific areas to explore on foot with the aid of San Francisco's public transportation system.

The 49-Mile Drive is marked by pastel pink-white-and-blue route signs that depict a seagull and have the number "49" in the upper right corner. Following them can sometimes be challenging. In some areas there are so many street signs that it can be hard to spot the scenic route signs. Buses in the right lane can hide them from view. In some places there's no sign for so many blocks that you may start to wonder whether you missed a turn. The last time we drove this route, we noticed that a couple of signs were missing. The city is reasonably diligent about keeping 49-Mile Drive well marked as a matter of

civic pride, but nothing can stop souvenir pirates from snatching the signs now and then.

This chapter is designed to give your navigator an extra tool when following the signs gets tricky. The driving directions that appear in italics at the beginnings of paragraphs will confirm that you're on the right track—or at least help you find your way back to it.

*T*he 49-Mile Drive tour route officially begins at the **Civic Center**, the architectural pride of the city. With its bird-whitened statues and gray-columned buildings, the Civic Center is the domain of powerbrokers and political leaders; ironically, its grassy plots and park benches also make it the haunt of the city's homeless.

The Civic Center is located between Hyde Street on the east and Van Ness Avenue on the west, between Grove Street on the south and McAllister Street on the north. Larkin Street takes you through it.

The long-ago city officials who declared the Civic Center the starting point for San Francisco's official driving tour clearly did not intend sightseers to drive off before taking in the other buildings surrounding City Hall. To take a look at the city's most impressive concentration of showpiece public architecture, after passing the piazza on Larkin Street, *turn left on McAllister Street and then left on Dr. Carlton B. Goodlett Jr. Place* (the two blocks of Polk Street within the Civic Center, recently renamed in honor of the San Francisco civil rights

Civic Center

FIFTIES
FLASHBACK ▬▬▬▬▬▬

A two-story motor court flanking a pool courtyard, spacious rooms and suites with a soft tropical motif, an aquatically-inspired restaurant and lounge . . . can this be the heart of San Francisco? It is, and it's the **Phoenix Hotel**, just a long block from Civic Center. Concierge services and the patronage of music-business mavens may make the Phoenix the hippest inn in town. ~ 601 Eddy Street; 415-776-1380, 800-248-9466, fax 415-885-3109; www.thephoenixhotel. com, e-mail phoenixhotel@jdvhospitality.com. MODERATE TO DELUXE.

leader who died in 1997). This will take you close in front of City Hall. *Drive the three blocks south to Grove Street, turn right, and go one more block to Van Ness Avenue.*

As you're waiting for the light on Grove at the Van Ness intersection, that ultramodern glass-and-granite building on your left across Van Ness is the **Louise M. Davies Symphony Hall**, home of the San Francisco Symphony. Through the semi-circle of green-tinted glass, you can peer into one of the city's most glamorous buildings. Or if you'd prefer to be on the inside gazing out, tours of the hall and its cultural cousins next door are given Monday from 10 a.m. to 12 p.m. Admission. ~ Van Ness Avenue and Grove Street; information, 415-552-8338.

Centerstage of the Civic Center is the **War Memorial Opera House**, on your right across Van Ness. Home of one of the world's finest opera companies as well as the San Francisco Ballet Company, the Opera House is considered by such performers as Placido Domingo to be one of the world's finest. Called "the most attractive and practical building of its kind in the U.S." by *Time*

OPERA, SYMPHONY, AND BLUES

September is the month for the sound of music. The openings of the San Francisco Opera and San Francisco Symphony bring out the stylish highbrows, while the annual Blues Festival and Opera in the Park draw a more laidback crowd.

magazine, the grandiose building's interior features lofty romanesque columns, a gold-leafed proscenium, and a five-story-high ceiling. Although conceived in 1918 as a tribute to the nation's World War I veterans, the opera house was not completed until 1932. Perhaps its finest moment came in 1945, when the opera house and adjacent Veterans Auditorium (now Herbst Theatre) hosted the signing of the United Nations Charter and the first official sessions of the U.N. ~ 301 Van Ness Avenue at Grove Street.

*To get there from Route 80 after crossing the Bay Bridge from Oakland, or from Route 101 coming north from San Jose, take the second exit on the San Francisco side of the bridge, marked "9th Street/ Civic Center." Follow 9th Street north (toward downtown) to Market Street, where the street forks. Keep left on Larkin and sud-*denly you're face to face with the city's own capitol dome, framed by the reflecting pool and formal gardens of **Joseph L. Alioto Performing Art Piazza**, an area often used for outdoor events and recently renamed in honor of one of San Francisco's most beloved mayors.

City Hall underwent a three-year, $300-million renovation during which it was lifted from its foundation and set on 600 steel-and-rubber base insulators designed to make it earthquake-proof. Its gold-leafed dome is 307 feet tall—the fifth-tallest domed building in the world, twenty feet taller than the U.S. Capitol. It also surpasses other government centers in technology, with interactive touch screens that let supervisors vote, call staff, and retrieve documents during meetings. Free guided tours of City Hall are offered daily. ~ 1 Dr. Carlton B. Goodlett Jr. Place. Guided tours of the Civic Center begin at the San Francisco Public Library. ~ Tour information, 415-557-4266.

JAPAN-TOWN FESTIVALS

During the April Cherry Blossom Festival, August Street Fair, Autumn Bon Dances, and the Aki Matsuri festival in September, Japantown turns out in splendid costumes for musical celebrations.

Across from City Hall and housed in a historic 1917 Beaux Arts building, the **Asian Art Museum** features major pieces from China, Tibet, Japan, Korea, Iran, Syria, and throughout the continent. This institution is the largest museum in the country devoted exclusively to Asian art. Some of the 14,000-plus pieces date back 6000 years. Admission. ~ 200 Larkin Street; 415-581-3500, fax 415-581-4700; www. asianart.org.

Across the street stands the main branch of the **San Francisco Public Library** in its $104.5-million head-quarters, which opened in 1996. Exemplifying the fact that libraries are not just about books anymore (in fact, critics charge that the architectural splendor and special features have resulted in a lack of shelf space), the main branch's facilities include 400 electronic workstations with free connection to the Internet. Among the library's 11 special-interest research centers are the San Francisco History Center, the Gay and Lesbian Center, and the Art and Music Center. ~ 100 Larkin Street; 415-557-4400, fax 415-557-4205; www.sfpl.lib.ca.us, e-mail info@sfpl.lib.ca.us.

Go five blocks north on Larkin Street from the Civic Center. Turn left onto Geary Street, which takes you past the stately stone First Unitarian Universalist Church on your left and then into Japantown. Center of culture for San Francisco's burgeoning Japanese population is **Japantown**, a self-contained area bounded by Geary and Post, Laguna and Fillmore streets. This

NOT YOUR AVERAGE SUSHI BAR

Tired of humdrum sushi bars? Bored with sea urchin platters? Then **Isobune** is the place for you. Here those fishy finger foods scud past you on wooden boats along a miniature canal. No joke —we're talking sushi on a stream. You simply sit at the counter and pluck off your favorite cargo as the boat goes by. There are numerous sushi selections, as well as soup and sashimi. ~ 1737 Post Street; 415-563-1030, fax 415-563-3337. MODERATE.

SHOPPING WITH FRANK LLOYD WRIGHT

One hidden place your car can't take you, where you'll want to visit while exploring the Union Square area on foot, is down **Maiden Lane**, headiest of the city's high-heeled shopping areas. This alleyway starts midblock across Stockton Street from Union Square and runs two blocks to the Financial District. Back in Barbary Coast days, when San Francisco was a dirty word, this two-block-long alleyway was wall to wall with bawdy houses. But today it's been transformed from red-light district to ultra-chic mall. Of particular interest among the galleries and boutiques lining this pedestrian-only thoroughfare is the building at **140 Maiden Lane**. Designed by Frank Lloyd Wright in 1948, its circular interior stairway and other unique elements foreshadow the motifs he later used for the famous Guggenheim Museum in New York. Among the notable Maiden Lane shops is **Xanadu Gallery Folk Art International**, offering icons, folk sculptures, baskets, pottery, and other crafts from Africa, Oceania, and Latin America. Europe and Asia are also represented with antique jewelry from India and gem-quality Baltic amber from Poland and Denmark. Closed Sunday. ~ FLW building, 140 Maiden Lane; 415-392-9999, fax 415-984-5856; www.folkartintl.com, e-mail info@folkartintl.com.

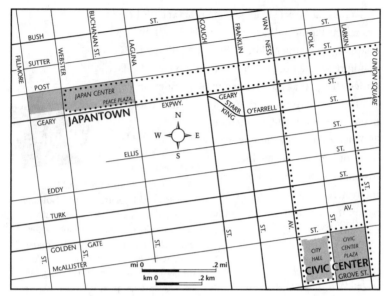

Civic Center to Japantown

town-within-a-city consists of two sections: the old part, where residential housing is located, and a newer commercial area.

Japan Center, designed by architect Minoru Yamasaki, is a five-acre monstrosity. Built in 1968, it epitomizes the freeway architecture of the era. There are, nonetheless, fascinating knickknack shops, bookstores, and outstanding restaurants located in this Asian mall.

NIPPON NOVELS AND MORE

Japantown's **Kinokuniya Bookstore** is a warehouse of a store, chockablock with volumes on Japanese language and culture. Among the works in both English and Japanese are books on history, travel, and cooking. ~ 1581 Webster Street; 415-567-7625; www.kinokuniya.com.

You'll also encounter special features here and there—like the Peace Pagoda, a five-tiered structure designed by world-renowned architect Yoshiro Taniguchi as an expression of friendship and goodwill between the people of Japan and America. Nihonmachi Mall has a cobblestone pathway and lovely Ruth Asawa origami fountains. There are also park benches featuring bas-reliefs done by local children.

Turn right on Webster Street, go one block and turn right again onto Post Street, which takes you downhill through the heart of Japantown. You may notice that this

PUBLIC TRANSPORTATION WITH PANACHE

Following 49-Mile Drive in your car, it takes two hours to travel from the Civic Center area to Ghirardelli Square. The **Hyde–Powell Cable Car** can get you there in half the time—even allowing for an average one-hour wait in line. As you may suspect by now, cable cars are *the* way to see this city of perpendicular hills. This venerable system covers a ten-mile section of downtown San Francisco.

The cable car was invented in 1873 by Andrew Hallidie and works via an underground cable that travels continuously at a speed of nine and a half miles per hour. Three of the system's original twelve lines still operate year-round. The Powell–Mason and Powell–Hyde cars travel from the downtown district to Fisherman's Wharf; the California Street line runs east to west and passes through Chinatown and Nob Hill. Built partially of wood and furnished with old-style running boards, these open-air vehicles are slow and stylish. Edging up the city's steep heights, then descending toboggan-run hills to the Bay, they provide many of San Francisco's finest views. Half the joy of riding, however, comes from watching the operators of these antique machines. Each has developed a personal style of gripping, braking, and bell-ringing. In addition to the breathtaking ride, they will often treat you to a clanging street symphony.

Asian enclave has become cosmopolitan, with many signs in Korean and some in Vietnamese. Continue on Post all the way to **Union Square**, a tree-dotted plot in the heart of the downtown hotel and shopping district. Lofty buildings bordering the area house major department stores while the network of surrounding streets features many of the city's poshest shops and plushest hotels.

Union Square is quite simply *the* center for shopping in San Francisco. First of all, this grass-and-hedgerow park (located between Post and Geary, Stockton and Powell streets) is surrounded by department stores. **Macy's** is located along one border. ~ 170 O'Farrell Street; 415-397-3333. **Saks Fifth Avenue** guards another. ~ 384 Post Street; 415-986-4300. **Neiman-Marcus**, the Texas-bred emporium, claims one corner. ~ 150 Stockton Street; 415-362-3900. Once the haven of European specialty boutiques, Union Square is becom-

DEEP-SEA DINING

In addition to being a dining extravaganza, **Farallon** is a total immersion experience. Step into this uniquely designed restaurant and it's like plunging beneath the waves; every aspect of the decor reflects an aquatic motif. Light fixtures resembling jellyfish hang suspended two stories overhead, handrails look like tendriling kelp, and bar stools stand on octopus tentacles. The Gothic arches in the dining room (called, naturally, the "Pool Room") sport mermaid mosaics and sea urchin light fixtures. After easing into a booth, you can order from a menu laden with seafood dishes. The menu, which changes every few weeks, might feature Atlantic black bass, poached sea scallops, parchment roasted monkfish, or, for those who don't get the point—grilled filet of beef. No lunch on Sunday and Monday. ~ 450 Post Street; 415-956-6969; www.farallon restaurant.com, e-mail jellyfsh@farallonrestaurant.com. ULTRA-DELUXE.

ing a hot address among sport-shoes shops, entertainment-company merchandising centers, and mass-appeal clothing stores.

Union Square's most intriguing role is as San Francisco's free-form entertainment center. On any day you may see a brass band high-stepping through, a school choir singing the world's praises, or a gathering of motley but talented musicians or mimes passing the hat for bus fare home.

Clanging **cable cars** from the nearby turnaround station at Powell and Market streets climb halfway to the stars en route to Nob Hill and Fisherman's Wharf, and you'll be crisscrossing their route as you make your way across town to these destinations.

From Post Street, one block past Union Square turn left onto Grant Avenue, passing through the famous Chinatown Gate and climbing this steep, congested main street of **Chinatown**. San Francisco's oldest street, today Grant Avenue is an ultramodern thoroughfare lined with Chinese arts-and-crafts shops, restaurants, and Asian markets. It's also one of the most crowded streets you'll ever squeeze your way through. Immortalized in a song from the musical *Flower Drum Song*, Grant Avenue, San Francisco, California, U.S.A., is a commotion, a clatter, a clash of cultures. At any moment,

HIDDEN ALLEYS OF CHINATOWN

For an in-depth visit to this fascinating neighborhood, you might want to come back later and explore the hidden heart of Chinatown on foot. First take a stroll along **Stockton Street**, which runs parallel to, and one block above, Grant Avenue. It is here, not along touristy Grant Avenue, that the Chinese shop.

The street vibrates with the crazy commotion of Chinatown. Open stalls tumbling with vegetables cover the sidewalk, and crates of fresh fish are stacked along the curb. Through this maze of merchandise, shoppers press past one another. In store windows hang Peking ducks, and on the counters are displayed pigs' heads and snapping turtles. Rare herbs, healing teas, and chrysanthemum crystals crowd the shelves.

The local community's artwork is displayed in a fantastic **mural** that covers a half-block between Pacific and Jackson streets.

To further explore the interior life of Chinatown, turn down Sacramento Street from Stockton Street, then take a quick left onto **Hang Ah Street**. This is the first in a series of alleyways leading for three blocks from Sacramento Street to Jackson Street. When you get to the end of each block, simply jog over to the next alley.

A universe unto themselves, these alleyways of Chinatown are where the secret business of the community goes on, as it has for over a century. Each door is a barrier beyond which you can hear the rattle of mah-jong tiles and the sounds of women bent to their tasks in laundries and sewing factories.

Along Hang Ah Street, timeworn buildings are draped with fire escapes and colored with the images of fading signs. As you cross Clay Street, at the end of Hang Ah Street, be sure to press your nose against the glass at **Grand Century Enterprise**. Here the ginseng and other precious roots sell for hundreds of dollars a pound. ~ 858 Clay Street; 415-392-4060, fax 415-392-4063.

The next alley, **Spofford Lane**, is a corridor of painted doorways and brick facades humming with the strains of Chinese melodies. It ends at Washington Street, where you can zigzag over to **Ross Alley**. This is the home of the **Golden Gate Fortune Cookie Factory**. At this small family establishment you can watch your fortune being made. ~ 56 Ross Alley; 415-781-3956.

The last segment in this intriguing tour will take you back to **Waverly Place**, a two-block stretch leading from Washington Street to Sacramento Street. Readers of Dashiell Hammett's mystery story, *Dead Yellow Women*, will recall this spot. It's an enchanting thoroughfare, more alley than street. At first glance, the wrought-iron balconies draped along either side of Waverly evoke images of New Orleans. But not even the French Quarter can boast the beauty contained in those Chinese cornices and pagoda swirl roof lines.

Prize jewel in this architectural crown is **Tian Hou Temple**. Here Buddhists and Taoists worship in a tiny temple overhung with fiery red lanterns. There are statues portraying battlefields and country landscapes; incense smolders from several altars. From the pictures along the wall, Buddha smiles out upon the believers. They in turn gaze down from the balcony onto Chinatown's most magical street. ~ 125 Waverly Place.

CHECK OUT
YOUR FORTUNE ▬▬▬▬▬

A favorite dim sum restaurant is tucked away in an alley above Grant Avenue. Personalized but unpretentious, more cozy than cavernous, **Hang Ah Tea House** is a rare find. Enter the dining room with its Chinese wood carvings and fiberglass tables. Serving full Mandarin cuisine as well as dim sum portions, it warrants an exploratory mission into the alleys of Chinatown. Open late for dessert. ~ 1 Hang Ah Street; 415-982-5686. BUDGET.

a rickety truck may pull up beside you, heave open its doors, and reveal its contents—a cargo of chinaware, fresh produce, or perhaps flattened pig carcasses. Elderly Chinese men lean along doorways smoking fat cigars, and Chinatown's younger generation sets off down the street clad in leather jackets.

At the corner of California Street, where cable cars clang across Grant Avenue, rises the lovely brick structure of **Old St. Mary's Church**. Dating to 1854, this splendid cathedral was originally built of stone quarried in China. Just across the way in **St. Mary's Square**, there's a statue of the father of the Chinese Republic, Dr. Sun Yat Sen, crafted by San Francisco's foremost sculptor, Beniamino Bufano. You might take a hint from the crowds of businesspeople from the nearby financial center who bring their picnic lunches to this tree-shaded plaza.

Turn left onto California Street, follow it four blocks to the top of the hill, and turn right on Taylor Street through the Nob Hill district. Perhaps the most famous of all the knolls casting their loving shadows on San Francisco is a prominent prominence called **Nob Hill**, a monument to San Francisco's crusty rich.

Downtown & Chinatown

Once the domain of the city's wealthiest families, Nob Hill now is home to the city's finest hotels. Strung like pearls along California Street, a doorman's whistle from the Fairmont, are three luxurious hotels. Fittingly, the **Stanford Court Hotel**, **Mark Hopkins Inter-Continental Hotel**, and the **Huntington Hotel** were built upon the ruins of the mansions for whose owners the hotels are named. That tree-dotted resting place across the street, *naturalement*, is **Huntington Park**. The hotels and the park are perched in a gilded nest known sarcastically among local folks as "Snob Hill."

Nob Hill's **Grace Cathedral**, half a block west of Taylor Street on California Street, marks San Francisco's attempt at Gothic architecture. Consecrated in 1964 and constructed of concrete, it's not exactly Notre Dame. But this mammoth, vaulting church does have its charm. Foremost are the doors atop the cathedral steps: they represent Lorenzo Ghiberti's "Doors of Paradise," cast in bronze from the artist's original work in Florence. The church interior is graced with a series of wall murals and tiers of stained-glass windows that picture such latter-day luminaries as labor leader John L. Lewis, social worker Jane Addams, and astronaut John Glenn. In addition to these architectural adornments, the cathedral is filled with objects as dear as they are sacred—a 15th-century carved oak altar piece, a 13th-century Spanish crucifix, a 16th-century

The Nabobs of Nob Hill

Originally known as California Street Hill, Nob Hill was nicknamed after the "nabobs" (slang for hoi poloi) who built their homes there. In the 19th century, misters James G. Fair, Collis P. Huntington, Mark Hopkins, and Leland Stanford—the tycoons who built the transcontinental railroad—chose Nob Hill as the place to honor themselves. They all built estates on top of the 338-foot rise, each more ostentatious than the other. It became, as Robert Louis Stevenson described it, "the Hill of palaces." At least until 1906: the fire that followed the great earthquake burned Nob Hill's mansions to the ground. One of the few surviving remnants of early-day Nob Hill is Golden Gate Park's Portals of the Past, part of the A. N. Towne mansion that originally stood at the corner of California and Taylor streets.

Belgian tapestry, and an organ boasting 7000 pipes. ~ 1051 Taylor Street.

Turn right on Washington Street, which takes you plunging down yet another of San Francisco's notoriously steep hills. The one-way Washington mysteriously reverses directions as it crosses the cable car tracks, so you need to *turn right again on Powell, then left on Clay Street*. This takes you through Chinatown again on a steep descent with a great view of the 48-story pyramidal **Transamerica Tower**, the most striking feature along San Francisco's skyline, straight ahead. Street signs are in both English alphabet and Chinese characters. *Go three blocks down Clay and turn left on Kearny, then left on Broadway.*

**NIGHTLIFE
NORTH BEACH
STYLE**

The corner of Broadway and Montgomery streets, a neon arabesque after dark, has long been San Francisco's answer to Times Square, a tawdry avenue that traffics in sex of the look-but-don't-touch variety. (There's little overt prostitution here; that's to be found in the Tenderloin district near the Civic Center.) On Broadway you'll find strip joints, peekaramas, and X-, Y-, and Z-rated theaters—a modern-day Barbary Coast. But if lap dances aren't your thing, you can still sample this area's curious version of the performing arts at **Club Fugazi**, where the outlandish musical revue *Beach Blanket Babylon* has become a San Francisco institution. The scores and choreography are good, but the costumes are great. The hats—elaborate, multilayered confections—make Carmen Miranda's adornments look like Easter bonnets. Cover. ~ 678 Green Street (a.k.a. Beach Blanket Babylon Boulevard); 415-421-4222; www.beachblanketbabylon.com.

*E*stablished in 1953 by poet Lawrence Ferlinghetti, **City Lights Bookstore** is the old hangout of the Beat poets. Back in the heady days of the '50s, a host of "angels"—Allen Ginsberg, Jack Kerouac, Gary Snyder, and Neal Cassady among them—haunted its book-lined rooms and creaking staircase.

Poet-bookseller Lawrence Ferlinghetti's influence on American culture reached beyond providing a safe haven for the Beat movement. In 1956, when his small press, City Lights Books, published *Howl* by Allen Ginsberg, the city prosecuted Ferlinghetti for publishing an obscene poem. The controversy surrounding the case stimulated a new concept of what the constitutional freedom of expression meant and ultimately inspired the Free Speech Movement across the Bay at the University of California at Berkeley, now recognized as the prototype for student activism in the 1960s.

Today the place remains a vital cultural scene and gathering point. It's a people's bookstore where you're invited to browse, carouse, or even plop into a chair and read a while. You might also check out the paintings and old photos, or perhaps the window display. Fifty years after the Beats, the inventory here still represents a who's who in avant-garde literature. ~ 261 Columbus Avenue; 415-362-8193, fax 415-362-4921; www.citylights.com, e-mail staff@citylights.com. **Vesuvio Café** next door was another hallowed Bohemian retreat. ~ 255 Columbus Avenue; 415-362-3370; www.vesuvio.com.

Turn right on Grant Street, heading toward Coit Tower, and you'll pass **Caffe Trieste**, on your left at the corner of Vallejo Street. With its water-spotted photographs and funky espresso bar, the place has changed little since the days when bearded bards discussed cool jazz and Eisenhower politics. ~ 601 Vallejo Street; 415-392-6739, fax 415-982-3045; www.caffetrieste.com.

You're on "upper Grant," North Beach, heart of the old Beat stomping grounds and still a major artery in the city's Italian enclave. Chinatown is at your back now, several blocks behind, but you'll see from the Chinese script adorning many shops that the Asian neighborhood is sprawling into the Italian. Still remaining, however, are the cafés and delicatessens that have lent this area its Mediterranean flair since the Italians moved in during the late 19th century.

Named for the semaphore station located on its height during the 1850s, **Telegraph Hill**—the steep hill you're now climbing on Grant

DECIDE FOR YOURSELF

by the way...

Built in 1934, the fluted Coit Tower was named for Lillie Hitchcock Coit, a bizarre character who chased fire engines and became a fire company mascot during the 1850s. Lillie's love for firemen gave rise to stories that the phallic tower was modeled after a firehose nozzle. Architectural critics scoff at the notion.

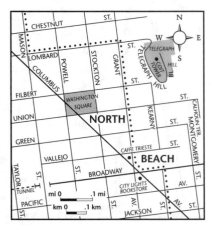

North Beach

Street—was a Bohemian haunt during the 1920s and 1930s. Money has since moved the artists out; today, this hillside real estate is among the most desirable, and most expensive, in the city. Poking through the top of Telegraph Hill is the 180-foot-high **Coit Tower**. Some of the nation's most outstanding WPA murals decorate the tower's interior. Done as frescoes by New Deal artists, they sensitively depict the lives of California laborers. An elevator takes you to an observation platform where San Francisco spreads before you. Parking is limited. Admission for elevator.

Turn left on Lombard Street for a steep three-block descent; then turn right on Mason Street and continue for six blocks to Jefferson

THE "REAL" FISHERMAN'S WHARF

To find sights worth seeing amid the commercialism of Fisherman's Wharf, you need to follow a basic law of the sea—hug the shoreline. **Pier 45**, for instance, is a working wharf, bleached with bird dung and frequented by fishing boats. From here it's a short jog to the docks on Jefferson Street, located between Jones and Taylor streets. The remnants of San Francisco's fishing fleet lies gunnel to gunnel here. The *Nicky-D, Ocean Star, Daydream, Phu Quy, Hai Tai Loc,* and an admiralty of others cast off every morning around 4 a.m. to return in late afternoon. With their brightly painted hulls, Christmas tree rigging, and rough-hewn crews, they carry the odor and clamor of the sea.

Street, where you'll find yourself on the waterfront at **Fisherman's Wharf**. Places have a way of becoming parodies of themselves—particularly if they possess a personal resonance and beauty or have some unique feature to lend the landscape. People, it seems, have an unquenchable need to change them. Such is the fate of Fisherman's Wharf. Back in the 19th century, a proud fishing fleet berthed in these waters and the shoreline was a quiltwork of brick factories, metal canning sheds, and woodframe warehouses. Genoese fishermen with rope-muscled arms set out in triangular-sailed *feluccas* that were a joke to the west wind. They had captured the waterfront from the Chinese and would be supplanted in turn by Sicilians. They caught sand dabs, sea bass, rock cod, bay shrimp, king salmon, and Dungeness crab. Salt caked their hands; wind and sun gullied their faces.

Today the woodplanked waterfront named for their occupation is hardly a place for fishermen. It has become "Tourist's Wharf," a bizarre assemblage of shopping malls and penny arcades that makes Disneyland look like the real world. The old waterfront is an amusement park with a wax gallery, a Ripley's museum, and numerous trinket shops. The **Musée Mécanique** is also located here and houses a collection of vintage mechanical amusements dating to a simpler time. You can put in your change and see them still do their thing (415-386-1170, fax 415-381-5637).

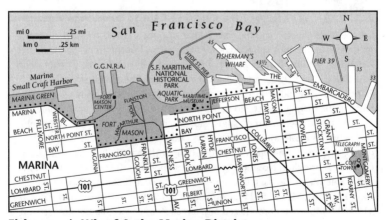

SIDEWALK SEAFOOD

Dining at Fisherman's Wharf usually means spending money at Fisherman's Wharf. The neighborhood's restaurants are overpriced and over-touristed. If you look hard enough, however, it's possible to find a good meal at a fair price in a fashionable restaurant. Of course, the easiest way to dine is right on the street, at one of the **seafood cocktail stands** along Jefferson Street. An old wharf tradition, these curbside vendors began years ago by feeding bay fishermen. Today they provide visitors an opportunity to sample local catches like crab, shrimp, and calamari—at budget prices.

The architecture subscribes to that modern school that makes everything look like what it's not—there's pseudo-Mission, ready-made antique Victorian, and simulated falsefront. But salt still stirs the air here and fog fingers through the Bay. There are sights to visit along "the Wharf." It's a matter of recapturing the past while avoiding the plastic-coated present.

Fish Alley is a nostalgic nook. Just duck into the narrow corridor next to Castagnola's Restaurant on Jefferson Street and walk out towards Scoma's Restaurant. Those corrugated metal sheds lining the docks are fish-packing operations. The fleet deposits its daily catch here to be processed for delivery to restaurants and markets. This is an area of piers and pilings, hooks

Fisherman's Wharf & the Marina District

and hawsers, flotsam and fish scales, where you pay a price to recapture the past: as you work further into this network of docks, approaching nearer and nearer the old salty truths, you'll also be overwhelmed by the putrefying stench of the sea.

by the way...

From 1920 on, as tuna grew scarce, the biggest catches for San Francisco's fishing fleet became sardines and anchovies. When air transport made it possible to ship fresh and frozen fish, the demand for canned sardines dwindled. Meanwhile, petroleum-based oils replaced the industrial fish oil that was the main use for anchovies. Today, San Francisco has less commercial fishing than other major West Coast ports such as San Diego, Los Angeles, and Seattle. The fishing fleet's main stock in trade is crab, lobster, and various fish, most of which is served in local restaurants.

Turn left onto Hyde Street and, a block later, right onto Beach Street. You'll pass **Hyde Street Pier**, where history is less offensive to the nose. Docked along the length of this wharf are the **Historic Ships**. Part of the San Francisco Maritime National Historical Park, they include a wood-hulled, three-masted schooner, *C. A. Thayer*, which once toted lumber along the California coast. You can also board the *Eureka*, an 1890 paddlewheeler that ferried commuters between San Francisco and Sausalito for almost 30 years. Currently the largest floating wooden structure on earth, it has served as police headquarters for the crime-fighting crew on TV's *Nash Bridges*. To walk this pier is to stride back to San Francisco's waterfront at the turn of the 20th century. Salt-bitten lifeboats, corroded anchors, and old coal engines are scattered hither-thither. The *Eppleton Hall* is an old paddlewheeler and the *Alma* a "scow schooner" with a

A HOSTEL WITH A TOUCH OF CLASS ━━━━━━

Say the word "hostel" and the first pictures to come to mind are spartan accommodations and shabby surroundings. At **Hostelling International–San Francisco–Fisherman's Wharf** that simply is not the case. Set in Fort Mason, an old military base that is now part of a magnificent national park, the hostel overlooks San Francisco Bay. In addition to eye-boggling views, the facility is within walking distance of the Marina district and Fisherman's Wharf. The hostel itself is contained in a World War II–era infirmary and features a living room, a kitchen, and a laundry, as well as a café with stunning views of the bay. The rooms, carpeted and quite clean, are dorm-style with 8 to 12 bunk beds in each. Rates also include a continental breakfast. No smoking or alcohol-imbibing; strict noise curfew at midnight. Free walking tours, music, and movies are offered. Reservations recommended. ~ Fort Mason, Building 240, Bay and Franklin streets; 415-771-7277, fax 415-771-1468; www.norcalhostels.org, e-mail sfhostel@norcalhostels.org. BUDGET.

STARRING
GARY DANKO

Dinner at **Gary Danko**, one of San Francisco's top-rated restaurants, is an extravaganza. The eponymous owner, who once built stage sets, envisions each evening as a "performance" featuring a "multi-act meal." The restaurant setting is certainly dramatic enough—with contemporary paintings on taupe walls and a decor that combines oak panels, plantation-style shutters and pin-spot lights to create an intimate but active atmosphere. The seasonal cuisine focuses on freshness and includes signature dishes like lamb loin and roast lobster. They also boast an exceptional wine cellar, special tea service, and a cheese service for which they are renowned. It's a special place for special occasions. Highly recommended. Dinner only. ~ 800 North Point Street; 415-749-2060, fax 415-775-1805; www.garydanko.com, e-mail info@garydanko.com. ULTRA-DELUXE.

---

flat bottom and square beam. A three-masted merchant ship built in Scotland in 1886, the *Balclutha* measures 301 feet. This steel-hulled craft sailed around Cape Horn 17 times in her youth. She loaded rice in Rangoon, guano in Callao, and wool in New Zealand. Today the old ship's cargo consists of a below-deck maritime museum and a hold full of memories. Admission. ~ 415-556-3002, fax 415-556-1624; www.nps.gov/safr.

Together with the **San Francisco National Maritime Museum**, it's enough to make a sailor of you. The museum, in case you mistook it for a ferryboat run aground, is actually an art-deco building designed to resemble the bridge of a passenger liner. Onboard there's a weird collection of body parts from old ships plus models, scrimshaw displays, and a magnificent photo collection. ~ Beach and Polk streets; 415-561-7100.

All these nautical showpieces are anchored in **Aquatic Park**, which sports a lovely lawn that rolls down to one of the Bay's few sandy beaches. A mélange of sounds and spectacles, the park has a bocce ball court where you'll encounter old Italian men exchanging stories and curiously eyeing the tourists. There are street vendors galore. If that's not enough, you can catch an eye-boggling glimpse of San Francisco Bay. Alcatraz lies anchored offshore, backdropped by one of the prettiest panoramas in this part of the world.

At Hyde and Beach streets, you'll see the northern terminal for the **Hyde–Powell Cable Car**—a good thing to know about when you return to explore this part of the city later on as a pedestrian. Be sure to stop at **Ghirardelli Square**, an old chocolate warehouse that has been converted into an open-air shopping courtyard. ~ 900 North Point Street; 415-775-5500; www.ghiradellisq.com.

If you check your watch and your odometer as you leave the Fisherman's Wharf area, you'll find that you've covered the first nine miles of 49-Mile Drive—in about two hours. Fortunately, the tour is about to take you out of the downtown area and into less congested realms.

From Beach Street, turn left up Polk Street for one block, then turn right on Bay Street past **Fort Mason Center**, a complex of old wharves and tile-roof warehouses that was once a major military embarkation point. Fort Mason today is the cultural heart of avant-garde San Francisco. This National Historic Landmark houses theaters, museums, and a gourmet vegetarian restaurant, and hosts thousands of programs and events. ~ Marina Boulevard and Buchanan Street; 415-979-3010, fax 415-441-3405; www.fortmason.org, e-mail contact@fortmason.org.

A VEGETARIAN'S DELIGHT

One of San Francisco's most popular vegetarian restaurants is incongruously situated in an old waterfront warehouse. With pipes exposed and a metal superstructure supporting the roof, **Greens at Fort Mason** possesses the aura of an upscale airplane hangar. But this eatery, run by the Zen Center, has been deftly furnished with burlwood tables, and there's a view of the Golden Gate Bridge out of the warehouse windows. The lunch menu includes vegetable brochettes fired over mesquite charcoal, pita bread stuffed with hummus, grilled tofu, soups, and daily specials. The dinner menu is à la carte Monday through Friday, pre-set on Saturday. The menu changes daily: a typical multicourse repast would be fougasse with red onions; spinach linguine with artichokes, shiitake mushrooms, pine nuts, rosemary, and parmesan; Tunisian salad; eggplant soup; Gruyère tart; lettuce salad; tea; and dessert. Reservations recommended for lunch and dinner. No lunch on Monday, no dinner on Sunday. ~ Fort Mason, Building A; 415-771-6222, fax 415-771-3472. MODERATE.

greens
RESTAURANT

Nearly all the arts and crafts are represented—several theater groups are housed here; there is an ongoing series of workshops in dance, creative writing, painting, weaving, printing, sculpture, music, and so on. A number of environmental organizations also have offices in the center. As one brochure describes, "You can see a play, stroll through a museum or gallery, learn how to make poetry films, study yoga, attend a computer seminar, or find out about the rich maritime lore of San Francisco."

At the **San Francisco Craft and Folk Art Museum** exhibitions range from Cook Island quilts to San Simeon architect Julia Morgan's craftware. You'll also want to visit the gift shop where they sell native and tribal goods, as well as a wide variety of jewelry and contemporary crafts. Closed Monday. Admission. ~ Building A; 415-775-0990, fax 415-775-1861; www.mocfa.org.

Museo Italo Americano presents samplings of Italian artistry. The museum is dedicated to the works of Italian and Italian-American artists and culture. The permanent collection features the work of several artists, some of whom have made San Francisco their home for years. There are also temporary exhibits ranging from 1930s photos of Italy to a pictorial display of contemporary Italian cinematographers like Francis Ford Coppola, Dino De Laurentiis, Michael Cimino, and Martin Scorsese. Closed Monday and Tuesday. Admission. ~ Building C; 415-673-2200, fax 415-673-2292; www.museoitaloamericano.org, e-mail museo@firstworld.net.

For a look at the rich arts and cultures of our neighbors to the south, visit the **Mexican Museum**. There are rotating exhibits of pre-Columbian art, Mexican Colonial art, and Chicano contemporary art and art of the Americas. Exhibits in the galleries change every several months. Closed Sunday through Tuesday. Admission. Note: the museum will be moving to a new location on Mission Street in 2004; call ahead for info. ~ Building D; 415-202-9700, fax 415-441-7683; www.mexicanmuseum.org, e-mail emmalouise@mexicanmuseum.org.

After passing Fort Mason on Bay Street, turn right on Laguna, which takes you past the Marina with its small craft harbor and yacht basin. There, the sign for 49-Mile Drive directs you *left into Marina parking area* for a great view of **Golden Gate Bridge**. Nearby **Marina Green**, a stretch of park paralleling the Bay, is a landlubber's haven. Bicyclers, joggers, jugglers, sunbathers, and a world of others inhabit it. The most interesting denizens of that small green rectangle of park are the kitefliers who fill the blue with a rainbow of soaring colors. Continue on past a line-up of luxury toys—boats with names like *Haiku*, *Sea Lover*, *Valhalla*, and *Windfall*.

When leaving the Marina parking lot, go straight (or, from Marina Boulevard, turn left) on Scott Street. Continue for two blocks on Scott and turn right on Beach Street. That magnificent Beaux-Arts monument looming before you is the **Palace of Fine Arts**, a domed edifice built of arches and shadows that houses the **Exploratorium**. A great place to bring children, this "hands-on" museum, with imaginative exhibits demonstrating the principles of optics, sound, animal behavior, etc., was once deemed "the best science museum in the world" by *Scientific American*. It's an intriguing place with constantly changing temporary exhibits and permanent displays that include a "distorted room" lacking right angles and an illusionary mirror into which you seemingly pass. Also check out the Tactile Dome (reservations

sights

THE PALACE BY THE POND

Adorned with molded urns and bas-relief figures, the **Palace of Fine Arts**, with its neoclassical Corinthian collonaded gallery and domed octagonal temple, is the only surviving structure from the 1915 Panama–Pacific International Exposition. It began to crumble in the 1960s, but fortunately, architect Bernard Maybeck had located it on the bank of a sun-shivered pond populated by mallards and swans, as well as pintails and canvasbacks from out of town. Together, the pool, the pillars, and surrounding park make this one of the city's loveliest spots for sitting and sunning, so under preservationist pressure the city chose to rebuild it with stronger materials rather than tear it down.

required), an enclosed crawlspace of textural adventures. Closed Monday. Admission. ~ Marina Boulevard and Lyon Street; 415-561-0360, fax 415-561-0370; www.exploratorium.edu.

Past the palace, it's your navigator's moment to shine: *turn left on Baker Street, then left again on Bay Street for one block, right on Broderick for two blocks, and right on Chestnut. Jog a block left on Lyon, turn right on Lombard Street to enter the Presidio, and turn right on Presidio Boulevard.* What was previously the oldest active military base in the country is now part of the country's largest urban national park. **The Presidio** is also a National Historic Landmark. It was established by the Spanish in 1776 and taken over by the United States in 1846. Civil War troops trained here, and the Sixth Army established the base as its headquarters. Even when it was a military base, the Presidio had the feel of a country retreat. Hiking trails snake through the 1400 acres of undulating hills sprinkled with acacia, madrone, pine, and redwood trees, and there are expansive bay views. Although still under development, there are plans for new hiking trails, museums, education centers, and conference facilities.

Much of the Presidio's grounds form one of San Francisco's natural areas. There's **El Polin Spring** where, as the brass plaque proclaims, "the early Spanish garrison attained its water supply." History has rarely been made in a more beautiful spot. The spring is set in a lovely park surrounded by hills upon which eucalyptus trees battle with conifers for strategic ground. Hiking trails lead down and outward from this enchanted glade. ~ Located at the end of MacArthur Avenue.

THE LAST STAND

The battle lines are drawn at **Lover's Lane**. March, or even stroll, along this narrow pathway, and review these armies of nature. On one side, standing sentinel straight, out-thrust arms shading the lane, are the eucalyptus. Mustered along the other front, clad in darker uniforms, seeming to retreat before the wind, are the conifer trees. Forgetting for a moment these silly games soldiers play, look around. You are standing in an awesome and spectacular spot, one of the last forests in San Francisco. ~ In the southeast corner of the Presidio.

GOLFING WITH THE GOVERNMENT

The 18-hole **Presidio Golf Course**, one of only a few golf courses in a U.S. national park, was originally built in 1895 for army officers to use and doubled as a drill field for troop reviews. Opened to civilians in 1995, it has quickly gained a reputation as one of the finest public courses in Northern California. Cart and club rentals are available. ~ Presidio; 415-561-4664, fax 415-561-4667; www.presidiogolf.com.

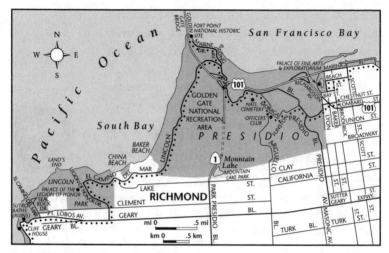

Presidio & Land's End

Mountain Lake Park, stationed along the Presidio's southern flank, is another idyllic locale. With grassy meadows and wooded walkways, it's a great place to picnic or stroll. The lake itself, a favorite watering hole among ducks visiting from out of town, is skirted with tule reeds and overhung with willows. ~ Lake Street between 8th and Funston avenues.

The base's prettiest walk is actually in civilian territory along the **Presidio Wall** bordering Lyon Street. Starting at the Lombard Street Gate, where two cannons guard the fort's eastern entrance, walk uphill along Lyon Street. That wall of urbanity to the left is the city's chic Union Street district, breeding place for fern bars and antique stores. To the right, beyond the Presidio's stone enclosure, are the tumbling hills and towering trees of the old garrison.

A right turn on Moraga takes you to the **Officers' Club**, a tile-roof, Spanish-style structure that includes part of the original 1776 Presidio, one of the first buildings ever constructed in San Francisco. ~ Moraga Avenue. The club temporarily houses the **William Penn Mott, Jr. Visitor Center**. The folks here are very knowledgeable; they'll provide you with a map and information about free public programs. ~ Building 50, Moraga Avenue; 415-561-4323, fax 415-561-4310; www.nps.gov/prsf.

Go one block on Montgomery, then turn left on Sheridan Avenue, which becomes Lincoln Boulevard as it winds through the woods, past the **National Cemetery**. San Francisco's salute to the nation's war dead has rows of tombstones on a grassy knoll overlooking the Golden Gate Bridge. ~ Lincoln Boulevard.

A road turns off on your right to **Fort Point National Historic Site**. Modeled on Fort Sumter and completed around the time Confederate forces opened fire on that hapless garrison, this was the only brick fort west of the Mississippi. With its collection of cannons and Civil War–era exhibits, it's of interest to history buffs. Call for information on guided tours and special programs. Open Friday through Sunday. ~ End of Marine Drive; 415-556-1693, fax 415-556-8474; www.nps.gov/fopo.

From Fort Point, a footpath leads up to the observation area astride the **Golden Gate Bridge**; if driving, take Lincoln Boulevard to the vista point. By whichever route, you'll arrive at "The Bridge at the End of the Continent." Aesthetically, it is considered one of the world's most beautiful spans, a medley of

sidetrips

CRUISE TO THE ROCK

From several vista points along Lincoln Boulevard, it's easy to see why **Alcatraz** was nicknamed "The Rock." Even today, after almost four decades under the protection of the National Park Service, the notorious former prison island still has almost no greenery, just gray stone cliffs that plunge into the chilly waters of the Bay. Originally a fort and then a military prison, Alcatraz became a federal maximum security prison in 1934. Al Capone, "Machine Gun" Kelly, and Robert "Birdman of Alcatraz" Stroud were among its best-known inmates. The prison closed in 1963; then in 1969 a group of American Indians occupied the island for almost two years, claiming it as Indian territory. Today Alcatraz is part of the Golden Gate National Recreation Area.

If you'd like a closer look, **Blue and Gold Fleet** sponsors Alcatraz trips from Pier 41. ~ 415-773-1188. The highlight is a National Park Service tour in which you'll enter the bowels of the prison, walk the dank corridors, and experience the cage-like cells where America's most desperate criminals were kept. Be sure to tune in to the audio-cassette tour of former guards and prisoners remembering their time at The Rock.

splayed cable and steel struts. Statistically, it represents one of the longest suspension bridges anywhere—6450 feet of suspended concrete and steel, with twin towers the height of 65-story buildings and cables that support 200 million pounds. It is San Francisco's emblem, an engineering wonder that has come to symbolize an entire metropolis. If you're game, you can walk across, venturing along a dizzying sidewalk out to one of the most magnificent views you'll ever experience. The Bay from this height is a toy model built to scale; beyond the bridge, San Francisco and Marin, slender arms of land, open onto the boundless Pacific.

The Golden Gate Promenade ends at the bridge, but Lincoln Boulevard continues along the cliffs that mark the ocean side of San Francisco. There are **vista points** overlooking the Pacific and affording startling views of the bridge and Alcatraz. After about a mile you'll reach the turnoff to **Baker Beach**, a wide corridor of white sand. Ideal for picnicking and sunbathing, this lovely beach is a favorite among San Franciscans. ~ Off Lincoln Boulevard on Gibson Road.

Adventurers can follow this strand, and the other smaller beaches with which it connects, on a fascinating walk back almost all the way to the Golden Gate Bridge. With the sea unfolding on one side and rocky crags rising along the other, it's definitely worth a little sand in the shoes. As a final reward, there's a **nude beach** on the northern end, just outside the bridge.

BIKING

Though some of San Francisco's hills are almost too steep to walk and downtown traffic can be gruelling, there *are* places that are easy to ride and beautiful as well. Golden Gate Park, the Golden Gate Promenade, and Lake Merced all have excellent bike routes. Among the city's most dramatic rides is the bicyclists' sidewalk on the Golden Gate Bridge. For bike rentals, visit **Avenue Cyclery** near the southeast corner of Golden Gate Park; they rent mountain bikes, tandems, hybrids, and kids' bikes. ~ 756 Stanyan Street; 415-387-3155.

*S*tay on Lincoln Boulevard as it transforms into El Camino del Mar, which winds through **Sea Cliff**, one of San Francisco's most affluent residential neighborhoods. This exclusive area has something to offer the visitor in addition to its scenic residences—namely **China Beach** (formerly known as James Phelan Beach). More secluded than Baker, this pocket beach is backdropped by a rocky bluff atop which stand the luxurious plate-window homes of Sea Cliff. The beach, named for the Chinese fishermen who camped here in the 19th century, has a dilapidated beach house and restroom facilities. (To reach it, turn right on 25th Avenue, left on Sea Cliff Avenue, then follow the street until it dead ends.)

Continuing on El Camino del Mar as it sweeps above the ocean, you'll come upon San Francisco's prettiest museum. With its colonnaded courtyard and arching entranceway, the **California Palace of the Legion of Honor** is modeled after an edifice of the same name in Paris. In fact, a mini-pyramid mirroring the one at the Louvre sits in the courtyard, letting light into the gallery below. Appropriately, it specializes in European art and culture. The exhibits trace European aesthetic achievements from ancient Greek and Roman art to the religious art of the Middle Ages to Renaissance painting, the Baroque and Rococo periods, and the Impressionists of the 19th and 20th centuries. Drink in the splendid view of city and Bay from the museum grounds. Closed Monday. Admission. ~ Lincoln Park, 34th Avenue and

An Unlikely Philanthropist

California's Palace of the Legion of Honor was given to the city by Adolph Spreckels, a scion of a wealthy San Francisco family that made its money in Hawaiian sugar and went into competition against the city's public utilities with its own gas, light, and power companies and even a private streetcar line. Known for his hot temper, Adolph was most remembered for shooting *San Francisco Chronicle* editor M. H. de Young, whose newspaper had accused him of stock fraud. Spreckels' gift of the palace, made soon after his marriage at age 50 in 1926, did much to restore his reputation.

Clement Street; 415-750-3600, fax 415-750-3656; www.legionofhonor.org, e-mail guestbook@famsf.org.

Head downhill on 34th Avenue past the Lincoln Park Municipal Golf Course, then turn right on Geary Boulevard, which becomes Point Lobos Avenue; turn right onto El Camino del Mar and follow it to the end. (Yes, this is the same street you were on earlier; no, I'm not leading you in circles. It seems that years ago landslides collapsed the midriff of this highway, leaving among the survivors two dead-end streets known forever by the same name.)

A NOTE OF CAUTION

If you decide to go hiking on the footpaths around Land's End, **be careful!** The area is plagued by landslides and foolish hikers. Remain on the trails. Exercise caution and this exotic area will reward you with eye-boggling views of Marin's wind-chiseled coast.

This is **Land's End**, a thumblike appendage of real estate that San Francisco seems to have stolen from the sea. It is the nearest you will ever come to experiencing San Francisco as the Costanoan Indians knew it. Hike the trails that honeycomb the hillsides hereabout and you'll enter a wild, tumbling region where winds twist cypress trees into the contours of the earth. The rocks offshore are inhabited by slithering sea creatures. The air is loud with the unceasing lash of wave against shoreline. Land's End is San Francisco's grand finale—a line of cliffs poised at the sea's edge and threatening imminently to slide into eternity.

INSIDE A CONTROVERSIAL CAMERA

A controversy surrounds the **Camera Obscura**, the camera-shaped kiosk near the Cliff House. The National Park Service, which leases the land on which this venerable old-time tourist attraction stands, wants to tear the building down and move the camera's inner workings to a yet-to-be-built visitors center. You can stand inside this dark chamber and watch as a rotating lens and mirror, based on a 16th-century design by Leonardo da Vinci, projects a panoramic view that takes in the Cliff House, the Sutro Baths and the Golden Gate Bridge, and Seal rocks, which lie just offshore. Camera Obscura is closed during the Cliff House renovations; call 415-239-2366 for updates.

From the parking lot located at the end of El Camino del Mar, walk down the steps that begin at the U.S.S. *San Francisco* Memorial Flagpole, and head east on the trail to the water. That dirty blonde swath of sand is a popular **nude beach**, perfectly situated here in San Francisco's most natural region.

Continuing down Point Lobos Avenue, at the corner where the road turns to parallel the Pacific Ocean, rest

**DINNER ON
THE ROCKS**

Try as you might to escape the trodden paths, some places in
the world are simply inevitable. Such a one is the **Cliff House**,
a historic structure at the edge of the sea that is positively inundated with tourists.
Upstairs at the Cliff House offers a great view in a café-cum-formal setting.
The breakfast and lunch menu boasts 20 kinds of omelettes as well as soups and
sandwiches. At dinner the waitstaff changes into nicer clothes, the linen goes on
the tables, and the café morphs into a formal dining room. There are pasta dishes,
several seafood selections, and a few chicken, steak, and lamb entrées. ~ 1090
Point Lobos Avenue; 415-386-3330, fax 415-387-7837; www.cliffhouse.com,
e-mail info@cliffhouse.com. MODERATE TO DELUXE.

For a tad less expensive meal, head uphill a few steps to **Louis'**, a cliffside
café that's been family-owned since 1937. The dinners, served with soup or salad,
include New York steak, prawns, scallops, and hamburger steak. Breakfast and
lunch are similar all-American affairs. Add a postcard view of the Sutro Baths and
Seal Rocks and you have one hell of a bargain. No dinner in winter. ~ 902 Point
Lobos Avenue; 415-387-6330. MODERATE.

---

the ruins of the **Sutro Baths**. From the configuration of
the stones, it's a simple trick to envision the foundation of Adolf Sutro's folly; more difficult for the mind's
eye is to picture the multitiered confection that the San
Francisco philanthropist built upon it in 1896. Sprawling across three oceanfront acres, Sutro's baths could
have washed the entire city. There were actually
six baths total, Olympian in size, as well as
three restaurants and 500 dressing rooms—
all contained beneath a stained-glass dome.

Towering above them was the **Cliff
House**, a Gothic castle that survived the
earthquake only to be consumed by fire the
next year. Following several reincarnations, the Cliff
House is a rather bland structure housing several restaurants and tourist shops. From this crow's nest you
can gaze out over a sweeping expanse of ocean. Due to
major renovations, the Cliff House is currently open
only for dining. To check on the progress of other portions, call 415-239-2366. ~ 1090 Point Lobos Avenue.

Below the Cliff House, extending to the very end of
vision, is the Great Highway. The salt-and-pepper
beach beside it is **Ocean Beach**, a slender ribbon of
sand that decorates three miles of San Francisco's
western perimeter. Remember, this is San Francisco—
land of fog, mist, and west winds—beachwear here

STEAK BY THE LAKE

Out in San Francisco's southwest corner, in Harding Park on the shores of Lake Merced, you'll discover a spiffy dining room: **The Boathouse Sports Bar and Restaurant**. With pretty views, it offers a lunch and dinner menu of steak, seafood, sandwiches, and salad. They take their sports themes seriously. Corridor walls are lined with photos of local athletes and every corner (as in all four) has a television to keep you posted on the latest scores. If you're out here to begin with, it's probably to go golfing, boating, hiking, or hang gliding, so the athletic ambience shouldn't bother you. Saturday and Sunday brunch. ~ 1 Harding Park Road; 415-681-2727, fax 415-681-3067. MODERATE.

---

more often consists of sweaters than swimsuits. The water, sweeping down from the Arctic, is too cold for mere mortals; only surfers and polar bear swimmers brave it. Watch for surf warnings. Nevertheless, to walk this strand is to trek the border of eternity. American Indians called San Francisco's ocean the "sundown sea." If you take the time some late afternoon, you'll see that the fiery orb still settles nightly just offshore.

Located on Skyline Boulevard at the far end of Ocean Beach, **Fort Funston** is the prettiest stretch to stroll. The fort itself is little more than a sequence of rusting gun emplacements, but there is an environmental education center and a half-mile nature trail here that winds along cliffs overlooking the sea. It's a windblown region of dune grass and leathery succulent plants, with views that span San Francisco and alight on the shore of Marin. Hang gliders dust the cliffs of Fort Funston, adding another dramatic element to this spectacle of sun and wind. (If you pass Fort Funston while following 49-Mile Drive, though, you've missed your turn.)

Across from Ocean Beach, on your left, where the city's Golden Gate Park (not to be confused with the federal Golden Gate Recreation Area) almost reaches the Pacific, you'll see the **Dutch Windmill**, a regal structure built in 1903. With its wooden struts and scale-like shingles, it stares into the face of the sea's inevitable west winds. The Dutchman's cousin, **Murphy**

Windmill, an orphan with broken arms, lives several hundred yards down the coast, barely glimpsed through the trees. On your right are dunes covered in sea grass. The rough pavement of the Great Highway suggests the fury of past storms, and in places sand drifts over the edges of the road.

Farther along the Great Highway, you'll encounter the **San Francisco Zoo**. A walk-through exhibit completed in an ambitious six-year rebuilding program, Puente al Sur ("bridge to the south") brings together such South American species as the giant anteater, the tapir, and the capybara. Other unique exhibits include Gorilla World, one of the world's largest gorilla habitats; Koala Crossing, one of the few zoo habitats of this teddy bear–like marsupial; and the Primate Discovery Center, a home for rare and endangered apes, monkeys, and lemurs. More than most zoos, this one goes out of its way to prove it's not just for kids. Besides a full calendar of events for children and families, the zoo sponsors adults-only mating season parties, including a popular Valentine's Day Sex Tour. Admission. ~ 45th Avenue and Sloat Boulevard; 415-753-7080; www.sfzoo.org, e-mail guestservices@sfzoo.org.

At a stoplight the road splits without much warning. *Bear left on John Muir Drive.* (If you reach the San Mateo county line you've missed the turn.) John Muir Drive takes you around the south end of **Lake Merced**, a U-shaped reservoir that has the unusual distinction of once having been salt water. Bounded by hiking trails and the 27-hole **Harding Park Golf Course**, considered to be one of the finest public courses in the country, the lake provides a pretty spot to picnic. There are rowboats and canoes for rent at the clubhouse here, and the lake is stocked with catfish and trout. ~ 415-661-1865.

From John Muir Boulevard, turn left onto fast, four-lane Lake Merced Boulevard. This is a T-intersection with a stop sign, not much visibility, and lots of pedestrians to watch out for, so making the turn may take some time.

*L*eaving the lake, Merced Boulevard becomes Sunset Boulevard, a broad, tree-lined thoroughfare that leads you directly into **Golden Gate Park**. The official 49-Mile Drive route turns *left off Martin Luther King Jr. Drive*, taking you west to the Chain of Lakes, where a *right turn on John F. Kennedy Drive* takes you back east past the long, narrow park's museums and gardens. Both main drives run the full four-mile length of the park. This is one place where you can be casual about following the tour route. Explore the park's side roads, confident that you'll pick up 49-Mile Drive again at the east entrance.

It is the Central Park of the West. Or perhaps we should say that Central Park is New York's answer to Golden Gate Park. It extends from the ocean all the way to the Haight-Ashbury neighborhood, across nearly half the width of the city. With its folded hills and sloping meadows, lakes, and museums, Golden Gate is everyone's favorite park.

Once an undeveloped region of sand dunes, the park today encompasses over 1000 acres of gardens, lawns, and forests. The transformation from wasteland to wonderland came about during the late 19th and early 20th centuries through the efforts of a mastermind

GLOBAL SAVORY SAMPLES

Haig's Delicacies, a long-established specialty food shop, is where many chefs from San Francisco's finest restaurants go for unusual and hard-to-find ingredients from around the world, such as Indian chutneys, Turkish olive oil, Israeli soup mixes, and Lebanese hot red-pepper sauce. There are a few tables where old-timers linger over cups of Turkish coffee and diners can eat on the premises (but why not pick up the makings for a classy picnic and head up to Golden Gate Park?). The hummus and tabbouleh come highly recommended. Closed Sunday. ~ 642 Clement Street; 415-752-6283. BUDGET TO MODERATE.

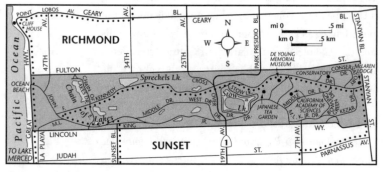

Golden Gate Park

named John McLaren. A gardener by trade, this Scotsman could rightly be called an architect of the earth. Within his lifetime he oversaw the creation of the world's largest human-made park.

What he wrought was a place that has something to suit everyone: there are tennis courts; lawn bowling greens; hiking trails; byways for bicyclists, rollerskaters, skateboarders, even unicyclists; a nine-hole golf course; an archery field; flycasting pools; playgrounds; fields for soccer and football; riding stables; and even checker pavilions. Facilities for renting bikes and skates are located just outside the park along Haight and Stanyan streets.

Along Martin Luther King, Jr. Drive in Golden Gate Park, you'll find **Strybing Arboretum**, a place specially made for garden lovers. Strybing is a world within itself, a 70-acre flower quilt stitched together by pathways. Over 7000 species peacefully coexist here—dwarf conifers and sprawling magnolias, as well as plants from Asia, the Andes, Australia, and America. There is a "redwood trail" devoted to native California plants, a "garden of fragrance" redolent of flowers, and a Japanese strolling garden. It's a kind

INLINE SKATING

When Sunday rolls around, several hundred folks are apt to don inline skates and rollerskates and careen along the sidewalks and streets of Golden Gate Park. John F. Kennedy Drive, on the east side of the park, is closed to cars on Sunday and holidays. Rentals are available at **Skates on Haight**. Closed Sunday in winter. ~ 1818 Haight Street; 415-752-8376; www.skates.com.

of park within a park, a glorious finale for your visit to this park within a city. ~ 415-661-1316, fax 415-661-7427; www.strybing.org.

Immediately beyond is the **Chain of Lakes**, a string of three reservoirs stretching the width of the park, perpendicular to John F. Kennedy Drive. Framed by eucalyptus trees, they offer hiking paths around each shoreline. As you circumnavigate these baby lakes, you will notice they are freckled with miniature islands. Each lake possesses a singular personality: North Lake is remarkable for its hip-deep swamp cypress; Middle Lake features an island tufted with willows; and South Lake, tiniest of the triplets, sprouts bamboo along its shore. **Spreckels Lake** is home to ducks, seagulls, and model sailboats.

ROW, ROW, ROW YOUR BOAT

For an afternoon on the water with kids in tow, head for Stow Lake's rowboats, pedalboats, or electric motorboats. For the always-hungry munchkins, there's also a small snack bar to sate their appetites.

Next along John F. Kennedy Drive you'll pass a chain of meadows, a kind of rolling green counterpoint to the chain of lakes that lies ahead. **Speedway Meadow** and **Lindley Meadow** offer barbecue pits and picnic tables; both are fabulous areas for sunbathing. These are followed close on by **Rainbow Falls**. The monument at the top, from which this cascade appears to spill, is **Prayerbook Cross**, modeled after an old Celtic cross.

Continue on John F. Kennedy Drive to **Stow Lake**, a donut-shaped body of water with an island as the hole in the middle. From the island's crest you can gaze across San Francisco from Bay to ocean. Or, if an uphill is not in your day's itinerary, there's a footpath around the island perimeter that passes an ornate Chinese pagoda.

Just beyond Stow Lake beats the cultural heart of Golden Gate Park. Located around a tree-studded concourse are the De Young Museum, Academy of Sciences, and Japanese Tea Garden. The **M. H. De Young Memorial Museum** houses an impressive collection. Exhibits trace the course of American art from colonial times to the mid-20th century, including an important collec-

tion of colonial-era art donated by the Rocke-
fellers. The Art of the Americas gallery features ancient art from Central and South
America as well as North American art of the
past 400 years. There's also an intriguing display of works from Africa and Oceania. The
De Young has one of the largest collections in
the nation. The museum will be closed for renovations until 2005. ~ 415-750-3600, fax 415-750-7386;
www.thinker.org, e-mail guestbook@famsf.org.

It takes a facility like the **California Academy of
Sciences**, called the "Smithsonian of the West," to
even compete with a place like the De Young Museum.
Here you will find a planetarium where the stars rise
all day, an array of African animals grouped in jungle
settings, and a "roundabout" aquarium in which you
stand at the center of a circular glass tank while creatures of the deep swim around you. A tremendous
place for kids, this natural history museum also features numerous hands-on exhibits. The museum will
be moving, sans planetarium, to 875 Howard Street in
December 2003; it will return to its current location in
mid-2008. Call for details. Admission. ~ 415-750-
7145, fax 415-750-7346; www.calacademy.org, e-mail
info@calacademy.org.

If you're like me, it won't be more than an hour or
two before museum fatigue sets in and dinosaur verte-
brae start looking like rock for-
mations. It's time to visit the
Japanese Tea Garden. Here you
can rest your heavy eyes on carp-
filled ponds and hand-wrought
gateways. A stroll through this
charming garden brings you to
arch footbridges, cherry trees,
bonsai gardens, and, of course, a
tea house. Admission. All these cultural gathering
places cluster around a **Music Concourse**.

**A TASTE OF
JAPAN**
A popular spot for
respite and refresh-
ment is the **Japanese Tea Garden**, where
kimono-clad servers bring jasmine tea
and cookies to guests. Are you sure
you're in San Francisco?

Farther along John F. Kennedy Drive lies **Rhododendron Dell**. A lacework of trails threads through
this 20-acre garden; if you're visiting in early spring,

when the rose-hued bushes are blooming, the dell is a concert of colors. The startling glass palace nearby is the **Conservatory**. Built in 1879 and Victorian in style, it's being restored after sustaining severe damage in a 1995 winter storm. Although it's not open until fall 2003, the Conservatory still makes for a stunning photo op. ~ www.conservatoryofflowers.org.

That red-tile building near the park's east entrance is **McLaren Lodge**, park headquarters and home base for maps, brochures, pamphlets, and information. ~ Stanyan and Fell streets; 415-831-2700, fax 415-221-8034; www.parks.sfgov.org, e-mail elizabeth_goldstein @ci.sf.ca.us.

*L*eaving the east side of Golden Gate Park, turn right on Stanyan Street, climbing up a formidable hill, and turn right on Parnassus Street, which takes you through the grounds of the **University of California at San**

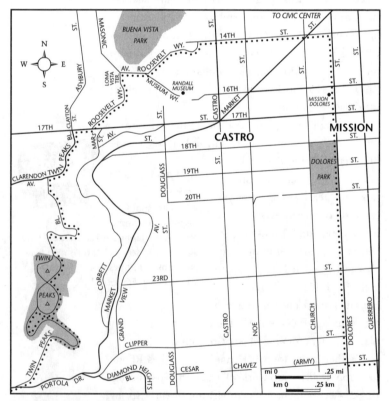

Twin Peaks & the Mission

Francisco. If this massive hillside complex appears more like a hospital than a college campus, it's no coincidence: UCSF is the medical school for the whole vast University of California, the world's largest university system.

Descending from the campus on Parnassus, turn left on 7th Avenue, then left again on Laguna Honda, which takes you up to the saddle ridge between two hills higher than any you've encountered on this tour. *From there, a left turn on Portola, followed by a left on Twin Peaks Boulevard,* leads you up a winding road one and a half miles along wooded slopes to an overlook near the broadcast towers atop **Twin Peaks**, San Francisco's second-highest mountain. (Mount Davidson, the peak to the southwest with the huge cross on top, stands six feet higher.) Atop these bald knobs rising 922 feet above the city, the eye traces a circle around the entire Bay.

As ever-taller broadcast towers are built on the summits of Twin Peaks, activists greet each new tower with stronger opposition. Besides worrying that radiation from the towers may threaten the health of residents in nearby neighborhoods, many fear that an earthquake could send the towers toppling down the steep slope and into the streets of the Castro district directly below.

The Golden Gate Bridge becomes a mere corridor that opens onto a mountain range called Marin. The Bay is a pond inhabited by sailboats. The cityscape lies before you, and buildings appear as out of the wrong end of a telescope. Jostled and teeming, civilization stretches to the west, only to pile up at the Pacific's edge. It is a view for travelers who can wander back in the mind to the days before humankind when wind and water were all the land could see.

Descending from the overlook on Twin Peaks Boulevard, turn right on Clarendon, bear left on Clayton, and then immediately turn right on 17th Street. Then turn left on Roosevelt Way (careful—the route marker is easy to miss). Here you'll

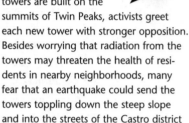

FUN AT THE MUSEUM
The Randall Museum offers free audience-participation animal feeding sessions every Saturday at noon. Kids get a chance to pet and help feed birds, lizards, mice, snakes, and an owl. The museum is also the meeting place for many San Francisco special-interest clubs, including the Audubon Society, the mycological society, hobby beekeepers, and natural science illustrators. Lectures and slide shows by guest naturalists are presented on the fourth Thursday of each month at 7:30 P.M.

come to the **Randall Museum**, a city-owned children's museum that contains animal exhibits, native arts and crafts of Northern California, and science displays. There's a playground adjacent to the museum. ~ 199 Museum Way; 415-554-9600; www.randallmuseum. org, e-mail info@randallmuseum.org.

*C*ontinuing downhill, Roosevelt runs into 14th Street. After crossing Market Street, turn right on Dolores Street*, which takes you past San Francisco's most beautiful reminder of its Spanish Colonial origins. **Mission San Francisco de Asís**, or Mission Dolores, completed in 1791, was one of the 21 Spanish missions built along the California coast by Franciscans. Its thick adobe walls (and perhaps a few prayers) helped the church survive the 1906 earthquake and fire; today it is the city's oldest building. Here you can wander back to the last great days of the Spanish empire: the tabernacle door came from Mexico, the ceiling design was borrowed from Costanoan Indians—all unfortunate subjects of 18th-century Spain. There's a mini-museum behind the chapel and a massive 20th-century basilica next door. Admission. ~ 415-621-8203; e-mail mdolores@earthlink.net.

The most intriguing feature on the Mission Dolores grounds is the **cemetery**. Studded with yew trees and tombstones, it is the last resting place of several famous (and infamous) San Francisco figures. Captain Louis Antonio Arguello, California's first Mexican governor, and Father Francisco Palou, the mission's architect, are interred here. So are Charles Cora and James Casey, a notorious pair who died at the hands of San Francisco's Vigilance Committee.

Continue downhill on Dolores Street, one of San Francisco's prettiest boulevards. Bordered on either side by bay-window homes, its proudest feature is the grassy median planted with stately palm trees. Better still, this marvelous promenade opens onto **Dolores Park**, between Dolores and 20th streets, a rectangle of rolling hills dotted with magnolia and pepper trees. If you make a stop here, you can stroll the sinuous walkways

The Names of the Mission

Although it was officially named after Saint Francis, founder of the Franciscan religious order whose gray-robed padres established all of California's Spanish Colonial missions, Mission San Francisco de Asís has always been better known as **Mission Dolores**. The original log chapel with its thatched roof was built beside Arroyo de los Dolores, an intermittent stream named by conquistador Juán Bautista de Anza in honor of Our Lady of Sorrows. The unofficial name stuck even when the present church was built several blocks from the original site—and even when the Arroyo de los Dolores was filled in and forgotten. In 1846, when California became United States territory, the city of San Francisco was named after the mission—even though most of the residents at the time were Mormons. In Spanish Colonial times, the main town on the peninsula was called Yerba Buena ("good herb"), the Spanish name for peppermint, which grew wild in the area.

down to the tennis courts or head for the high ground and a luxurious view of the city.

Turn left on Cesar Chávez Boulevard (renamed in 1995 and still shown on some maps as Army Street) and follow this thoroughfare all the way to the freeway.

Now you're on the home stretch. *Take Interstate 280 north to King Street.* If you get a chance to take your eye off the traffic for a moment, notice **Pacific Bell Park**, San Francisco's new baseball stadium, off to your right. Nicknamed even before it opened in spring 2000, "PacBell Park" is situated on the south side of the South of Market warehouse district, along the China Basin waterfront and readily accessible from the Embarcadero or Interstate 280. The San Francisco Giants left 3Com Park (known as Candlestick Park until a Silicon Valley conglomerate bought the naming rights) in favor of the more cost-efficient new PacBell Park, which has just over one-half the seating capacity. The $319-million ballpark features classic architecture inspired by Wrigley Field and Fenway Park, together with state-of-the-art lighting and electronics and an innovative seating alignment that provides the best possible views of the field from all seats.

Speaking of views, fans also find themselves surrounded by a panorama of the San Francisco skyline, the Bay, and the distant East Bay Hills. Just outside the stadium, a wharfside promenade near center field lets passersby view ball games knothole-style. A kids' slide in the shape of a giant Coca-Cola bottle gives a touch of commercialism to the ballpark's classic silhouette. Tours, offered daily at 10:30 a.m. and 12:30 p.m. except game days, include looks at the press box and the dugout. ~ King Street between 2nd and 3rd streets; 415-972-2400.

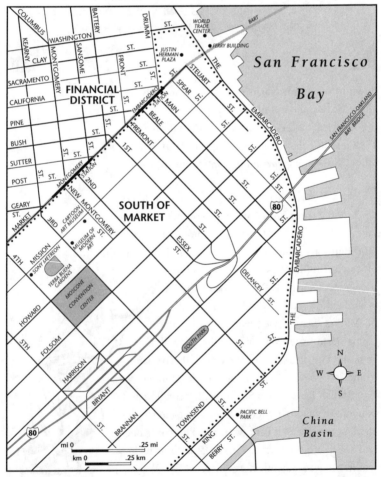

The Embarcadero, South of Market (SOMA), and China Basin

TWIST
AND SLEEP

As soon as you spot the Twister sculpture on the lobby wall—complete with life-sized mannequin assuming the position—you know you've entered the land of the terminally hip. The **W Hotel** provides trendy types upscale accommodations done in sleek Euro-Asian style. Rooms are spacious enough to launch a start-up inside. ~ 181 3rd Street; 415-777-5300, 888-627-8391, fax 415-817-7823; www.whotels.com. ULTRA-DELUXE.

King Street curves around to become **The Embarcadero**, bringing you to the **Ferry Building**, whose clock tower was San Francisco's answer to the Statue of Liberty at the turn of the 20th century, when it was as well-known a landmark as the Golden Gate Bridge is today. Back then there were no bridges, and 100,000 ferryboat commuters a day poured through the portals of the world's second-busiest passenger terminal. Built in 1896, the old landmark is now making a comeback. Sleek, jet-powered ferries stream into refashioned slips, and plans are afloat to space age the entire complex with the help of noted architect I. M. Pei.

The **World Trade Center**, on Embarcadero at the foot of Market Street, is lined with Covarrubias' murals that were preserved from the 1939 Golden Gate International Exposition. They look like those maps in your old sixth-grade social studies book: one vividly depicts "the people of the Pacific" with aborigines sprouting up from the Australian land mass and seraped Indians guarding the South American coast. Another pictorial geography lesson features the Pacific economy with salmon swimming off the North American shore and rice bowls growing in China.

Finally, turn left on Washington Street, then left on Drumm Street, and right on Market Street, which takes you back to the Civic Center. Along the way, you'll pass one block from **Moscone Convention Center**. Named for George Moscone, the San Francisco mayor who was assassinated in 1978, the mammoth convention center extends across 11 acres. With restaurants, hotels, apartments, and stores encircling it like satellites, the center is the dominant feature in San Francisco's fastest-changing district: South of Market (SOMA). ~ Howard Street between 3rd and 4th streets, center of the city's Internet

FEAST *ALL* YOUR SENSES

There's another side to San Francisco beyond the bridge-dotted skyline and bustling capitalism; past the elaborate Victorians and winding streets; behind the inline skaters and Sunday strollers. It's a world of camp and fashion, where the drinks are mixed, the music is intoxicating, the clothing is sleek, and the men are women. Welcome to **AsiaSF**. Make no mistake, the food is good: lots of grilled seafood, chicken satay, "baby got back" ribs and other Asian-influenced entrées. But no one comes for the food. They come for the "gender illusionists"—men you'd swear on your partner were women—performing cabaret numbers on a red runway when they're not filling water glasses. After dinner, work off the calories in the state-of-the-art dance-club downstairs. ~ 201 9th Street; 415-255-2742; www.asiasf.com. DELUXE.

industry, commonly known as Multimedia Gulch. Between Market and the convention center is **Yerba Buena Gardens**, a project that was 30 years in the making but is proving to be worth the wait by providing a forum for the visual and performing arts as well as some much-needed green space.

One component of the ten-acre complex located on top of the underground Moscone Convention Center is the **Yerba Buena Center for the Arts**; one of its two buildings is designed by the acclaimed Japanese architect Fumihiko Maki. The Center includes three galleries devoted to visual arts and high-tech installations, and there's also a screening room for video and film. A large multi-purpose room called "The Forum" hosts special events. In addition, a 755-seat theater offers a diverse lineup of music, dance, and performance art. Closed Monday. Admission. ~ 415-978-2787, fax 415-978-5210; www.yerbabuenaarts.org.

The **San Francisco Museum of Modern Art**'s popularity soared after it moved to its current SOMA location in early 1995, and it is now one of the top-ten most visited museums in the United States. The building, designed by Swiss architect Mario Botta, is a Modernist work of art in itself, distinguished by a tower finished in alternating bands of black and white stone. Inside are three large galleries and more than twenty smaller ones, totaling 50,000 square feet. The second floor displays selections from the museum's permanent collection. The third-floor gallery features photos and works on paper. The top two gallery floors accommodate special exhibitions and large-scale art from the museum's collection. Closed Wednesday. Admission. ~ 151 3rd Street; 415-357-4000, fax 415-357-4037; www.sfmoma.org.

A peculiar blend of theme park and shopping mall, the **Metreon** combines San Francisco's largest motion-picture complex (15 screens plus an IMAX theater), nine restaurants, play areas based on children's books, a futuristic video arcade, and nine retail stores, plus plenty of high-tech advertising. The self-styled "entertainment center" looks like a giant concrete cube from the outside and stands four stories tall to accommodate the 50-by-100-foot IMAX screen. ~ 4th and Market streets; 415-537-3400, 800-638-7366; www.metreon.com.

Just over a second-floor walkway from the Metreon, on top of the Moscone Convention Center, the **Rooftop at Yerba Buena Gardens** presents another

by the way...

Softening the contemporary hard edges of Yerba Buena Center is a five-and-a-half-acre esplanade of gardens and outdoor public art. A focal point of Yerba Buena Gardens is the Martin Luther King Jr. Memorial, a graceful waterfall spilling over Sierra granite. Behind the waterfall are a series of eight thick-glass panels etched with quotations drawn from speeches Dr. King made in San Francisco. Each quote is paired with a translation in a different language, representing the origins of the city's major ethnic groups, including Chinese, Spanish, Hebrew, Swahili, and others.

INSIDE THE CUBE

If you're traveling with kids, the Metreon is a must-see—sort of. Among the multimedia "tie-ins" is the 175-seat Action Theatre featuring anime movies and live performances, and Where the Wild Things Are, a live-action adventure based on Maurice Sendak's book. Another Sendak children's book is the basis for the family-friendly Night Kitchen restaurant. You gotta be a teen to fully appreciate Portal 1, an arcade designed by French comic artist Moebius (Heavy Metal) that features expensive video games played against opposing teams instead of against the computer. A standout here is HyperBowl, where players use actual bowling balls in interactive environments that simulate the streets of San Francisco, the surface of an alien planet, or the rocking deck of an ancient sailing ship. Meanwhile, mom and dad can play with the latest high-tech toys at the Sony and Microsoft retail outlets. If the Metreon, with its ubiquitous interactive videoscreens, seems a little like being trapped inside a giant TV ad, bear in mind that it's the crowning achievement of Sony's entertainment and technology empire, and many of the management team members are veterans of Disney.

collection of family-oriented attractions, this time created not by megacorporations but by the San Francisco Redevelopment Agency. The high-tech draw here is **Zeum**, an art-and-technology center that offers hands-on, behind-the-scenes experiences in animation, video production, digital photography, web-page design, 3-D modeling, and stage set design and production. Admission. ~ 4th and Howard streets; 415-777-2800; www.zeum.org. In striking contrast to the futuristic Zeum is the antique **1906 Charles Looff Carousel**, originally the centerpiece of San Francisco's former Playland-at-the-Beach amusement park. The large, beautifully restored carousel has all-white horses that gleam like new. Admission. ~ 4th and Howard streets; 415-541-0312. In addition, the rooftop complex includes the **Yerba Buena Ice Skating Center** (admission), an Olympic-size ice rink with huge windows overlooking the San Francisco skyline to create the feel of skating outdoors, and the adjoining 12-lane **Yerba Buena Bowling Center**. ~ 750 Folsom Street; 415-777-3727.

Explore the area surrounding Yerba Buena Gardens and you'll discover plenty of proof that the visual arts are alive and well.

The **Cartoon Art Museum** is also located in the Yerba Buena neighborhood. The museum features rotating exhibits of cartoon art in all its various incarnations: newspaper strips, political cartoons, comic books, and animation are amply represented. Highlights include a children's gallery and a bookstore. One of only two museums of its kind in the United States, this rare treat should not be missed. Closed Monday. Admission. ~ 655 Mission Street; 415-227-8666, fax 415-243-8666; www.cartoonart.org, e-mail office@cartoonart.org.

Continue up Market Street for several blocks to return to the Civic Center, where this tour began.

SOMA
AFTER DARK ━━━━━━━━━━━━━━━━━━━━━━━━━━━

SOMA is the new epicenter of San Francisco's nightclub scene, and "something for everybody" seems to be the motto. Not sure what you're in the mood for tonight? Then head to **Ten 15**, a SOMA club with three floors and five separate dance environments, each featuring a different sound from house to trance to techno. Open after-hours, often going on until 7 a.m. Open Friday and Saturday. Cover. ~ 1015 Folsom Street; 415-431-1200; www.1015.com, e-mail 1015@1015.com.

Other clubs take turns sharing the same dancefloor, like the one at 715 Harrison Street at 3rd Street: **The X** features alternative music on Friday night; on Saturday **City Nights** jumps to the sound of hip-hop, R&B, and house in the same location; and on Thursday, it's gay and lesbian night at **Club Faith**. Cover. ~ 415-546-7938; www.sfclubs.com, e-mail sharonsfclubs@aol.com.

The most unusual club in the neighborhood, **Brain Wash** offers live acoustic sounds from local bands and deejay-spun jazz. There's always something happening at this hip café that also doubles as a . . . laundromat! Wednesday is "spoken word" night, and Friday features female comedians. Thursday is comedy night. ~ 1122 Folsom Street; 415-861-3663; www.brainwash.com, e-mail getlost@brainwash.com.

If you find SF's nightlife options overwhelming, **3 Babes and a Bus** allows you a 45-minute taste of different scenes, from '70s disco and Top-40 to salsa and R&B. For a flat fee, this nightclub-touring company takes care of the driving and cover charges while ensuring priority entry to a number of clubs on this four-hour tour. Reservations recommended. ~ 800-414-0158; www.threebabes.com, e-mail info@threebabes.com.

From there, proceeding south on 10th Street will take you back to the junction of I-80 (which takes you to the Bay Bridge) and Route 101 (which takes you to Silicon Valley).

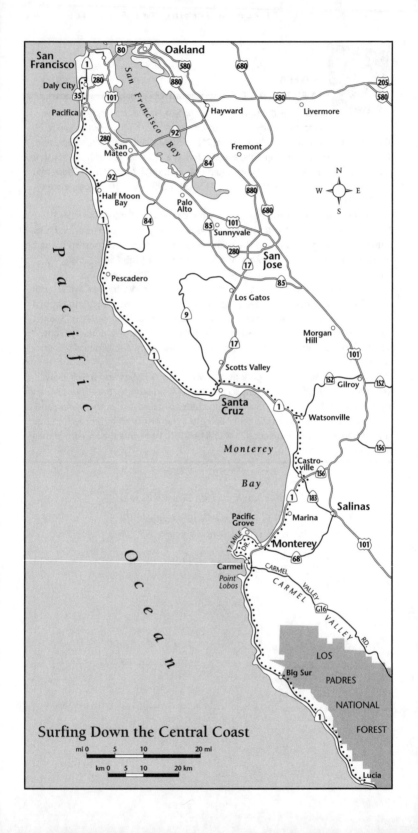

Surfing Down the Central Coast

3 SURFING DOWN THE CENTRAL COAST

Route 1 South from San Francisco

If Route 1 from San Francisco to Big Sur were an oil painting, it would portray a surf-laced shoreline near the bottom of the frame. Pearly beaches and bold promontories would occupy the center, while forested peaks would rise in the background. After adding a patch-work of hills, headlands, farmland, and a swath of redwoods, the painter's impossible task would have only just begun. This stretch of highway will never be captured—on canvas, in print, or in the camera's eye. It cuts through a region of unmatched beauty and extraordinary diversity.

Due south of San Francisco is Half Moon Bay, a timeless farming and fishing community

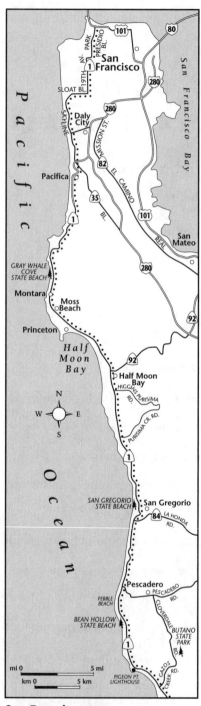

**San Francisco to
Pigeon Point Lighthouse**

founded by Italians and Portuguese during the 1860s. In the seaside town of Santa Cruz, on the other hand, you'll encounter a quiet retirement community that has been transformed into a dynamic campus town. Different still is the Monterey Peninsula, a fashionable residential area including the towns of Monterey, Pacific Grove, and Carmel. The wealthy enclave is a far cry from bohemian Santa Cruz. Farther south lies Big Sur, the most unique region of all. Extending from the Monterey Peninsula south along Route 1 for 90 miles along the coast and backdropped by the steep Santa Lucia Mountains, it is one of America's most magnificent natural areas, a rugged region of bald crags and flower-choked canyons.

The road you'll find is full of surprises. You might see a gray whale pod, watch sea lions, or discover one of the rural towns that dot this shoreline. The area along Route 1 between San Francisco and Big Sur sports numerous beaches, bed-and-breakfast inns, and country roads that lead up into the mountains or down to the sea.

Your journey follows the highway as it leaves San Francisco, cuts through **Pacifica** and curls into the hills. The transformation when you leave Pacifica is a dramatic one—the flat urban landscape gives way to a curving roadway, with the ocean rolling to your right and sharp rockfaces towering to the left. As the road rises above a swirling coastline you'll be entering a geologic hotspot. The **San Andreas Fault**, villain of the 1906 earthquake, heads back into shore near Pacifica. As the road cuts will reveal, the sedimentary rock along this area has been twisted and warped into bizarre shapes. At **Devil's Slide**, several miles south of Pacifica, unstable hillsides periodically collapse into the sea.

Though sometimes a little scary from behind the wheel, this is an area not to be missed. Drive carefully and you'll be safe to enjoy the outstanding ocean vistas revealed at every hairpin turn in this winding roadway. Rocky cliffs, pocket beaches, and erupting surf open to view. Sea stacks lie offshore and, in winter, gray whales cruise the coast.

Nick's Restaurant has been operated by the same family for more than seven decades and is still pulling in the Pacifica crowds. Wood sculptures of sea life decorate the walls, but the main attraction is the million-dollar view of Rockaway Beach. Nick's is known for its grilled crab sandwiches, sautéed prawns, and fettuccine angelina. ~ 100 Rockaway Beach, Pacifica; 650-359-3900, fax 650-359-5624. DELUXE.

The first pocket beach you'll come to is aptly named **Gray Whale Cove**. Located along Route 1 three miles south of Pacifica (watch for the parking lot on

MOSS BEACH RESTAURANT

For dinner overlooking the ocean, there's nothing quite like **Moss Beach Distillery**. The place enjoys a colorful history, dating back to Prohibition days, when this area was notorious for supplying booze to thirsty San Francisco. Today it's a bustling plate-glass restaurant with an adjoining bar. The menu includes gulf shrimp, calamari sauté, cioppino, steak, and grilled pork loin medallions with wild mushroom ragout. The bootleggers are long gone, but those splendid sea views will be here forever. Just don't be too surprised if an invisible dinner guest rattles your glass—a ghost known as the Blue Lady has supposedly been haunting the place since she missed a rendezvous with her lover here in those rum-hazy days of the '30s. Brunch served on Sunday. ~ Beach Way and Ocean Boulevard, Moss Beach; 650-728-5595; www.mossbeachdistillery.com. MODERATE TO DELUXE.

the east side of the highway, then cautiously cross the highway and proceed down the staircase to the beach), this white-sand crescent is tucked discreetly beneath steep cliffs. The only facilities are toilets. Day-use fee, $6.50. ~ 650-728-5336.

Continuing seven miles south on Route 1 you will come to the village of **Montara**, where you will pass an old lighthouse whose utility buildings have been converted into a youth hostel.

As the road descends over the next mile precipitous rockfaces give way to gentle slopes and placid tidepools.

Each October, the free, fun-filled **Great Art and Pumpkin Festival** in Half Moon Bay features bountiful pumpkin patches, harvest-inspired arts and crafts, live music, specialty foods, a Great Pumpkin Parade, a haunted house, giant pumpkins, contests, and events galore. ~ 650-726-9652.

Approximately 25 miles south of San Francisco and 6 miles north of Half Moon Bay you'll come upon **Moss Beach**, a small community on the San Mateo County coastline. In addition to Moss Beach being a perfect spot for a leisurely meal with a view, it offers one of the best locations to explore the ocean's natural treasures. **James V. Fitzgerald Marine Reserve**, with its sandy beach and excellent tidepools, is a great place to while away the hours watching crabs, sea urchins, and anemones. There's also restrooms and a picnic area. ~ 650-728-3584.

Continuing south, you come to the first sizable town along the coast. **Half Moon Bay** is what happens when the farm meets the sea. It's a hybrid town, half landlubber and half old-salt. While local farmers grow prize vegetables, commercial fishing boats comb the entire coast for salmon, herring, tuna, anchovies, and cod. They are as likely to sell artichokes here as fresh fish. Main Street, Half Moon Bay, could as easily be spelled Main Street America. It has all the classic qualities (brick-built City Hall, falsefront stores, Victorian houses) plus a few modern accouterments (cappuccino bars, gourmet restaurants).

Barbara's Fishtrap in Half Moon Bay is set in and around a small woodframe building smack on the bay. This unpretentious eatery features several fresh fish dishes daily; they're liable to be serving sea bass, halibut, and salmon, as well as shellfish and steak sandwiches. Calamari rings are a specialty. Friendly, relatively inexpensive, and highly recommended. ~ 281 Capistrano Road, Princeton-by-the-Sea; 650-728-7049. MODERATE TO ULTRA-DELUXE.

The town was named for its crescent beach, but oceanside farms are so bountiful that Half Moon Bay dubs itself the pumpkin capital of the world. At times the furrowed fields seem a geometric continuation of ocean waves, as if the sea lapped across the land and became frozen there. It is Half Moon Bay's peculiar schizophrenia, a double identity that lends an undeniable flair to the community.

The farming plus fishing spirit of Half Moon Bay prevails as Route 1 continues south. Take La Honda Road a short distance inland off the highway and you will encounter **San Gregorio**, a weather-beaten little town. Once a resort area, today it reveals a quaint collection of sagging roofs and unpainted barns. Be sure to stop

A MEDITERRANEAN FEAST
IN HALF MOON BAY

If you're in the mood for raw oysters, fresh produce and hearty Mediterranean dishes stop by **Cetrella** for dinner (or Sunday brunch). This bistro/café is a mix of the contemporary and the traditional, with its open, stainless-steel kitchen, roaring fireplace, and exposed-truss ceiling. Along with a tempting selection from the raw bar, they offer up intriguing appetizers from their cheese-and-charcuterie room. The menu changes daily: I started with shrimp ceviche and ended with a vanilla *panna cotta* and fresh cherries; my main course was milk-braised lamb shank with aromatic Moorish spices. ~ 845 Main Street, Half Moon Bay; 650-726-4090; www.cetrella.com. DELUXE TO ULTRA-DELUXE.

by the **San Gregorio General Store** at the corner of Stage Road, a classic that's been around for over a century. ~ 650-726-0565; www.sangregoriostore.com.

Right on the roadside of Route 1 is **San Gregorio State Beach**, a white-sand strand framed by sedimentary cliffs and cut by a small creek. Star of the show, though, is the nearby private **nude beach** (admission) several hundred yards north of the state beach, reputedly the first beach of its type in California. Among the nicest of the state's nude beaches, it features a narrow sand corridor shielded by high bluffs. There are picnic areas and toilets at the state beach, but no facilities at the nude beach. Day-use fee, $4. ~ 650-726-7245. 🏃 🏊 🏄 🚣

PESCADERO KIDS

Famous for rare heirloom beans (people from all over the world bring their ancestors' seeds here), **Phipps Ranch** is a family-owned farm open to the public that hooks kids with its child-friendly barnyard zoo. Summertime U-pick berries are also a big hit. ~ 2700 Pescadero Road, Pescadero; 650-879-0787.

Pescadero represents another timeworn inland town hidden on a short detour off Route 1 on Pescadero Creek Road. It's a woodframe hamlet of front-porch rocking chairs and white-steeple churches. The name translates as "fisherman," but the Portuguese and Italian residents are farmers planting artichokes, Brussels sprouts, beans, and lettuce in the patchwork fields surrounding the town.

The 1896 wreck of the Pacific Mail Steamship *Columbia* (the first ship with electricity on board, wired by Edison himself—though what role the new technology played in the ship's demise will never be known) contributed to Pescadero's once-prim New

HIGGINS–PURISIMA ROAD

On the southern outskirts of Half Moon Bay, watch for the Higgins–Purisima Road, a country lane that offers a great detour that curves for eight miles into the Santa Cruz Mountains before returning right back to Route 1. This scenic loop passes old farmhouses and sloping pastures, mountain meadows, and redwood-forested hills. Immediately upon entering this bumpy road, you'll spy a stately old New England–style house set in a plowed field. That will be the James Johnston House, a saltbox structure with a sloping roof and white clapboard facade. Dating back to 1853 and built by an original '49er, it is the oldest house along this section of coastline. The house is rarely open to the public; during the summer, it occasionally opens on the third Saturday of the month.

Pigeon Point Lighthouse History

The importance of maritime disasters along this coast is memorialized by Pigeon Point's name as well as its beacon. Don't look for dirty little doves here—the place was named after the *Carrier Pigeon*, a clipper ship that wrecked on the rocks in 1853. In the 19 intervening years before the lighthouse began operating, a dozen more ships went down. The powerful Fresnel lens that finally arrived in 1872 had already served in lighthouses on the New England and south Atlantic coasts, and had spent the Civil War years buried in the sand to keep it out of Confederate hands. These days an automated aerobeacon helps keep sailors oriented.

England look in an opportune way: the town's inhabitants salvaged the *Columbia*'s cargo of white paint and applied it liberally to every wall in sight, giving Pescadero the reputation of being "the whitest town in California." The appellation stuck around a bit longer than the paint did, though fortunately it faded well before the term took on suspicious overtones.

About 21 miles south of Half Moon Bay, the small sandy beach at **Bean Hollow State Beach** is bounded by rocks, so sunbathers go elsewhere while tidepool watchers drop by. Particularly interesting is nearby (about one mile north of Bean Hollow State Beach) **Pebble Beach**, a coarse-grain strand studded with jasper, serpentine, carnelians, and agates. The stones originate from a quartz reef offshore and attract rockhounds by the pack. But don't take rocks away—it's illegal. Also not to be missed is the blufftop trail between Bean Hollow and Pebble Beach, from which you can spy seals and whales in season. Facilities include a picnic area and toilets. ~ 650-879-2170.

SPORTFISHING

The Central Coast is renowned for its open-sea fishing. If you want a chance to test your skill in chasing down salmon or cod, contact **Captain John's Fishing Trips**. They operate four boats ranging from 55 to 65 feet and head out to the Farallon Islands. ~ 21 Johnson Pier, Princeton-by-the-Sea; 650-726-2913.

BUTANO STATE PARK

Several miles inland from the coast, Butano State Park provides a welcome counterpoint to the beach parks. In its 3600 acres, it features a deep redwood forest, including stands of virgin trees; hiking trails traverse the territory. Not as well known as other nearby redwood parks, Butano suffers from less human traffic. The park has picnic areas and restrooms. Day-use fee, $4. Camping by reservation only (800-444-7275) from Memorial Day to Labor Day. ~ From Route 1, go 20 miles south of Half Moon Bay; turn left (east) on Pescadero Road, and then right on Cloverdale Road about four miles to the park.

The beacon several miles south is **Pigeon Point Lighthouse**, a 110-foot sentinel that's one of the nation's tallest lighthouses. The point gained a nasty reputation during the 19th century when one ship after another smashed on the rocks. The lighthouse went up in 1872, and originally contained a 1000-piece lens. Doubling as a youth hostel, it now warns sailors while welcoming travelers.

Route 1 cruises along, paralleling each curve and stretch of the shoreline perhaps 50 feet above sea level; to one side red rock and white ocean spray, on the other a broad expanse of green edges up to humpbacked hills and distant forest.

Miles of sand dunes border **Año Nuevo State Reserve**, a lovely park containing an offshore island where two-ton elephant seals breed in winter. With its exotic bird population, sea lions, and harbor seals, the

Elephant Seals

Reaching two tons and 16 feet, adorned with the bulbous, trunklike snouts for which they are named, these mammals are unique. Back in 1800, elephant seals numbered in the hundreds of thousands; by the end of the century, they were practically extinct; it's only recently that they have achieved a comeback. When breeding, the bulls stage bloody battles and collect large harems, creating a spectacle that draws crowds every year. During breeding season, docents lead two-and-a-half-hour tours, which must be booked eight weeks in advance (650-879-2025). Be forewarned that it's a three-mile roundtrip walk from the parking lot to the rookery.

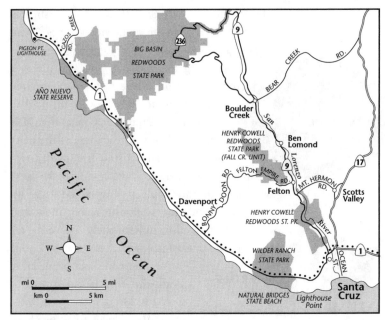

Pigeon Point Lighthouse to Santa Cruz

reserve is a natural playground. The Ohlone Indians highly valued the region for its abundant fish and shellfish population. It was here the Ohlone had the first encounter with whites in 1769 when Juan Gaspar de Portolá trekked through Año Nuevo en route to his discovery of San Francisco Bay. Awesome in its beauty and abundant in wildlife, this park is one of the most spectacular on the California coast. It consists of a peninsula heaped with sand dunes. A miniature island lies just offshore. There are tidepools to search and a nature trail for exploring. Seals and sea lions inhabit the area; loons, hawks, pheasants, and albatrosses have all been spied here. But most impressive of all the denizens are the elephant seals, those lovably grotesque creatures who come here between December 15 and March 31 to breed. Also be aware: the elephant seal population makes this beach attractive to sharks. The only facilities are toilets. Closed the first two weeks of December. Day-use fee, $4. ~ 650-879-2025; www.anonuevo.org.

HIKING

To explore Año Nuevo after mating season, you can hike on your own past sand dunes, tidepools, and sea caves. Follow **Año Nuevo Trail** (2.5 miles), beginning at the west end of the parking lot, to Año Nuevo Point.

From Año Nuevo to Santa Cruz, Route 1 streams past bold headlands and magnificent seascapes. There are excellent beaches to explore and marvelous vista points along the way. You will also discover rolling farmlands where giant pumpkins grow at the edge of the sea.

You will have traveled 30 miles from Half Moon Bay when you reach one of the most secluded and beautiful strands around: **Greyhound Rock**. There are startling cliffs in the background and a gigantic boulder—Greyhound Rock—in the foreground; the area is a favorite among those who love to fish. It is also, unfortunately, a favorite for thieves. Keep your valuables with you and lock your car. Restrooms and picnic areas are the only facilities. ~ 831-462-8333.

DISCOVERING THE OCEAN

Why not let the kids see how ocean scientists really work? That's the mission of the **Seymour Marine Discovery Center**, a University of California facility that introduces visitors to the human side of scientific research. Not a museum or aquarium in the typical sense (though plenty of strange-looking animals live in the tanks here), the center gives kids an unusual glance into the life of a watery lab. To get here, leave Route 1 in Santa Cruz, and as you drive toward Natural Arches State Park, you'll come to Delaware Avenue; drive north a couple of blocks to the end of this street to find the Long Marine Laboratory and Seymour Discovery Center. The 40-acre facility overlooks marine terraces landscaped with native coastal flora. Closed Monday. Admission. ~ 831-459-3800; www.seymourcenter.ucsc.edu.

About two miles north of Santa Cruz on Route 1 you'll discover **Wilder Ranch State Park**. This 6500-acre spread has 30 acres that have been designated a "cultural preserve" because of the Ohlone Indian shell mounds and historic ranch complex on the property. Hiking trails allowing horses and bikes wind throughout. In addition to an 1839 adobe, the complex features a Greek Revival farmhouse dating to 1859 and an 1897 Queen Anne Victorian. You can also tour the outlying barns and workshops portraying life on a turn-of-the-20th-century dairy farm, which this once was. Go on a weekend to see living history demonstrations. Open Thursday through Sunday. Parking fee, $5. ~ 831-426-0505.

Route 1 veers slightly inland on reaching **Santa Cruz**. In town it first turns into Mission Street then becomes a freeway that speeds past all the attractions of Santa Cruz and sends you careening down the coast. That means it's time to find a different waterfront drive.

Exploring Santa Cruz reveals one of California's original missions, a very popular beach scene, and a University of California campus. This town of 51,000 is in many respects one big playground. It enjoys spectacular white-sand beaches, entertaining nightlife, and an old-style boardwalk amusement park. The city faces south, providing the best weather along the Central Coast. Santa Cruz continues to boast 300 sunny days a year. Explorers once complained of foggy summers and rainy winters, but like today's travelers, they were rewarded with beautiful spring and fall weather. Arts and crafts flourish here, and vintage houses adorn the area. When the University of California opened a school here in the 1960s, it created a new role for this ever-

Most Santa Cruz restaurants can be found near the Boardwalk or in the downtown area, with a few others scattered around town. Of course, along the Boardwalk the favorite dining style is to eat while you stroll. Stop at **Hodgie's** for a corn dog, Italian sausage sandwich, or fried zucchini; sit down to a bowl of clam chowder or crab salad at the **Fisherman's Galley**; or pause at the **Barbary Coast** for cheeseburgers, baked potatoes, or chicken nuggets. Old-time arcade specialties—caramel apples, ice cream, cotton candy, popcorn, and saltwater taffy—hold up as after-dinner treats.

One-Eyed Charley, Charlotte?

One-eyed Charley Parkhurst had a reputation all along the coast and up into the Sierras as a daring, skillful, and resourceful stagecoach driver—"one of the most celebrated whips of the early days"—as well as for a foul mouth legendary even among this rough-riding bunch. Chin perpetually stained by tobacco juice, an eyepatch concealing on old injury (kicked by a horse)—Charley's beardless face and taciturn ways were well known on Wells Fargo's Santa Cruz to Watsonville stage route.

Not much is known of Parkhurst's early life, but the details show a determination that lasted a lifetime: born Charlotte Parkhurst in New Hampshire around 1812, the young girl was abandoned by her parents at an early age. She escaped from an orphanage disguised as a boy and found it suited her. She spent years in the livery trade along the Eastern Seaboard, working her way up from the stables to carriage driver. In 1851 she made her way to San Francisco and for nearly 20 years One-eyed Charley drove all over California and, in spite of a surly attitude, was known as one of the most reliable drivers in the region. That no one suspected "his" secret until Charley died in 1879 seems astounding, but we may presume anyone getting close enough to find out was probably drunk or similarly addled.

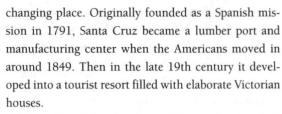

changing place. Originally founded as a Spanish mission in 1791, Santa Cruz became a lumber port and manufacturing center when the Americans moved in around 1849. Then in the late 19th century it developed into a tourist resort filled with elaborate Victorian houses.

To explore Santa Cruz, turn off Route 1 at the north end of town where you see signs for **Natural Bridges State Beach**. All but one of the sea arches here have collapsed, leading local wags to dub the spot "Fallen Arches." Northernmost of the Santa Cruz beaches, Natural Bridges State Beach is a small park with a half moon–shaped beach and tidepools. This is an excellent spot to watch monarch butterflies during their annual winter migration (from October to late February). During these months there are weekend guided tours of the eucalyptus groves. Facilities include picnic areas, a visitors center, a bookstore, and restrooms. Day-use fee, $5. ~ 831-423-4609.

On the south side of Natural Bridges State Beach is the place to pick up **West Cliff Drive**, which sweeps the Santa Cruz waterfront. The shoreline is a honeycomb of tiny coves, sea arches, and pocket beaches. From **Lighthouse Point** on a clear day, the entire 40-mile curve of Monterey Bay silhouettes the skyline. Even in foggy weather, sea lions cavort on the rocks offshore, while surfers ride the challenging "Steamer Lane" breaks.

Testament to the surfers' talent is the tiny **Santa Cruz Surfing Museum** situated in the lighthouse at Lighthouse Point. Here vintage photos and antique boards re-create the history of the Hawaiian sport that landed on the shores of Santa Cruz early in the 20th century. Closed Tuesday year-round and Wednesday in winter. ~ 408-429-3429.

Heading down from the lighthouse on West Cliff Drive, you can pick up **Beach Street**, which continues this coast-hugging route to **Santa Cruz Municipal Pier**, a half-mile-long wharf lined with bait shops, restau-

SURFING

Catching a wave when the surf's up near Lighthouse Point just north of the Santa Cruz wharf is a surfer's dream. Known as "Steamer Lane," this stretch of coastline hosts many international surfing competitions. Surfing lessons and surfboard, body board and wetsuit rentals are available at **Club Ed** on Cowell Beach next to the Santa Cruz wharf. ~ 831-459-9283, 800-287-7873.

rants, and fishing charters. Those early-morning folks with the sun-furrowed faces are either fishing or crabbing. They are here everyday with lawn chairs and tackle boxes. When reality overcomes optimism, they have been known to duck into nearby fresh fish stores for the day's catch. The pier is a perfect place to promenade, soak up sun, and seek out local color. It also provides a peaceful counterpoint to the next attraction.

Santa Cruz Beach Boardwalk is Northern California's answer to Coney Island. Pride of the city, it dates back to 1907 and sports several old-fashioned rides. The penny arcade features vintage machines as well as modernistic video games. You'll find shooting galleries and candy stalls, coin-operated fortune tellers and do-it-yourself photo machines.

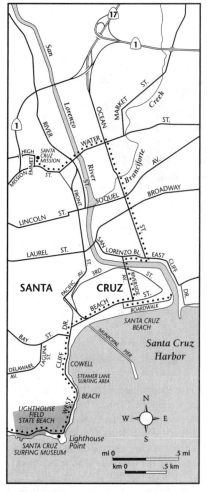

Santa Cruz

SLEEP TIGHT IN AN OLD VICTORIAN

A stroll near the Boardwalk and beach might lead you to believe that Santa Cruz specializes in neon motels. Don't be convinced. A welcome exception is the Beach Hill neighborhood's **Cliff Crest Bed & Breakfast Inn**, a five-bedroom establishment in a historic 1887 Victorian home. The yard was designed by the architect of San Francisco's Golden Gate Park and the house features a sunny belvedere perfect for soaking up the sounds of the ocean. A complimentary full breakfast is presented in the solarium. Rooms vary in cost from a small room with a private bath to the spacious Rose and Empire rooms, which have fireplaces and other cozy trappings. In any case, the decor you're apt to find includes patterned wallpaper and an antique bed. ~ 407 Cliff Street; 831-427-2609, 800-427-2609, fax 831-427-2710; www.cliff crestinn.com. MODERATE.

Shops sell everything from baubles to bikinis. Then there are the ultimate entertainments: a slow-circling Ferris wheel with chairs suspended high above the beach; antique merry-go-round, a whirl of mirrors and flashing color; a funicular whose brightly painted cars reflect the sun; rides with names that instantaneously evoke childhood memories— bumper cars, tilt-a-whirl, haunted castle; and that soaring symbol of amusement parks everywhere, the roller coaster. Closed December and most nonsummer weekdays. ~ 400 Beach Street; 831-423-5590; www.beachboardwalk.com.

Of the major beaches extending along the Santa Cruz waterfront, **Santa Cruz Beach** is the most popular, most crowded, and most famous. All for a very simple reason: the Santa Cruz Boardwalk, with its amusement park and restaurants, runs the length of the sand, and the Santa Cruz Municipal Pier anchors one end of the beach. This, then, is the place to come for crowds and excitement. Facilities at Santa Cruz Beach include restrooms, showers, seasonal lifeguard, volleyball, restaurants, and groceries. ~ Located along Beach Street; access from the Municipal Wharf and along the Boardwalk; 831-429-5747.

ALL ABOARD!

During the summer you can climb aboard the full-size Santa Cruz, Big Trees and Pacific Railway for a scenic eight-mile journey from the Santa Cruz boardwalk to the hillside town of Felton. In Felton you can catch the area's locomotive superstar, the **Roaring Camp & Big Trees Pacific Railroad**. This vintage steam engine whistles through redwood stands en route to Bear Mountain. Passengers are invited to picnic on the mountain, hike the area, then return on a later train. ~ Graham Hill Road, Felton; 831-335-4400; www.roaringcamp.com.

After cruising the Boardwalk and tanning on the beach, head across downtown to the **Santa Cruz Mission**, a half-scale replica of the 1791 structure. Closed Monday. ~ To get there from the Boardwalk, follow Beach Street to Riverside Avenue and make a right over the bridge. At San Lorenzo Boulevard, turn right and then left on Ocean Street. Turn left on Water Street. At the top of the hill turn right onto Emmet Street. The mission is at the corner of Emmet and High streets; 831-426-5686.

From Santa Cruz, coastal Route 1 turns to freeway as it speeds past the beach towns of Capitola and Aptos in a freeway stretch that gets you to Watsonville in

SANTA CRUZ REDWOODS SIDETRIP

For a hawk's-eye view of the coast and a close-up look into the redwood forest, head off on Highway 9 from downtown Santa Cruz up into the mountains.

A short way up the windy road you will come to **Henry Cowell Redwoods State Park**. An 1800-acre park on the San Lorenzo River with 18 miles of hiking trails, picnic areas, a mini-museum, a bookstore, restrooms, and showers, it's a favorite among locals. It features a short nature trail (three-quarter-mile loop) through a redwood forest. One of the goliaths here measures 285 feet; there are also stands of Douglas fir and madrone. Day-use fee, $5. ~ 831-335-4598.

▲ There are 111 sites in a campground on Graham Hill Road three miles from the park center; $14 to $16 per night; information, 831-438-2396.

Continuing up Route 9, you will pass through Felton, Ben Lomond, and Boulder Creek. These rustic towns don't offer much, but they do house numerous antique stores and crafts shops. There is also one rather marvelous spot—the **Felton covered bridge**. To find it, turn right off Route 9 onto Graham Hill Road in Felton and then right again onto Covered Bridge Road. A wood-plank span with a sagging shingle roof, the structure dates from 1892. Appropriately, it's set in a secluded spot along the San Lorenzo River.

HIKING

There are hikes for everyone along the 60 miles of trails in Big Basin Redwoods State Park. **Redwood Trail** is a half-mile self-guiding nature trail easy enough for the entire family. On the other extreme is the **Berry Creek–Sunset Loop Trail**, a ten-mile trek through the most beautiful scenery in the park. Follow Redwood Trail, then pick up **Skyline-to-the-Sea Trail**, which will run into Berry Creek Trail. This trek climaxes at Lower and Upper Berry Creek Falls, which tumble more than 50 feet over sandstone cliffs. Return along Sunset Trail for the afternoon vistas to complete the six-hour journey.

Once in Boulder Creek, leave Route 9 and pick up Route 236, an even narrower and more sinuous thoroughfare. This road leads into **Big Basin Redwoods State Park**. California's oldest state park, this 18,000-acre expanse reaches from the ocean to a 2300-foot elevation. Within that domain are 2000-year-old redwoods, a sandy beach, 88 miles of hiking trails, 20 to 30 miles of mountain-biking trails, and a host of facilities. You'll also find Homo sapiens in tents, black-tailed deer, coyotes, bobcats, raccoons, and salamanders inhabiting the area, as well as over 250 bird species that either live here or drop by. It's highly recommended that you do also. There are picnic areas, a mini-museum, a snack bar, a grocery, a gift shop, restrooms, and showers. Day-use fee, $5. ~ Located at 21600 Big Basin Way (Route 236), nine miles north of Boulder Creek; 831-338-8860. ▲ 🚶 🚴 🏇 There are 183 designated sites plus several hike-in sites; $16 per night. Also, four-person tent cabins are available for $49 per night; call 800-874-8368 for reservations. (Two especially recommended campsites near park headquarters are the Blooms Creek and Huckleberry campgrounds.)

a hurry. Popular with visitors for decades, **Capitola** is a well-known resort community. Seafood restaurants line its shore and boutiques flourish within blocks of the beach. It's also a great place for families because of the adjacent facilities and a coastline that is well protected for water sports.

For a more enjoyable drive from Capitola to Watsonville, take the Larkin Valley and San Andreas Road exit off Route 1 just outside of Santa Cruz and follow **San Andreas Road**. This rural side trip carries you past miles of farmland before rejoining Route 1 near Watsonville. Follow San Andreas Road, which tunnels through forest, then opens into rich agricultural acres. Intricately tilled fields roll down to the sea and edge up to the foot of the mountains. The entire stretch of coastline is flanked by high sand dunes, a wild and exotic counterpoint to the furrowed fields nearby.

Along San Andreas Road is the park turn off for **Manresa Uplands State Beach**. Here you'll find a strip of white sand bookended by blufftop homes. Popular with surfers, it provides a sweeping view of Monterey Bay. A bit more removed than other nearby beaches, Manresa nevertheless can be quite popular on summer afternoons. Facilities include restrooms, lifeguards (in summer), picnic tables, fire pits, and showers. There are 64 walk-in tent sites in Manresa Uplands Campground next to the beach.

Located a little farther south on San Andreas Road is the marked turn off for **Sunset State Beach**, where over three miles of beach and sand dunes create one of the area's prettiest parks. There are bluffs and meadows behind the beach as

Santa Cruz to Carmel

well as Monterey pines and cypress trees. This 324-acre park is a popular spot for fishing. Surfing is also done here but the break is powerful—exercise caution. But remember, there's more fog here and farther south than in the Santa Cruz area. There are picnic areas, restrooms, and showers. Camping is permitted in 90 sites; each beach has a day-use fee of $5 (one fee covers both beaches); 831-763-7062. Camping at each beach costs $13 to $16 per night; a hiker/biker camp is available ($2 per person). Call 800-444-7275 for reservations.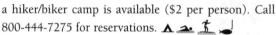

When you get to the end of San Andreas Road, follow Beach Street east into **Watsonville**, where you will meet up with Route 1 again. Central to the surrounding farm community, Watsonville is the world's strawberry-growing capital. It's also rich in **Victorian houses**, which you can tour with a printed guide available from the **Chamber of Commerce**. ~ 444 Main Street, Watsonville; 831-724-3900.

Walk down Main Street and you're liable to hear more people speaking Spanish than English. Mexican gentleman in cowboy hats relax in the town's landscaped plaza and Hispanic school kids play around the bandstand. Set in the heart of Pajaro ("Bird") Valley, Watsonville is a major source of apples, mushrooms, lettuce, and cut flowers.

Testament to this agricultural bounty are the roadside produce stands along Route 1 as you proceed south toward **Moss Landing**, a weather-beaten fishing harbor. With its antique stores, one-lane bridge, brightly painted boats, and unpainted fish market, the town has a warm personality. There is one eyesore, however—a huge power plant with twin smokestacks that stand out like two sentinels of an occupying army. Otherwise the place is enchanting, particularly nearby

Elkhorn Slough National Estuarine Research Reserve, a 1400-acre world of salt marshes and tidal flats. Within this delicate environment live some 400 species of invertebrates, 80 species of fish, and 300 species of birds (among them red-shouldered hawks, peregrine falcons, and acorn woodpeckers) as well as harbor seals, oysters, and clams. Guided tours are available on the weekend. To get to the visitors center from Route 1, follow Dolan Road for three miles, go left on Elkhorn Road, and proceed two more miles. Closed Monday and Tuesday. Admission. ~ 1700 Elkhorn Road, Watsonville; 831-728-2822; www.elkhornslough.org, e-mail esf@elkhorn slough.org.

by the way...

WORLD'S BEST SAND

Washed down the Salinas River, then turned to beach by the bay's surf and piled into dunes by the coastal wind, the sand along the east shore of Monterey Bay is exceptionally soft and fine. These qualities make it desirable for beach reconstruction projects throughout California and all around the Pacific Rim. Once the largest dune system on the West Coast, reaching several miles inland, the sand hills have been mined and exported until only vestiges remain.

Next in this parade of small towns is **Castroville**, "Artichoke Center of the World." Proud of its product, this community of a little over 5000 people has made that alien-looking pod its central image. There's an Artichoke Inn, several "Artichoke" restaurants and cafés, and even a giant artichoke near the center of town. So plan on enjoying at least one helping of deep-fried artichokes on your way through.

To the south lies a cluster of towns—Marina, Sand City, and Seaside—that probably represent the sand capitals of the world. The entire area rests on a sand dune that measures up to 300 feet in depth, and extends ten miles along the coast and as much as eight miles inland. From here you can trace a course into Monterey along wind-tilled rows of sand.

From Castroville, Route 1 passes through more flat agricultural land as it crosses the wide mouth of the Salinas River and angles toward the ocean. The highway finally meets the shore six miles to the south at the bedroom community of Marina, where the main attraction is **Marina State Beach**. The tall, fluffy sand dunes at this 170-acre park are unreal. They're part of a giant dune covering 50 square miles throughout the

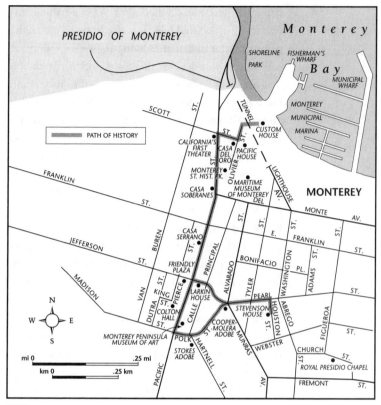

Monterey

area. A boardwalk takes you through the sand to the beach and gives you an up-close view of the unique vegetation. There are marvelous views of Monterey here, plus a chance to fish or sunbathe. It is also the perfect place to try out hang gliding with tandem rides for first-time gliders and hang-gliding rentals for the more experienced. Swimming is allowed, though rip tides do occur. Regarding surfing, there's a great beach break in summer but it's dangerous in winter. The only facilities are restrooms and a snack bar. ~ Route 1; 831-384-7695; e-mail nbeaches@mbay.net. Nine more miles along the fast four-lane highway will bring you into the Monterey metro area.

Over two million travelers visit the Monterey area every year. Little wonder. Its rocky coast fringed with cypress forests, its hills dotted with palatial homes—the area is unusually beautiful. In **Monterey** itself are historic homes, an old Spanish presidio, Fisherman's Wharf, and Cannery Row. Set in a natural amphitheater of forested hills, it is also home to one of the richest marine sanctuaries along the entire California coast. Little wonder that this town, with a population that numbers 32,000 people, has served as inspiration for Robert Louis Stevenson and John Steinbeck. With a downtown district that reflects small-town America and a waterfront that once supported a rich fishing and canning industry, Monterey remains one of the most vital spots on the Central Coast.

For a tour of Monterey Peninsula, exit Route 1 at Del Monte Avenue, which leads past Monterey State Beach and into the heart of the historic district. On your right, you'll pass **Municipal Wharf #2**, all that remains from the heyday of Monterey's fishing fleet. Here broad-hulled boats still beat at their moorings while land-lubbing anglers cast from pierside. Gulls perch along the handrails, sea lions bark from beneath the pilings, and pelicans work the waterfront. On one side is the dilapidated warehouse of a long-defunct freezer company. At the end of the dock, fish companies still operate. It's a primal place of cranes and pulleys, forklifts, and conveyor belts. There are ice boxes and old packing crates scattered hither-thither, exuding the romance and stench of the industry. ~ Located at the foot of Figueroa Street.

Del Monte Avenue continues to **Monterey State Historic Park**. History in Monterey is a precious commodity that in most cases has been carefully preserved.

ROMANTIC DINING

Small and personalized with an understated elegance is the most fitting way to describe **Fresh Cream**. Its light green and gray walls are decorated with French prints and leaded glass. One wall is floor-to-ceiling windows that provide a great view of the bay. Service is excellent and the menu, printed daily, numbers among the finest on the Central Coast. On a given night you might choose from beef tournedos in Madeira sauce, sautéed veal loin, blackened ahi tuna, duckling in black currant sauce, and rack of lamb. That's not even mentioning the appetizers, which are outstanding, or the desserts, which should be outlawed. Four stars. Dinner only. ~ Heritage Harbor, Pacific and Scott streets; 831-375-9798; www.freshcream.com, e-mail dining@freshcream.com. ULTRA-DELUXE.

Ancient adobe houses and Spanish-style buildings are
so commonplace that some have been converted into
shops and restaurants. In the **Maritime Museum of
Monterey** you'll find model ships, a World War II exhibit, and a two-story-tall rotating lighthouse lens.
Closed Monday. Admission. ~ 5 Custom House Plaza;
831-375-2553, fax 831-655-3054; www.mntmh.org.

Many of Monterey's historic buildings can be seen—
and in most cases toured—along the two-mile **Path of
History**. The best place to begin is the **Custom House**
(c. 1827) across from Fisherman's Wharf. In 1846, Commodore Sloat raised the American flag here, claiming
California for the United States. Today the stone and
adobe building houses displays from an 1830s-era
cargo ship. ~ 1 Custom House Plaza.

Across the plaza rises **Pacific House** (c. 1847), a
two-story balconied adobe with a luxurious courtyard.
The exhibits inside trace California's history from
American Indian days to the advent of Spanish settlers
and American pioneers. ~ 10 Custom House Plaza; 831-
649-7118, fax 831-647-6236; www.mbay.net/~mshp,
e-mail mshp@mbay.net.

Just behind Pacific House sits **Casa
del Oro**, a tiny white 1840s adobe that
now houses the Joseph Boston Store, an
old-fashioned mercantile shop selling
Early American items. Closed Monday
through Wednesday. ~ Olivier and Scott
streets; 831-649-3364. Diagonally across
the intersection on Olivier Street behind
an office complex stands the **Whaling Station**, an adobe with a balcony from which the early
whalers spotted their migrating bounty.

California's First Theater, a block up the street, is
still used to stage 19th-century melodramas that are per-
formed by America's oldest continually operating theater troupe. The theater is undergoing renovations; call
ahead for information. ~ Scott and Pacific streets;
831-375-4916.

A left on Pacific Street leads to **Casa Soberanes**, a
Monterey-style house with red-tile roof and second-

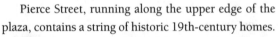

HISTORIC NIGHTS

Located in the downtown district, **Merritt House Inn** is not only an overnight resting place but also a stopping point along Monterey's "Path of History." Part of this lovely inn rests in a vintage 1830 adobe home. Accommodations in the old house (three lavish suites) and the adjoining modern (with 22 guest rooms) are furnished with hardwood period pieces and feature vaulted ceilings, fireplaces, and balconies. The garden abounds with magnolia, fig, pepper, and olive trees. Continental breakfast is served. ~ 386 Pacific Street, Monterey; 831-646-9686, 800-541-5599, fax 831-646-5392; www.merritthouse inn.com, e-mail info@merritthouseinn.com. DELUXE TO ULTRA-DELUXE.

story balcony. Completed in the 1840s, this impressive structure was built by a warden at the Custom House. ~ 6 Pacific Street; 831-649-7118. **Casa Serrano** (c. 1843) contains wrought-iron decorations over its narrow windows. Once home to a blind Spanish teacher, it is now open for touring only on weekends. For more information contact the Monterey History and Art Association. ~ 412 Pacific Street; 831-372-2608; www.mntmh.org.

Pierce Street, running along the upper edge of the plaza, contains a string of historic 19th-century homes.

A JOLT OF JAVA

Need a little pick-me-up after a hard day of sightseeing? Enjoy a cuppa java in a coffee shop quite unlike any you've ever visited before. At **Plume's Coffee** they grind the beans for each cup and brew it individually. So that your own special cup of coffee is not mistakenly served to someone else, you pick up your order under a picture of, say, a waterfall or sunset. Plume's also serves cheesecake, fruit tarts, custard eclairs, and other sweet treats from the best bakeries in the area. ~ 400 Alvarado Street; 831-373-4526. BUDGET.

Colton Hall, site of California's 1849 constitutional convention, displays memorabilia from that critical event. The squat granite **Old Jail** next door, with wrought-iron bars across the windows, dates back to the same era. ~ Pacific Street at Jefferson and Madison streets.

After exploring the plaza, turn left onto Madison Street from Pacific Street, then left again along Calle Principal to one of the town's most famous homes, the **Larkin House**. Designed in 1834 by Thomas Larkin, it is now a house museum filled with period pieces. Admission. ~ 510 Calle Principal; 831-649-7118, fax 831-647-6236.

A right on Jefferson Street and another quick right on Polk takes you past a cluster of revered historic houses, including the **Cooper-Molera Adobe** with its 19th-century museum and a "historic garden" of herbs and vegetables of the Mexican era. Visit by guided tour (call for information). Admission. ~ 525 Polk Street; 831-649-7118.

Backtrack along Polk Street to the five-way inter-section, take a soft right onto Pearl Street, walk a few short blocks, then turn right on Houston Street to the **Stevenson House**, Robert Louis Stevenson's residence for several months in 1879. In addition to its period furniture and Early California decor, the house features personal belongings, original manuscripts, and first editions, all of which can be viewed on a guided tour (call for tour information). Admission. ~ 530 Houston Street; 831-649-7118.

Nearby spreads **Friendly Plaza**, a tree-shaded park that serves as a focus for several important places. The **Monterey Peninsula Museum of Art** exhibits works and artifacts by early and contemporary California artists. Closed Monday and Tuesday. Admission. ~ 559 Pacific Street; 831-372-7591; www.montereyart.org.

After finishing the Path of History, return to the Custom House. Jutting out over the water at the north edge of Monterey State Historic Park, **Fisherman's Wharf**, like its San Francisco namesake, has been transmogrified into what the travel industry thinks tour-ists think a fishing pier should look like. Something was lost in the translation. Few fishing boats operate from the wharf these days; several charter companies sponsor glass-bot-tom boat tours and whale-watching expeditions. Other-wise the waterfront haven is just one more mall, a macadam

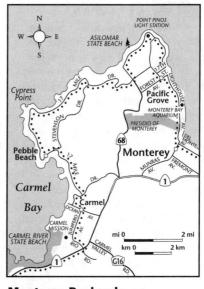

Monterey Peninsula

corridor lined on either side with shops. There are ersatz art galleries, shops vending candy apples and personalized mugs, plus a school of seafood restaurants. A few outdoor fish markets still sell live crabs, lobsters, and squid, but the symbol of the place is the hurdy-gurdy man with performing monkey who greets you at the entrance.

KAYAKING

To experience the thrill of sea kayaking on Monterey Bay, stop by **Adventures by the Sea**. They have 150 double and single kayaks for rent. A two-and-a-half-hour tour is led by a marine biologist who tells the history of Cannery Row. ~ 299 Cannery Row; 831-372-1807; www.adventuresbythesea.com.

Actually this is only the most recent in the wharf's long series of role changes. The dock was built in 1846 to serve cargo schooners dealing in hides. Within a decade the whaling industry took it over, followed finally by Italian fishermen catching salmon, cod, and mackerel. During the Cannery Row era of the '30s, the sardine industry played a vital part in the life of the wharf. Today all that has given way to a bizarre form of public nostalgia.

The **Royal Presidio Chapel** is a graceful expression of the 18th-century town. Decorative molding adorns the facade of the old adobe church while the towering belfry, rising along one side, makes the structure asymmetrical. Heavy wooden doors lead to a long, narrow chapel hung with dusty oil paintings. This was the mission that Father Junípero Serra founded in 1770, just before moving his congregation a few miles south to Carmel. ~ 550 Church Street.

CRUISING WITH CETACEANS

Whale watching along the Central Coast offers a chance to see the amazing giants of the sea from mid-June to September and mid-December to mid-March. For a close look at these migrating mammals and other marine life—sea lions, seals, otters, sea birds—catch a cruise with **Randy's Fishing Trips**. They can accommodate up to 68 people, and the two-hour trip is fully narrated by a marine biologist. ~ Fisherman's Wharf; 831-372-7440; www.randysfishingtrips.com. Also offering glimpses of blue whales, humpbacks, and dolphins from aboard their 65-foot vessel is **Monterey Sport Fishing and Whalewatching**. Trips last about three hours, and sonar equipment is used to help locate whales. ~ 96 Old Fisherman's Wharf #1; 831-372-2203; www.montereybay whalecruise.com.

Behind the wheel again, from Del Monte Avenue, turn north (right) on Pacific Street, which becomes Lighthouse Avenue. On your left, the **Presidio of Monterey** sits on a hill near the northwest corner of town. Established as a fort by the Spanish in 1792, it currently serves as a foreign language institute for the military. There are cannons banked in a hillside, marking the site of

Fort Mervine, built by the Americans in 1846. The Presidio is also the site of an ancient Costanoan Indian village and burial ground. And a granite monument at the corner of Pacific and Artillery streets marks the spot where in 1602 the Spanish celebrated the first Catholic mass in California. In addition to historic points, the Presidio grounds enjoy marvelous views of Monterey. You can look down upon the town, then scan along the bay's curving horizon. ~ Pacific and Artillery streets; 831-242-5555, fax 831-242-5464; www.dli-army.mil.

The same visionary who turned Fisherman's Wharf into a sightseeing attraction appears responsible for the resurrection of **Cannery Row**, located along Foam and Wave streets a few blocks northwest of Lighthouse Avenue, the main thoroughfare. Made famous by John Steinbeck's feisty novels *Cannery Row* and *Sweet Thursday*, this oceanfront strip has been transformed into a neighborhood of wax museums and dainty antique shops. As Steinbeck remarked upon returning to the old sardine canning center, "They fish for tourists now."

Cannery Row of yore was an unappealing collection of corrugated warehouses, dilapidated stores, seedy hotels, and gaudy whorehouses. There were about 30 canneries, 100 fishing boats, and 4000 workers populating the place. The odor was horrible, but for several decades the sardine industry breathed life into the Monterey economy. The business died when the fish ran out just before *Cannery Row* was published in 1945. Before the entire oceanfront strip was developed in the early 1980s, you could still capture a sense of the old Cannery Row. A few weather-beaten factories remained. Rust stained their ribbed sides, windows were punched, and roofs had settled to an inward curve. In places, the

MONTEREY'S MAGNIFICENT MUSIC FESTIVAL

With a budget of $6700 and a roster of world-renowned artists such as Louis Armstrong, Gerry Mulligan, Billie Holiday, and Max Roach, the **Monterey Jazz Festival** came to fruition in 1958. Still going strong, the three-day event begins in mid-September on a Friday night and continues through Sunday, providing 13 hours of music a day, as well as the requisite souvenirs and international food. The festival now concentrates on jazz and boasts over 500 musicians on seven stages playing to 40,000 fans. Big names include Lou Rawls, Dave Brubeck, and Diane Reeves. ~ 925-275-9255, fax 925-866-9597; www.montereyjazzfestival.org.

A Little Monterey History

As early as 1542, Juan Rodríguez Cabrillo, a Portuguese explorer in Spanish employ, set anchor off Pacific Grove. Then in 1602 Sebastian Vizcaíno came upon the peninsula again and told a whale of a fish story, grandly exaggerating the size and amenities of Monterey Bay.

His account proved so distorted that Gaspar de Portolá, leading an overland expedition in 1769, failed to recognize the harbor. When Father Junípero Serra joined him in a second journey the next year, they realized that this gentle curve was Vizcaíno's deep port. Serra established California's second mission in Monterey, then moved it a few miles in 1771 to create the Carmel Mission.

By the 1820s, Yankee merchant ships were plying Monterey waters, trading for hides and tallow. This early American presence, brilliantly described in Richard Henry Dana's classic *Two Years Before the Mast*, climaxed in 1846 during the Mexican War. Commodore John Sloat seized the town for the United States. By 1849, the adobe town of Monterey had become the site of California's constitutional convention.

Monterey became a tourist mecca during the 1880s. Of course the old Spanish capital also developed into a major fishing and canning region during the early 20th century. But despite industrialization and real estate development, the most important elements of the Monterey Peninsula—its foaming ocean, open sky, and wooded heights—are still here, waiting for the traveler with a bold eye and robust imagination.

stone pilings of old loading docks still stood, haunted by sea gulls. Now only tourists and memories remain.

At the other end of the Row, Steinbeck aficionados will find a few literary settings. **Kalisa's La Ida Café**, a funky restaurant and ice-cream parlor with Friday-night belly-dancing, still retains its same tumbledown appearance. This is also the home of Steinbeck's birthday party every February 27, now a recognized town holiday. ~ 851 Cannery Row; 831-644-9316. In the middle you'll encounter the scene of the malling of Cannery Row. Old warehouses were renovated into shopping centers, new buildings rose up, and the entire area experienced a face lift.

Perched on the waterfront at the end of Cannery Row is the **Monterey Bay Aquarium**, a state-of-the-art museum that re-creates the natural habitat of local sea life. Monterey Bay is one of the world's biggest submarine canyons, deeper than the Grand Canyon. At the aquarium you'll encounter about 100 display tanks representing the wealth of underwater life that inhabits this mineral-rich valley. For instance, the Monterey Bay Habitat, a 90-foot-long glass enclosure, portrays the local submarine world complete with sharks, brilliant reef fish, and creosote-oozing pilings. The Outer Bay Galleries contains, among other delights, a million-gallon tank filled with all kinds of native Californian species, including green turtles and jellyfish. Another aquarium contains a mature kelp forest crowded with fish. Don't forget the hands-on exhibits where you can pet bat rays and hold crabs, starfish, and sea cucumbers. Also be sure to wander upstairs to where the special exhibits are housed. One of the favorites is the jellyfish exhibit. Together the many displays and exhibitions make it one of the world's great aquariums. Don't miss the deep-sea video images beamed six to eight times a day live from research vessels in undersea Monterey Canyon, two miles beneath the surface of the bay. Admission. ~ Cannery Row and David Avenue; 831-648-4888, 800-756-3737, fax 831-644-7560; www.montereybayaquarium.org.

Lighthouse Avenue continues to the diminutive town of **Pacific Grove** on the northern tip of Monterey Peninsula; a more scenic way to get there is to pick up Ocean View Boulevard near Cannery Row and follow the road as it winds along Pacific Grove's surf-washed shores. Covering just 1700 acres, Pacific Grove is a quiet town with a lightly developed waterfront that offers paths that lead for miles along a rock-crusted shore. Costanoan Indians once dove for abalone in these waters. By the 19th century, Pacific Grove had become a religious retreat. Methodist Episcopal ministers pitched a tent city

The quaint, shingled **Red House Café** is a cozy place to join the locals for breakfast, lunch, or dinner. Morning brings Belgian waffles, frittatas, and croissant sandwiches, while the later meals feature oven-roasted chicken sandwiches and warm eggplant with fontina cheese. The freshly squeezed lemonade, which comes with free refills, is delicious. No dinner on Sunday. Closed Monday. ~ 662 Lighthouse Avenue, Pacific Grove; 831-643-1060, fax 831-372-1738. BUDGET TO MODERATE.

Author in Love

John Steinbeck was not the first author to find enchantment in the sights and sounds of Monterey Bay—and an ambivalent reception from its people. In 1880 Robert Louis Stevenson, the vivacious but sickly Scottish writer, sailed the Atlantic and traveled overland across the continent to visit his wife-to-be Fanny Osbourne in Monterey. Writing for local newspapers, depending in part upon the kindness of strangers for sustenance, the fragile wanderer fell in love with Fanny and Monterey both. From the surrounding countryside he drew inspiration for some of his most famous books, including *Treasure Island*. But local landlords refused to rent to him because of a temporary but unsightly skin disease he had contracted on his journey to California, and gossipmongers manufactured a scandal out of his relationship with Fanny, who was ten years older than Stevenson and not yet divorced from her former husband. Four months later, when her divorce became final, Fanny promptly married Stevenson, and the blissful couple moved away from Monterey, never to return.

and decreed that "bathing suits shall be provided with double crotches or with skirts of ample size to cover the buttocks." The town was dry until 1969. Given the fish canneries in Monterey and teetotalers in this nearby town, local folks called the area "Carmel-by-the-Sea, Monterey-by-the-Smell, and Pacific Grove-by-God."

Today Pacific Grove is a sleepy residential area decorated with Victorians, brown-shingle houses, and clapboard ocean cottages. The waterfront drive goes past rocky beaches to **Point Pinos Lighthouse**. When this beacon first flashed in 1855, it burned sperm whale oil. Little has changed except the introduction of electricity; this is the only early lighthouse along the entire California coast to be preserved in its original condition. The U.S. Coast Guard still uses it to guide ships; it is the oldest continually operating lighthouse on the West Coast. Two rooms have been restored to look as they did in Victorian times, and there's a short history of Emily Fish, the woman who ran the lighthouse in the 19th century. Open for self-guided tours from Thursday through Sunday. ~ North of Lighthouse Avenue; 831-648-3116.

Also of interest is the **Pacific Grove Museum of Natural History**, an excellent small museum with exhibits on native animals and early peoples, and a touch gallery for children. Closed Monday. ~ Central and Forest avenues; 831-648-3116; www.pgmuseum.org. The **ivy-cloaked cottage** (not open to the public) at 147 11th Street is where John Steinbeck lived and wrote *Tortilla Flat*, *In Dubious Battle*, and *Of Mice and Men*. **Gosby House Inn** is a century-old Victorian mansion decorated in period antiques. ~ 643 Lighthouse Avenue. Next door, the **Hart Mansion**, now a restaurant called Robert's White House on Lighthouse, is an elaborate old Victorian house. Closed Monday. ~ 649 Lighthouse Avenue; 831-375-9626.

Ocean View Boulevard curves around the point of the peninsula and turns south to become Sunset Drive as it continues along the sea to **Asilomar State Beach**.

SHOPPER'S DELIGHT

From designer fashions to gourmet cookware, the 50 shops at **American Tin Cannery Premium Outlets** are a shopper's paradise. A good place to look for luggage, books, shoes, housewares, and linens, this renovated two-story complex has a variety of outlet stores. If you're looking for bargains in the Monterey area, don't miss this gem. ~ 125 Ocean View Boulevard; 831-372-1442, fax 831-372-5707; www.premiumoutlets.com.

Here sand dunes mantled with ice plant front a wave-lashed shore. There are tidepools galore, plus beaches for picnics and trails that lead through the rolling dunes. The best surfing here is just off the main sandy beach. Since northern and southern currents run together here, the waters teem with marine life. Swimming is not recommended. If you're into algae, you'll

Butterfly Town, U.S.A.

Pacific Grove's major claim to fame lies in an area several blocks inland: around George Washington Park on Melrose Street and in a grove at 1073 Lighthouse Avenue. Every mid-October, brilliant orange-and-black **monarch butterflies** migrate to Pacific Grove, remaining until mid-March. Some arrive from several hundred miles away to breed amid the cypress and oak trees. At night they cling to one another, curtaining the branches in clusters that sometimes number over a thousand. Then, at first light, they come to life, fluttering around the groves in a frenzy of wings and color.

want to know that over 200 species congregate in the ocean here. Another species—Homo sapiens—gathers at the park's multifaceted conference center.

From Sunset Drive in Pacific Grove, **17 Mile Drive** leads to Pebble Beach, one of America's most lavish communities. This place is so exclusive that the rich charge a fee to anyone wishing to drive around admiring their homes. No wonder they're rich.

Galling as the gate fee might be, this is an extraordinary region that must not be missed. The road winds through pine groves down to a wind-combed beach. There are miles of rolling dunes tufted with sea vegetation. (The oceanfront can be as cool and damp as it is beautiful, so carry a sweater or jacket, or better yet, both.)

Among the first spots you'll encounter is **Spanish Bay**, where Juan Gaspar de Portolá camped during his 1769 expedition up the California coast. (The picnic area here is a choice place to spread a feast.) At **Point Joe**, converging ocean currents create a wild frothing sea that has drawn several ships to their doom. **Seal Rock** and **Bird Rock**, true to their nomenclature, are carpeted with sea lions, harbor and leopard seals, cormorants, brown pelicans, and gulls. Throughout this thriving 17 Mile Drive area are black-tail deer, sooty shearwaters, sea otters, and, during migration periods, California gray whales.

There are crescent beaches and granite headlands as well as vista points for scanning the coast. You'll also pass the **Lone Cypress**, the solitary tree on a rocky point that has become as symbolic of Northern California as perhaps the Golden Gate Bridge. The **private homes** en route are mansions, exquisite affairs fashioned from marble and fine hardwoods. Some appear like stone fortresses, others seem made solely of glass. They range from American Colonial to futuristic and were designed by noted architects like Bernard Maybeck, Julia Morgan, and Willis Polk. This is also home to sev-

GOLF

For golfers, visiting the Monterey Peninsula is tantamount to arriving in heaven. Pebble Beach is home to the annual AT&T National Pro-Am Golf Championship. Several courses rank among the top in the nation. With stunning views of the rugged coastline, **Pebble Beach Golf Course** is the most renowned. Three U.S. Open tournaments have been held here. The 7th, 8th, 17th, and 18th holes are legendary, highly difficult ocean holes. **Spyglass Hill Golf Course,** known as one of the toughest courses in the nation, has six of its holes by the ocean. Be prepared: Green fees at Pebble Beach and Spyglass are steep! ~ 800-654-9300.

eral of the world's most renowned **golf courses**—
Spyglass Hill, Cypress Point, and Pebble Beach—
where the AT&T National Pro-Am Championship
takes place each year. More than the designer
homes and their celebrity residents, these
courses have made Pebble Beach a place fabled for wealth and beauty.

The best part of the drive lies along
the coast between the Pacific Grove and
Carmel gates. Along the backside of 17
Mile Drive, where it loops up into Del
Monte Forest, there are marvelous
views of Monterey Bay and the San
Gabilan Mountains. Here also is
Huckleberry Hill, a forest of Mon-
terey and Bishop pine freckled
with bushes.

The south gate to 17 Mile
Drive lets you out on San Antonio Avenue in Carmel-by-the-
Sea. Follow this road to the intersection with Ocean Avenue
and you're at the municipal **Carmel Beach**, a snowy strand shadowed by cypress trees.

From Carmel Beach, take
Ocean Avenue east to Junipero
Avenue, turn right and drive south
until Junipero angles eastward to
become Rio Road. Here you'll
find Mission San Carlos Bor-

TOR HOUSE AND HAWK TOWER

Poet Robinson Jeffers' Tor
House and Hawk Tower seem drawn from
another place and time—perhaps a
Scottish headland in the 19th century. In
fact, the poet modeled the house after an
English-style barn and built the 40-foot-
high garret with walls six feet thick in the
fashion of an Irish tower. Completed
during the 1920s, the granite structures
include porthole windows that Jeffers
salvaged from a shipwreck. One-hour
tours of the house and tower are
conducted on Friday and Saturday by
reservation. No children under 12 years
allowed. Admission. ~ 26304 Ocean View
Avenue, Carmel; for information and
reservations, call 831-624-1813.

romeo del Rio Carmelo, better known as **Carmel Mission Basilica**. Established by Father Junípero Serra, this
mission is one of California's most remarkable. If the
holiness holds no appeal, there's the aesthetic sense of
the place. Dating back to 1793, its Old World beauty
captivates and confounds. The courtyards are alive with
flowers and birds. The adobe buildings have been dusted
with time—their eaves are hunchbacked, the tile roofs
coated in moss. The basilica is a vaulted-ceiling affair
adorned with old oil paintings and wooden statues of
Christ; its walls are lime plaster made from burnt sea-

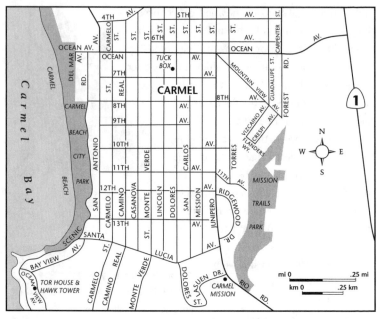

Carmel

shells. The exterior is topped with a Moorish tower and 11 bells. Junípero Serra lies buried in the sanctuary, his grave marked with a stone plaque. There are also museum rooms demonstrating early California life—a kitchen with stone hearth and rudimentary tools, the state's first library (complete with water-stained bibles), and the cell where Father Serra died, its bed a slab of wood with a single blanket and no mattress. Close by, in the cemetery beside the basilica, several thousand American Indians are buried. Admission. ~ Located on Rio Road just off Route 1; 831-624-3600.

South of the mission stretches **Carmel River State Beach**, a sandy corridor at the foot of Carmel Bay. This beach would be more attractive were it not upstaged by Point Lobos, its remarkable neighbor to the south. Nevertheless, there's a sandy beach here as well as a view of the surrounding hills. The chief feature is the bird refuge

THE SECRET FOREST

A secret that local residents have long withheld from visitors is **Mission Trails Park**. No signs will direct you here, so watch for an entrance at the corner of Mountain View and Crespi avenues. Within this forest preserve are miles of hiking trails. They wind across footbridges, through redwood groves, and past meadows of wildflowers en route to Carmel Mission. There are ocean vistas, deer grazing the hillsides, and an arboretum seeded with native California plants.

along the river. The marshes offer opportunities to view willets, sandpipers, pelicans, hawks, and kingfishers, plus an occasional Canadian snow goose. The beach has restrooms. ~ Carmelo Road; 831-624-4909.

Just two miles south of Carmel lies **Point Lobos State Reserve**, an incomparable natural area of rocky headlands and placid coves. In a region packed with uncommonly beautiful scenery, this park stands out as something special. A 1225-acre reserve, only 456 acres of which are above water, it contains over 300 species of plants and more than 250 species of animals and birds. This is a perfect place to study sea otters, harbor seals, and sea lions. During migrating season in mid-winter and mid-spring, gray whales cruise the coast. Along with Pebble Beach, Point Lobos is the only spot in the world where Monterey cypresses, those ghostly, wind-gnarled coastal trees, still survive in the wild. There are 80-foot-high kelp forests offshore, popular with scuba divers who know the reserve as one of the most fascinating places on the coast. The park features hillside crow's nests from which to gaze out along Carmel Bay.

A BAR WITH A VIEW

Possibly the prettiest place you'll ever indulge the spirits in is the **Lobos Lounge** at Highlands Inn. An entire wall of this leather-armchair-and-marble-table establishment is plate glass. And the picture on the other side of those panes is classic Carmel—rocky shoreline fringed with cypress trees and lashed by passionate waves. If that's not entertainment enough, there's a piano bar during the week and a three-piece jazz combo on weekends. ~ Route 1, about four miles south of Carmel; 831-620-1234, fax 831-626-1574; www.highlands-inn.com.

CARMEL'S OLDEST CARAVANSARY

The **Pine Inn** is not only Carmel's oldest hostelry, but also one of the town's most reasonably priced places. This 49-room hotel dates back to 1889 and still possesses the charm that has drawn visitors for decades. The lobby is a fashionable affair with red brocade settees, marbletop tables, and a brick fireplace. The less expensive accommodations are small but do have the antique reproductions, private baths, televisions, and phones common to all the rooms. Each room has decorative touches of both Europe and the Far East. Rather than a country inn, this is a full-service hotel with restaurant and bar downstairs as well as room service. ~ Ocean Avenue between Lincoln and Monte Verde streets; 831-624-3851, 800-228-3851, fax 831-624-3030; www.pine-inn.com. DELUXE TO ULTRA-DELUXE.

Every tidepool is a miniature aquarium pulsing with color and sea life. The water is clear as sky. Offshore rise sea stacks, their rocky bases ringed with mussels, their domes crowned by sea birds. The point also has a patina of history. Before Westerners arrived, the American Indians gathered mussels and abalone here. Later Point Lobos was a whaling station and an abalone cannery. Reservations to dive are necessary and can be made up to two months in advance by phone or e-mail. There are picnic areas and restrooms. Dogs are not allowed. Parking fee, $5. ~ Located on Route 1 about three miles south of Carmel; 831-624-4909, e-mail pt-lobos@mbay.net. 🏃 🚲 ⛵ 🚶

Rio Road quickly returns you to Route 1, which is no longer the traffic-packed divided freeway skirting Monterey Bay but a narrow two-lane blacktop highway wending its way among the evergreens.

*F*rom Point Lobos, the highway hugs the coastline as it snakes south toward Big Sur. Like Route 1 north of San Francisco, this is one of America's great stretches

SHOPPING WITH THE RICH AND FAMOUS

In Carmel, shopping seems to be the raison d'être. If ever an entire town was dressed to look like a boutique, this was the one. Its shops are stylish and expensive. The major shopping strip is along Ocean Avenue between Mission and Monte Verde streets, but the best stores generally are situated on the side streets. The **Doud Arcade** is a mall featuring artisan shops. Here you'll find leather merchants, potters, and jewelers. ~ Ocean Avenue between San Carlos and Dolores streets.

Most of the artists who made Carmel famous have long since departed, but the city still maintains a wealth of art galleries. While many are not even worth browsing, others are outstanding. The **Carmel Art Association Galleries**, owned and operated by artists, offer paintings and sculpture by local figures. ~ Dolores Street between 5th and 6th avenues; 408-624-6176; www.carmelart.org. Also of note is the **Chapman Gallery**, which features local artists as well. Closed Monday except by appointment. ~ 7th Avenue between Mission and San Carlos streets; 831-626-1766; www.chapmangallery.com.

Carmel is recognized as an international center for photographers. Two of the nation's most famous—Ansel Adams and Edward Weston—lived here. The **Weston Gallery** displays prints by both men, as well as works by other 19th- and 20th-century photographers. Closed Monday. ~ 6th Avenue between Dolores and Lincoln streets; 831-624-4453; www.westongallery.com. At **Photography West Gallery**, too, Weston and Adams are represented, as are Imogen Cunningham and Brett Weston. ~ Dolores Street between Ocean and 7th avenues; 831-625-1587.

TEA AND SCONES, ANYONE?

The **Tuck Box** is a dollhouselike creation with a swirl roof and curved chimney straight out of a fairy tale. *The* place to go for afternoon tea, the prim and tiny dining room also serves breakfast and lunch. The outdoor seating is particularly picturesque. During the noon meal there are omelettes, sandwiches, shrimp salad, and Welsh rarebit. Tea includes scones, muffins, and homemade pies. Jams and scone mix are available for purchase. ~ Dolores Street between Ocean and 7th avenues, Carmel; 831-624-6365; www.tuckbox.com. BUDGET TO MODERATE.

of roadway. Situated between the Santa Lucia Mountains and the Pacific, Route 1 courses about 30 miles from Carmel to Big Sur, then spirals farther south along the coast toward San Luis Obispo and Los Angeles.

The **Big Sur** district is where the Santa Lucia Mountains encounter the Pacific. Backed by the challenging Ventana Wilderness, the region is marked by sharp coastal cliffs and unbelievable scenery. Though it's hard to conceive, Big Sur may be even more beautiful than the other sections of the Central Coast.

Along Route 1, each turnout provides another glimpse into a magic-lantern world. Here the glass pictures a beach crusted with rocks, there a wave-wracked cliff or pocket of tidepools. The canyons are narrow and precipitous, while the headlands are so close to the surf they seem like beached whales. Trees are broken and blasted before the wind. The houses, though millionaire affairs, appear inconsequential against the backdrop of ocean and stone.

The broad swath of white sand at **Garrapata State Park** is particularly favored by local people, some of whom use it as a nude beach. Easily accessible, it's nevertheless off the beaten tourist path, making an ideal hideaway for picnicking and skinny dipping. There are no facilities. A rough current and lack of lifeguards make swimming inadvisable. The park entrance is along Route 1 about seven miles south of Carmel. Watch for the curving beach from the highway; stop at the parking lot just north of the Garrapata Creek

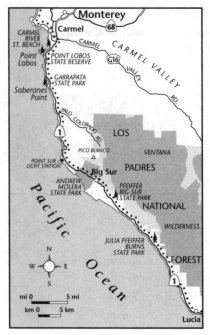

Carmel to Lucia

bridge. From here a path leads down to the beach. ~ 831-667-2315. 🏃 🛶 🚣 🏄

At **Soberanes Point**, eight miles south of Carmel, hiking trails lead out along the headlands. Here you can stand on a rock shelf directly above the ocean and gaze back at the encroaching hills.

Past the Point, the road straightens and the landscape broadens as it approaches the wall of mountains that separates the Monterey area from the Big Sur Valley. Ice plant and wildflowers tumble down the slopes to the rugged shoreline on your right. Scenic vistas look down on rocky coves sheltered from the surf that blasts and boils just beyond.

Thirteen miles south of Carmel you'll traverse **Rocky Point Bridge**, the first in a series of arched bridges that span deep canyons falling into the Pacific. Soon after comes the longer and more famous **Bixby Creek Bridge**, which stretches 714 feet from one cliff to another across an infernal chasm 260 feet above the ocean. Local legend cites it incorrectly as the world's longest concrete arch span. With fluted hills in the background and a fluffy beach below, it may, however, be the world's prettiest.

Route 1 climbs along **Hurricane Point**, a promontory blessed with sweeping views and cursed by lashing winds, and descends toward **Little Sur Beach**. This sandy crescent is bounded by a shallow lagoon. There are dunes and lofty hills all around, as well as shore birds. Another lengthy beach leads to **Point Sur Light Station**, set on a volcanic headland. This solitary sentinel dates back to 1889. The only way to visit this lighthouse is by a guided tour. Tours run Saturday at 10 a.m. and 2 p.m., and Sunday at 10 a.m. There are additional tours in summer, including a moonlight tour. Admission. ~ 831-625-4419.

An adventurer's hideaway beginning two miles south of Point Sur, 4800-acre **Andrew Molera State Park** rises from the sea to a 3455-foot elevation. It features three miles of beach and over 15 miles of hiking trails. The forests range from cottonwood to oak to redwood, while the wildlife includes mule deer, bobcat, harbor seals, and gray whales. Big Sur River rumbles through the landscape and surfers try the breaks on the beach. The only thing missing is a road: this is a hiker's oasis, its natural areas accessible only by heel and toe. The wilderness rewards are well worth the shoe leather. This is the only place in Big Sur where you can ride a horse; you can hire one from a concessionaire and ride on designated trails. Also check out Captain Cooper's

The Last Primeval Valley

Big Sur received its name from early Spanish settlers, who called the wilderness south of Carmel *El País Grande del Sur*, "the big country to the south." But this redwood eden protected by steep mountains, deep gorges, and wind-blasted coastal cliffs remained roadless and uninhabited through almost two centuries of Spanish and Mexican colonization.

It was not until the late 19th century that the federal government encouraged settlement in Big Sur Valley by opening it up to homesteaders, who could buy a 160-acre parcel of paradise for only $200. There was a catch, however. Since no road reached Big Sur, pioneers in the area were limited to those possessions they could carry on muleback through the rugged Santa Lucia Mountains or manufacture from local wood and stone.

Although California politicians proposed building a road to Big Sur as early as 1897, construction of the road that is now Route 1 did not begin until 1921. Fog, landslides, and high winds slowed progress on the ambitious project, which involved the building of 32 bridges across the chasms that had kept Big Sur Valley inaccessible for centuries. The road between Carmel and San Simeon was finally completed in 1938.

Later the area became a rural retreat, an artists' colony, and a mecca for unconventional writers such as Jack Kerouac, Henry Miller, and Richard Brautigan. Today the artists are being displaced by soaring land values, while the region is gaining increased popularity among visitors. It's not difficult to understand why as you cruise along its knife-edge cliffs and timbered mountainsides.

BIG SUR BACKCOUNTRY

sidetrips

For an intriguing excursion into those hills, head about six miles up **Palo Colorado Road**, which intersects with Route 1 a couple of miles south of Garrapata Creek. Though paved, this country road is one lane. The corridor tunnels through an arcade of redwoods past log cabins and rustic homes. If you're feeling adventurous, follow the twisting eight-mile road to its terminus at Los Padres National Forest.

For another incredible sidetrip, you can follow **Coast Road** for about 11 miles up into the Santa Lucia Mountains. Climbing along narrow ledges then corkscrewing deep into overgrown canyons, the road carries you past exquisite views of forests and mountain ridges. There are hawk's-eye vistas of the Pacific, the rolling Big Sur countryside, and Pico Blanco, a 3709-foot lime-rich peak. This is the old coast road, the principal thoroughfare before Route 1 was completed in the 1930s. Take heed: It is so curvy it makes Route 1 seem a desert straightaway; it is also entirely unpaved, narrow, rutted, and impassable in wet weather. But oh those views! Coast Road begins at Bixby Bridge and rejoins Route 1 at Andrew Molera State Park.

Cabin, a late-19th-century pioneer log cabin. Toilets are the only facilities. There are 24 hike-in sites (tents only); $7 per night. Though primitive facilities are the only amenities, water is available. Day-use fee, $5. ~ 831-667-2315.

by the way... The Pfeiffer family, whose descendents donated Big Sur's main parks to the state for conservation, arrived as homesteaders in the 1880s. In the early 1900s, widow Florence Brown married into the family. It was her idea to charge $3 a head for bed and breakfast at her husband's ranch, creating Big Sur's first tourist accommodations. When word reached San Francisco that travelers could at last get food and lodging in the pristine redwood valley to the south, the city's elite started heading to the Pfeiffer Ranch—a real adventure considering that the carriage trip from Monterey along a makeshift primitive road took ten hours—about the same time it would take to walk! To make Big Sur's development as a tourist destination more feasible, the Pfeiffer clan became active in persuading legislators to authorize the construction of Route 1 from Carmel to San Simeon.

Then the road enters the six-mile-long **Big Sur River Valley**, where a rural community of about 1000 people lives, and stretches the length of the valley. Lacking a town center, it consists of houses and a few stores dotted along the Big Sur River. The highway travels several miles inland from the ocean with its dank fog and punishing winds, and the weather often runs 20 degrees warmer.

One of California's southernmost coastal redwood parks, 800-acre **Pfeiffer Big Sur State**

Park is very popular, particularly in summer. With cottages, a restaurant, a grocery, a gift shop, picnic areas, restrooms, showers, and a laundromat on the premises, it's quite developed. However, nature still retains a toehold in these parts: the Big Sur River overflows with trout and salmon (fishing is prohibited, however), Pfeiffer Falls tumbles through a fern-banked canyon, and the park serves as the major trailhead leading to Ventana Wilderness. There are 218 sites for both tents and RVs (no hookups); $13 to $20 per night. For reservations, call 800-444-7275. Day-use fee, $5. ~ 831-667-2315.

For breakfast or lunch, try the outdoor **Café Kevah**, located on the lower level of Nepenthe Restaurant. They serve standard breakfast fare—waffles, omelettes—and lunch dishes with a Mexican twist. Their homemade pastries are the perfect companions for an afternoon gazing out at the ocean. Closed in January and February and when it rains. ~ 831-667-2344; www.nepenthebigsur.com. BUDGET TO MODERATE.

Just south of Pfeiffer Big Sur State Park is the valley's largest concentration of inns, restaurants, and services. Route 1 continues south past Big Sur's leading resorts, the Ventana Inn and Post Ranch Inn. The ocean comes into view in the distance as you approach the legendary Nepenthe Restaurant. Nearby is the **Henry Miller Memorial Library**. Miller lived here from 1947 until 1964, writing *Big Sur and the Oranges of Hieronymus Bosch*, *Plexus*, and *Nexus* during his residence. There's not much to the library, but somehow the

SLEEPING UNDER THE REDWOODS

For a variety of accommodations, consider **Big Sur Campground and Cabins**. Set in a redwood grove along the Big Sur River, this 13-acre facility has campsites, tent cabins, and A-frames. Camping out on the grounds costs $27 for two people and includes access to hot showers, a laundry, a store, a basketball and volleyball court, and a playground. The tent cabins, $55 per night, consist of woodframe skeletons with canvas roofs. They come with beds, bedding, and towels and share a bath house. The tent cabins are closed during the rainy season. The "cabins" along the river are actually mobile homes, neatly furnished but rather sterile. More intimate are the A-frame cabins with Franklin stoves and sleeping lofts. The newer modular units include pine floors with bedrooms as well as kitchens and private baths. ~ Route 1; 831-667-2322. BUDGET TO DELUXE.

HEAVENLY DINING

Cielo, part of the extraordinary complex that includes a prestigious inn, is one of the region's most elegant dining places. Resting on a hillside overlooking the mountains and sea, it's a perfect spot for a special meal. At lunch you'll be served salad, steak sandwiches, or fresh pasta, either inside the wood-paneled dining room, or alfresco on a sweeping veranda. For dinner you can start with oysters on the half shell or steamed artichoke, then proceed to such entrées as quail, rack of lamb, salmon, filet mignon, or fresh fish grilled over oak. ~ Route 1; 831-667-2331, 800-628-6500, fax 831-667-2419; www.ventanainn.com. DELUXE TO ULTRA-DELUXE.

unassuming nature of the place befits its candid subject. Occupying a small woodframe house donated by Miller's friend Emil White, the museum contains volumes from the novelist's library as well as his evocative artworks. The library's caretakers claim that it contains every word of Miller's published work; most of his books are also for sale. Closed Tuesday. ~ Route 1 about a mile south of Ventana Inn; 831-667-2574; www.henrymiller.org.

About a mile south past the entrance to Pfeiffer Big Sur State Park, turn right onto Sycamore Canyon Road (unmarked), which leads downhill two miles to **Pfeiffer Beach**. Of Big Sur's many wonders, this may be the most exotic. It's a sandy beach littered with boulders and bisected by a meandering stream. Behind the strand rise high bluffs that mark the terminus of a narrow gorge. Just offshore loom rock formations into which the sea has carved tunnels and arches. Little wonder poet Robinson Jeffers chose this haunting spot for his primal poem "Give Your Heart to the Hawks." The only

THE INN BEYOND BIG SUR

About 20 miles south of Big Sur, on the edge of an ocean cliff, sits **Lucia Lodge**. Perched 500 feet above a cobalt blue bay are ten cozy rooms offering otherworldly views along a curving sweep of shoreline. All of the accommodations are rustic and sufficiently removed from the highway to create a sense of natural living in this extraordinary landscape. An adjacent restaurant and store make it a convenient hideaway. (Call ahead to make sure the restaurant is open for all meals; it has been known to close early without notice.) ~ 62400 Route 1, Lucia; 831-667-2391. ULTRA-DELUXE.

facilities are toilets. Day-use fee, $5. ~ 831-667-2315.

Beyond Big Sur Valley, the highway twists crazily along the coastline with its dark granite cliffs plunging hundreds of feet down to the crashing surf. About ten miles farther south lies **Julia Pfeiffer Burns State Park**, a 3762-acre extravaganza that extends from the ocean to about 1500 feet elevation and is bisected by Route 1. The central park area sits in a redwood canyon with a stream that feeds through a steep defile into the ocean. Backdropped by sharp hills in a kind of natural amphitheater, it's an enchanting glade. A path leads beneath the highway to a spectacular vista point where 80-foot-high McWay Waterfall plunges into the ocean. Another path, one-and-eight-tenths miles north of the park entrance, descends from the highway to an isolated beach near Partington Cove that has been declared an underwater park (permit required). There are picnic areas and restrooms, as well as two hike-in environmental campsites for tents only ($11 to $14 per night with an eight-person maximum; reservations are required—call 800-444-7275). ~ 831-667-2315.

SHOP BIG SUR

Set in a circular wooden structure resembling an oversized wine cask (and made from old water tanks) is one of Big Sur's best known art centers. The **Coast Gallery** is justifiably famous for its displays of arts and crafts by local artists. There are lithographs by novelist Henry Miller as well as paintings, sculptures, ceramics, woodwork, handmade candles, and blown glass by Northern California craftspeople. An adjoining shop features a wide selection of Miller's books. ~ Route 1, 33 miles south of Carmel; 831-667-2301, fax 831-667-2303; www.coast galleries.com.

At this point you're midway between Carmel and San Simeon, publisher William Randolph Hearst's fabled castle. Ahead lie another 40 miles of look-but-don't-touch coastline guarded by formidable rock cliffs and punctuated only by the tiny villages of Lucia and Gorda. Here and there, rough unpaved roads turn inland, providing access to dozens of secluded campgrounds in the backcountry of Los Padres National Forest. Drive as far as you want past one eye-boggling vista after another; then turn back on Route 1 to the Monterey Peninsula, or continue on to another strange and exotic land—Southern California.

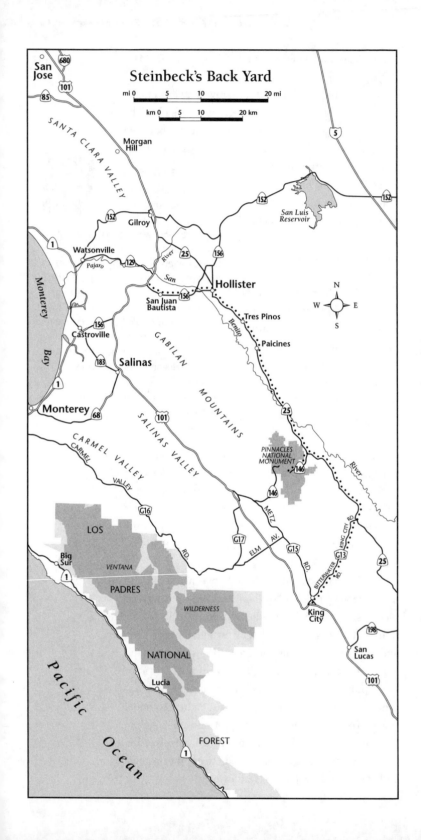

4 STEINBECK'S BACK YARD

Route 25 to Pinnacles National Monument

Along the entire 650-mile length of the earthquake fault known as the San Andreas Rift, there is no other geological area quite as spectacular as the Gabilan Mountains. Though only about 1200 feet tall and not vast in area, these mountains are unique. The entire mountain range is actually one half of the huge 23-million-year-old volcano that spewed the volcanic lava, pumice, and solidified ash that made the giant rock formations known as the Pinnacles. The volcano was sliced in two by shifting along the San Andreas Fault; the other half is 195 miles to the south in Los Angeles County!

The Gabilan Mountains wall off the east side of the Salinas Valley, the vast farming valley immortalized by John Steinbeck in his greatest novels, including *The Grapes of Wrath* and *East of Eden*. Route 101, the busy freeway that links San Francisco with Los Angeles, traces the west side of the Gabilans, but the east side is another story. Route 25, a two-lane asphalt highway running right on top of the San Andreas Rift, is a favorite motorcyclists' ride on weekends; during the week, it's one of California's most traffic-free stretches of road. Although this drive is only 73 miles from end to end, plan to make an all-day trip of it, allowing plenty of time to explore the strange maze of Pinnacles National Monument.

Route 25 exits Route 101 at the strawberry-growing town of Watsonville (see Chapter 3), but we recommend adding an extra dimension to your tour by continuing down the freeway for another nine miles to the San Juan Bautista exit. After you visit this placid village quaint with Spanish Colonial heritage, Route 156 will continue for eight miles and then join Route 25.

Anyone who has read Frank Norris' muckraking novel about the railroads, *The Octopus*, will recognize

HIDDEN HACIENDA ▬▬▬▬▬▬▬▬▬▬

Accommodations are scarce in San Juan Bautista, but **Posada de San Juan** offers comfortable rooms within walking distance of the mission and 3rd Street's shops and restaurants. The 33 rooms are equipped with wetbars, whirlpool bathtubs, and gas fireplaces. Decorated in a hacienda style, this inn reflects the distinctly Mexican flavor of San Juan Bautista. ~ 310 4th Street; 831-623-4030, fax 831-623-2378. MODERATE.

GARDEN DELIGHTS

Jardines de San Juan is recommended as much for its garden as its food. In addition to the usual tacos, burritos, and flautas, weekend specials get fancy: Veracruz-style red snapper served with crema on a bed of rice, or pollos borrachos cooked in sherry with ham and sausage. ~ 115 3rd Street; 831-623-4466; www.jardinesrestaurant.com, e-mail jardines@hollinet.com. BUDGET TO MODERATE.

San Juan Bautista and its thick, cool adobe church. And anyone who remembers the climax to Hitchcock's *Vertigo* will instantly picture the mission, even though the bell tower that Jimmy Stewart struggled to climb was a Hollywood addition that you won't see at the real San Juan Bautista.

Founded in 1797, the mission was completed in 1812. Today it ranks among California's most enchanting locales. With its colonnade and sagging crossbeams, the mission has the musty scent of history. The old monastery and church consist of a low-slung building roofed in Spanish tile and topped with a belfry. ~ 831-623-4528.

Our favorite spot in this most favored town is **Mission Cemetery**, a small plot bounded by a stone fence and overlooking valley and mountains. It's difficult to believe that over 4300 American Indians are buried here in unmarked graves. The few recognizable resting places are memorialized with wooden crosses and circling enclosures of stone. Shade trees cool the yard. Just below the cemetery, symbolic perhaps of change and mortality, are the old Spanish Road (*El Camino Real*) and the San Andreas Fault.

The mission rests on a grassy square facing **Plaza Hall**. Originally a dormitory for unwed American Indian women, this structure was rebuilt in 1868 and used as a meeting place and private residence. Peek inside its shuttered windows or tour the building and encounter a child's room cluttered with old dolls, a sitting room dominated by a baby grand piano, and other rooms containing period furniture.

Behind the hall sits a **blacksmith shop**, filled now with wagon wheels, oxen yokes, and the "San Juan Eagle," a hook-and-ladder wagon drawn by a ten-man firefighting crew back in 1869. Nearby **Plaza Stable** houses an impressive collection of buggies and carriages.

The **Plaza Hotel** (admission) lines another side of the square. Consisting of several adobe structures, the earliest built in 1814, the place once served as a stagecoach stop. Today its myriad rooms contain historic exhibits and 1860s-era furnishings. Similarly, the **Castro-Breen Adobe** located next door is decorated with Spanish-style pieces. Owned by a Mexican general and later by Donner Party survivors, it is a window into California frontier life. Nearby are **San Juan Jail**, an oversized outhouse constructed in 1870, and the **settler's cabin**, a rough log cabin built by East Coast pioneers in the 1830s or 1840s.

CHICANO CULTURE ON STAGE

A block away from San Juan Bautista State Historic Park is **El Teatro Campesino**, an excellent resident theater group. This Latino company originated *Zoot Suit*, an important and provocative play that was eventually filmed as a movie. With a penetrating sense of Mexican-American history and an unsettling awareness of contemporary Latino social roles, it is a modern expression of the vigor and spirit of this old Spanish town. From May to September summer productions are held in its theater; the Christmas show is staged in Mission San Juan Bautista. ~ 705 4th Street; 831-623-2444; www.elteatro campesino.com.

All are part of the **state historic park** that comprises San Juan Bautista. Like the plaza, 3rd Street is lined with 19th-century stores and houses. Here, amid porticoed haciendas and crumbling adobe, are antique stores, a bakery, restaurants, and other shops. Admission. ~ 831-623-4881.

Heading east from San Juan Bautista on Route 156, across flat farm country where the air is redolent with the scents of onions and mint, you'll come to the ranching and fruit-growing center of **Hollister**. Named for local rancher William Hollister, the first person to herd sheep across the American West to California in the 1850s, this prosperous town of 15,000 contains an impressive number of new car dealerships but little of interest to pleasure travelers. Route 156 meets Route 25 in the center of town. Turn right and follow Route 25 south through an older residential area with red-tile roofs and make a left turn at the south end of town

Other Uses for Grapes

While you'll see plenty of grapevines in the Hollister and Tres Pinos area, there are none of the wineries and tasting rooms found in other Northern California grape-growing regions. Some of these unidentified vineyards produce table grapes or juice grapes, while others grow generic wine grapes that will be blended with "noble" varietals in a 1-to-3 ratio to make less expensive mass-market wines. Most of the grapes from these vineyards, however, become raisins. The state's winemakers got into the raisin business to avoid bankruptcy during Prohibition; today California produces 90 percent of the raisins in the United States—and two-thirds of the entire world supply.

onto Sunny Slope Road, then right a couple of blocks later on McCray Street. Hollister is a larger community than first impression suggests. You'll pass shopping malls and sprawling modern housing developments, then fruit orchards interspersed with more new housing developments being built behind walls that shelter them from the highway. And at last you'll find yourself out on the open road.

Expect a fair amount of traffic on the road until you reach the upscale bedroom community of Tres Pinos, eight miles to the south. A sign warns that the handful of businesses in Tres Pinos—such as **Flapjacks Country Cafe**—are the last services for 76 miles. The restaurant serves up a bountiful breakfast and lunch. Look for steak sandwiches and chef salads. ~ 6851 Airline Highway, Tres Pinos; 831-628-3499.

CAMPING AT PINNACLES

Pinnacles National Monument is open for day use only and has no campground. The only place in the area to spend the night is **Pinnacles Campground Inc.**, a private facility just outside the park's east entrance. There are 103 tent sites and 36 RV sites with hookups for electricity but not water, which is in limited supply. Hot showers, a swimming pool, and campground activities are perks. A two-night stay may be required. Fees are $7 a night plus $4 for electric hookup and 50¢ per person lodging tax. Travelers with dogs (which are discouraged—they can't go on trails in the park and can't be left alone in the campground) must also pay a $10 leash deposit. Reservations recommended. Campfires are usually prohibited. ~ 2400 Route 146, Paicines; 831-389-4462; www.pinncamp.com.

At the southwest end of the Hollister Valley, just past the Bolado Park Golf Club, the road approaches gently rolling grassy hills, and soon steeper hills covered with piñon and juniper as it passes the San Benito County Fairgrounds, where there's a big rodeo arena.

On the left is a vineyard; then more vineyards appear on both sides of the road, filling the long, narrow valley. This is the tiny community of **Paicines**, with no roadside businesses and so few houses that it could easily be mistaken for a farm.

As you cross the San Benito River, very steep grassy hills close in. Here and there a farmhouse stands in the distance, often made more noticeable by tall, pointed cypress trees growing around it. Continuing to climb, you move into a mixed semi-arid forest interspersed with meadows where horses graze.

STEINBECK FESTIVAL

event Every August, Salinas' historical roots come alive with the four-day **Steinbeck Festival**. It's an intellectual event filled with walking tours, guest lectures, film screenings, and plays. Steinbeck aficionados will love the in-depth look at the area and bygone era. ~ National Steinbeck Center, 1 Main Street; 831-796-3828; www.steinbeck.org.

At last, 32 miles south of Hollister is the turnoff on the right to **Pinnacles National Monument**, the sole spectacular sightseeing highlight along Route 25. At the heart of the Gabilan Mountains, these sharp, dramatic volcanic crags, massive monolithic spires, sheer-walled canyons, and talus passages were shaped by mil-

sidetrips

JOHN STEINBECK'S HOME TOWN

It is fitting that you either begin or end your tour of "Steinbeck's Back Yard" at the center of the author's hometown, **Salinas**. The commercial center for the farmlands of the Salinas Valley, this community would boast nothing more interesting than produce warehouses, except that this is where the California novelist, who won the Nobel Prize for Literature in 1962, was born and raised. Steinbeck's best works were set in the Salinas Valley and around Monterey Bay, and today you can't go far in this part of the state without being reminded that you're in Steinbeck Country. For this reason alone, Salinas has achieved the status of a must-see for literary types.

Throughout his career, John Steinbeck had a love-hate relationship with the people of the Salinas Valley and Monterey Bay, the settings of his greatest novels. It started in 1938 with the publication of *The Grapes of Wrath*, which attacked the exploitation of farm workers in the valley. Steinbeck wrote, "The vilification of me out here from the large landowners and bankers is pretty bad. I'm frightened at the rolling might of this damned thing. It is completely out of hand—I mean a kind of hysteria about the book is growing that is not healthy."

Returning after World War II, Steinbeck bought a house in Monterey, but no one would rent him an office for writing, and he suffered continual harassment. He wrote, "This isn't my country any more. And it won't be until I am dead. It makes me very sad." He retreated to New York and there wrote *Cannery Row*, in which he immortalized Monterey. He returned again in 1948, this time to Pacific Grove, where he researched and wrote *East of Eden*, the book he considered his masterpiece. But once more local residents found the book objectionable. "Don't think for a moment that you will ever be forgiven for being what they call 'different,'" he wrote to an aspiring Salinas writer. "You won't! I still have not been forgiven. . . .The librarians at the Salinas Public Library, who had known my folks, remarked that it was lucky my parents were dead so that they did not have to suffer this shame."

John Steinbeck bade farewell to "Steinbeck Country" for the last time in 1960—an event recounted in his memoir *Travels with Charley In Search of America*—and died in New York eight years later. True to his prophecy, his ashes returned to be buried in Salinas, and 30 years later the town dedicated the National Steinbeck Center in his honor.

The **National Steinbeck Center**, opened in 1998 in the heart of Oldtown Salinas (the historic district surrounding the town plaza), houses photographic, multimedia, and interactive exhibits about the life and work of John Steinbeck. It also contains a research library (open by appointment) of more than 45,000 manuscripts, first editions, newspaper and magazine articles, reviews, letters, TV and radio scripts, theses, and historic photographs by and about Steinbeck and his works, along with art exhibitions depicting the Salinas Valley. One wing explores the history of Salinas Valley with hands-on displays and artifacts. Admission. ~ 1 Main Street; 831-796-3833; www.steinbeck.org.

The **Steinbeck House**, in which the author grew up, is located two blocks from the museum. It now serves as a restaurant, open for lunch Monday through Saturday. Reservations are essential and should be made a week in advance. ~ 132 Central Avenue; 831-424-2735. MODERATE.

John Steinbeck's grave is in the Garden of Memories cemetery—an irony in view of Steinbeck's observation that he would be welcome in Salinas "only when I am delivered in a pine box." ~ 768 Abbot Street.

lions of years of erosion, faulting, and tectonic plate movement.

In President Clinton's January 2000 proclamation expanding the park's area by 50 percent, the area is characterized as "one of the most complex and fascinating geological terrains in North America."

Sheer spires and solitary minarets vault 1200 feet from the canyon floor. These towering peaks challenge day hikers and technical rock climbers alike. Rock-

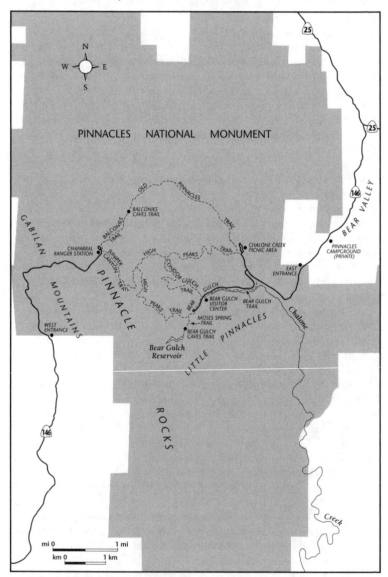

Pinnacles National Monument

climbing is a major activity here in fall (it's too hot in summer, and most climbers avoid crowded spring weekends, when the largest numbers of hikers come to experience the profusion of wildflowers). There are caves to explore (which are subject to seasonal closures due to flooding and "bat protection"), and more than 30 miles of trails leading through the remnants of the volcano.

Another road leads to the national monument on the west side, off Route 101. Don't be fooled by the fact that both entrance roads are designated as Route 146; they are connected by foot trails but not by a vehicle road. Because busy Route 101 carries hundreds of times as much traffic as lonely Route 25, one might think there would be more visitors on the west side; but the road on the west side is much more difficult—winding and narrow, in some places a single lane—so about the same number of people visit each side of the park.

The most popular time to visit is March through May, when the wildflowers bloom, or autumn; summer brings stifling heat to the area and winter carries rain. It's best to visit during the week if possible, since on weekends the limited parking areas can fill up quickly. In the spring, the park often reaches capacity by noon on weekends, and those who arrive too late are turned away at the gate.

HIKING BEYOND THE ROAD'S END

Most of the scenery at Pinnacles National Monument can only be seen from the more than 30 miles of interconnected hiking trails, which range from easy, near-level walks to strenuous climbs. For first-time visitors to the east side of the park, one of the prettiest trails—and the shadiest—is the **Old Pinnacles Trail**, which starts at the Chalone Creek parking lot and picnic area. It follows the creek for 3.9 miles to Balconies Caves. Half-hidden behind fallen boulders at the edge of the creek, the cave is inaccessible during rainy periods when the water is high.

Another good trail for a first visit, the **Moss Spring Trail**, which starts at the end of the road past the visitors center, is a .7-mile, moderate uphill hike that passes Bear Gulch Caves (closed to the public to protect the resident colony of rare Townsend's big-eared bats) and continues to Bear Gulch Reservoir, a picturesque little lake in a mountain basin surrounded by rocky crags. Wherever you hike in the park, bring durable, loose clothes, much more water than you think you'll need, and flashlights if you plan to explore Balconies Caves.

The east side of the park has an information center, picnic areas, and restrooms. The private campground near the park entrance has a grocery store, but restaurants are way back in Tres Pinos and Hollister. Day-use fee is $5; you may wish to save your receipt, which lets you re-enter either side of the park for the next seven days. ~ 831-389-4485; www.nps.gov/pinn, e-mail pinn_visitor_information@nps.gov. 🏃

by the way... WILDLIFE HAVEN

Wild boar, coyote, gray fox, and bobcat roam the region, while golden eagles, harriers, long-eared owls, and numerous species of hawks glide overhead. Pinnacles National Monument also provides habitat for three species of snake, of which only the western rattlesnake is a hazard to hikers, as well as eight lizard species—all harmless—including the strange-looking coast horned lizard. Amphibians in the park's creeks and reservoirs include the rare red-legged frog, whose status as a threatened species helped inspire the recent expansion of the park to save its watershed from being diverted to irrigate vineyards in the valley below.

*L*eaving Pinnacles, turn right (south) to continue down Route 25 between chaparral-covered slopes on the right and amber horse pastures on the left, backed by rocky arid hills that rise up almost vertically. Soon you're making a slow descent into another golden valley with no buildings in sight. The land grows greener and alfalfa fields appear. The steep hills to the east, with their thick covering of scrub and near-vertical white rockfaces, are privately owned ranchland with few roads. The turnoff for the Laguna Mountain, Condon Peak, and Clear Creek Road, which you'll pass on this stretch of highway, is the only public access road into the hills that can be driven easily in a passenger car.

tips SUCH A DEAL

At Pinnacles, as well as most other National Park units, you can buy a **National Parks Pass** for $50. It's good for free admission to all U.S. national parks and monuments for 12 months and will save you money if you visit several parks in a year. Admission at most of the 27 other National Park units in California is $10; at Yosemite, as well as other major parks like Yellowstone and the Grand Canyon, the entrance fee is $20. For $15 more, you can upgrade to a Golden Eagle Pass and avoid all federal land-use fees.

The best deal the park service offers is the **Golden Age Passport**. Available to people age 62 and older, it costs only $10, is good for free admission and a 50-percent discount on camping fees, and never expires during your lifetime. Unlike the National Parks Pass, you can't get this pass by phone, mail, or the Internet—only in person at a national park or monument.

Rather than staying on Route 25, which continues ten miles farther to the middle of nowhere to join Route 198 midway between San Lucas and Coalinga, it makes more sense to take a right turn on the road to King City. As you climb to the top of the hill, look off to the right and you can see the brown air-pollution haze that hangs over the south end of the Salinas Valley.

Crossing into Monterey County, you'll crest another hill and head down into **King City**, the farm center for the South Salinas Valley, surrounded by various kinds of vegetable fields. With a population of about 7600, King City seems to be made up almost entirely of low-income housing and giant aluminum-sided warehouses for different farming corporations—one, for instance, just for tomatoes. As devoid of charm as it is, driving through this "city" may forever change your understanding of where vegetables come from.

Just past King City, you'll join Route 101 a distance of 60 miles south of San Juan Bautista, where this tour began, and about 135 miles south of San Francisco.

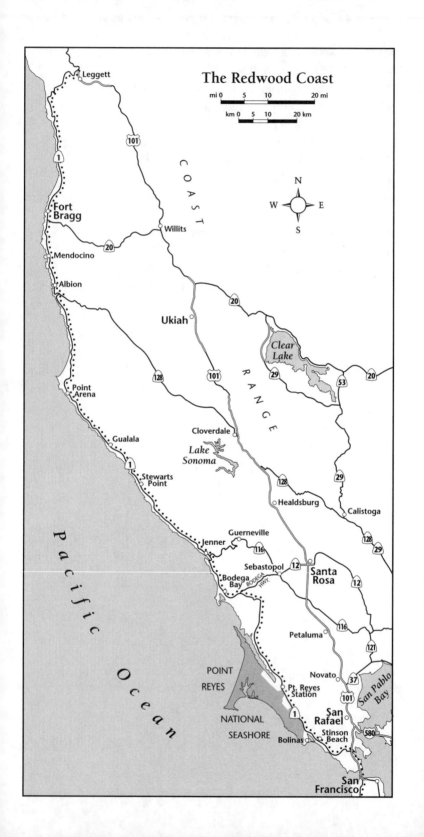

The Redwood Coast

mi 0 5 10   20 mi
km 0 5 10   20 km

N
W — E
S

Leggett

101

1

COAST

Fort
Bragg

Willits

20

Mendocino

Albion

20

Ukiah

Clear
Lake

29

53

20

R
A
N
G
E

128

101

Point
Arena

Gualala

Lake
Sonoma

Cloverdale

Stewarts
Point

128

29

Healdsburg

Calistoga

1

128

29

Guerneville

Jenner

116

Sebastopol

12

Santa
Rosa

Bodega
Bay

BODEGA
HWY.

12

Pacific

Petaluma

116

121

POINT
REYES

Novato

37

Pt. Reyes
Station

101

San Pablo
Bay

Ocean

NATIONAL
SEASHORE

1

San
Rafael

Stinson
Beach

580

Bolinas

San
Francisco

5 THE REDWOOD COAST

Route 1 North from San Francisco

With its wooded sanctuaries and ocean vistas, Route 1 is the quintessential hidden highway—even though it's enjoyed a uniquely legendary status among generations of road-trippers. This 198-mile route starts just over the Golden Gate Bridge from San Francisco and hugs the coastline north to the pretty Victorian town of Mendocino and its lumberjack big brother, Fort Bragg, before winding its way through coastal redwood forest to join Route 101, the main divided highway north from San Francisco. A sinuous road, Route 1 snakes along the seashore, providing a scenic—and slow—alternative to the freeway. In fact, it's so much slower that it's only used by motorists on pleasure trips and residents of the farms and villages along the way. Traffic is generally light on weekdays, even during the height of the summer season; you'll typically see two to four other vehicles on the road at any given time. Weekends are a different story; when the weather is nice, it can be bumper to bumper as thousands of city dwellers simultaneously decide to get back to nature.

PULL OVER— ENJOY THE VIEW

Almost all of Route 1 North is a no-passing zone. Even though traffic is usually light, it tends to bunch up in bumper-to-bumper clusters because area residents, who know the road well, generally drive as if the speed limit were 65 mph (which it isn't), whereas sight-seers—whether because of the fantastic views or the steep dropoffs—often drive half as fast. Both common courtesy and the law require that slower drivers use the paved turnouts provided at wide spots in the road. Locals know where these turnouts are and will often flash their headlights when one is coming up as a reminder to let them pass. If you do, they'll usually wave thanks as they zoom past. If you don't pull over, drivers behind you will grow more irate with each passing mile.

Scenically, the North Coast compares in beauty with any spot on Earth. There are the folded hills and curving beaches of Point Reyes, Sonoma's craggy coast and old Russian fort, plus Mendocino with its vintage towns and spuming shoreline. Along the entire seaboard, civilization appears in the form of fishing villages and logging towns. As a matter of fact, a lot of the prime real estate is saved forever from developers' heavy hands. California's Coastal Commission serves as a watchdog agency protecting the environment. Much of the coast is also preserved in public playgrounds.

Although 200 miles may not sound like much, it takes more than a single day to tour Route 1

North. Plan to spend a full day driving the coast highway to Mendocino, the most atmospheric of several
small towns along the route where you can spend the
night. For day trips, motorists can zip north on Route
101, bypassing Marin County, and shortcut over to the
coast on either of two hidden highways described elsewhere in this book. Route 116 from Sebastopol (see
Chapter 6) follows the Russian River to its mouth at
the little resort town of Jenner, the heart of the Sonoma
Coast, while Route 128 (see Chapter 7) rambles through
the Anderson Valley wine country before descending
to the sea at the mouth of the Navarro River, seven
miles south of Mendocino.

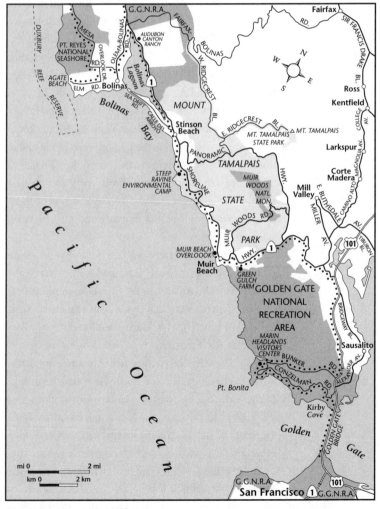

San Francisco to Bolinas

The Golden Horn

The Golden Gate Bridge was one of the engineering marvels of its day when it opened in 1937. Spanning 4200 feet, it has the largest suspension towers ever built—746 feet high—and 220 feet of vessel clearance beneath it.

Contrary to common belief, the Golden Gate (which the bridge spans) got its name three years before the California Gold Rush began. In naming it, explorer John C. Fremont was inspired by the Golden Horn, the name of the harbor entrance at the ancient, fabulously rich Turkish port city of Byzantium.

As frequently photographed as the Golden Gate Bridge, the coast of Marin County consists of rolling ranch lands and spectacular ocean bluffs. It extends from San Francisco Bay to Tomales Bay, offering groves of redwoods, meadows filled with wildflowers, and miles of winding country roads.

An exploration of this vaunted region begins immediately upon crossing the **Golden Gate Bridge** on Route 101. There's a vista point at the far north end of the bridge affording marvelous views back toward San Francisco and out upon the Bay. (If some of your party want to start off with an exhilarating walk across the bridge, drop them off at the vista point on the city side and pick them up here a little later.)

Once across the bridge, an easy detour from Route 101 leads you to a series of beaches and scenic vistas. Take the first exit, Alexander Avenue; then take an immediate left, following the sign back toward San Francisco. Next, bear right at the sign for **Marin Headlands** and follow Conzelman Road. For what is literally a bird's-eye view of the Golden Gate Bridge, go three-tenths of a mile uphill and stop at the first turnout on the left. From here it's a short stroll out and up, past deserted battery fortifications, to a 360° view point sweeping the Pacific and Bay alike. You'll practically be standing on the bridge, with cars careening below and the tops of the twin towers vaulting above you.

To view the Golden Gate Bridge from the opposite vantage point, stop at Kirby Cove, a pocket beach located at the end of a well-marked, one-mile trail from

THE PANORAMIC HIGHWAY

sidetrips   For a spectacular sidetrip through the redwood forest, when Route 1 forks after several miles, turn right on Panoramic Highway toward Muir Woods and Mt. Tamalpais. It's uphill and then down to **Muir Woods National Monument**, a 560-acre park inhabited by Sequoia sempervirens, the coast redwood. Though these forest giants have been known to live over two millennia, most enjoy a mere four-to-eight-century existence. In Muir Woods they reach 240 feet, while farther up the coast they top 350 feet (with roots that delve no deeper than ten feet!). It was designated a national treasure by President Theodore Roosevelt in 1908.

But facts can't convey the feelings inspired by these trees. You have to move among them, walk through Muir's Cathedral Grove where redwoods form a lofty arcade above the narrow trail. It's a forest primeval, casting the deepest, most restful shade imaginable. However, Muir Woods has the double-edged quality of being the redwood forest nearest to San Francisco: It can be horribly crowded. Since silence and solitude are vital to experiencing a redwood forest, plan to visit early or late in the day, and allow time to hike the more remote of the park's six miles of trails. There are also a snack bar, a gift shop, and restrooms. Day-use fee, $3. ~ 415-388-2596, fax 415-389-6957; www.nps.gov/muwo.

Back up on Panoramic Highway, the road continues through **Mt. Tamalpais State Park** en route to Mt. Tamalpais' 2571-foot peak. Mt. Tam, as it is affectionately known, represents one of the Bay Area's most prominent landmarks. Rising dramatically between the Pacific and the Bay, the site was sacred to Indians. Even today some people see in the sloping silhouette of the mountain the sleeping figure of an Indian maiden. So tread lightly up the short trail that leads to the summit. You'll be rewarded with a full-circle view that sweeps across the Bay, along San Francisco's miniature skyline, and out across the Pacific. Contrary to rumor, on a clear day you cannot see forever from Mt. Tam, but you can see north toward Redwood Country and east to the Sierras.

Every year since 1913 a mountain play has been staged in Mt. Tamalpais State Park's amphitheater. Past productions include "West Side Story," "Oliver," and "Bye Bye Birdie." Call 415-383-1100 for dates and times.

event

Spectacularly situated between Mt. Tamalpais and the ocean, 6300-acre Mt. Tamalpais State Park offers everything from mountaintop views to a rocky coastline. More than 50 miles of hiking trails wind past stands of cypress, Douglas fir, Monterey pine, and California laurel. Wildlife abounds. The park's facilities include picnic areas, restrooms, a refreshment stand, and a visitors center (open weekends only); ranger stations are located in various parts of the park. Parking fee, $4. ~ 415-388-2070, fax 415-388-2968. 🚶 🚵 🐎

Continue on Panoramic Highway as it corkscrews down to Stinson Beach. Better yet, take the longer but more spectacular route to Stinson: backtrack along Panoramic to where the fork originally separated from Route 1 (Shoreline Highway). Turn right and head north on Route 1.

Conzelman Road. The cove nestles literally in the shadow of the Golden Gate Bridge. The views from beachside are unreal: gaze up at the bridge's steel lacework or out across the gaping mouth of the Gate. When the fog's away, it's a sunbather's paradise; regardless of the weather, this cove is favored by those who like to fish. There are four campsites for tents only; $20 per night. Reservations are required; 415-561-4304. Closed November through March. ▲🏃🚴🐎⚓🎣

GOLDEN GATE BIRDING

Hawk Hill, the ridge just to the west of the Golden Gate Bridge, attracts birdwatchers by the hundreds in late summer and early fall for the annual hawk migration. Numerous hawk species native to Marin County, from tiny kestrels to red-tailed hawks (the largest hawks in North America) overcome their natural reluctance to fly over water; they take advantage of the strong thermal air currents that rise over the Marin Headlands at that time of year to carry them safely across the Golden Gate on their way to more southerly climes. The hawk migration reaches its peak on the first day of autumn, when as many as 3000 hawks cross the channel in a single day.

Farther along Conzelman Road you will pass a series of increasingly spectacular views of San Francisco. Ahead the road will fall away to reveal a tumbling peninsula, furrowed with hills and marked at its distant tip by a lighthouse. That is **Point Bonita**, a salient far outside the Golden Gate. After proceeding to the point, you can peer back through the interstices of the bridge to the city or turn away from civilization and gaze out on a wind-tousled sea.

Nature writes in big letters around these parts. As you reach the top of the climb, you enter the **Marin Headlands** section of **Golden Gate National Recreation Area**, an otherworldly realm of spuming surf, knife-edge cliffs, and chaparral-coated hillsides. From Point Bonita, follow Field Road, taking a left at the sign for the **Marin Headlands Visitors Center**, where you can pick up maps and information about the area, or make a camping reservation. ~ 415-331-1540, fax 415-331-6963; www.nps.gov/goga.

Bunker Road leads through a long tunnel and out of the Marin

SAVING SEA LIONS

Not far from the Marin Headlands Visitors Center, **California Marine Mammal Center** harbors seals, sea lions, and other marine mammals who have been found injured or orphaned in the ocean and brought here to recuperate. Center workers conduct rescue operations along 600 miles of coastline, returning the animals to the wild after they have gained sufficient strength. ~ Conzelman Road; 415-289-7325; www.tmmc.org.

Headlands. At the end of the lazy loop you'll emerge near an entrance to Route 101. Follow this north a few miles, then pick up Route 1. You'll be on the northern leg of one of the most beautiful roads in America.

It's startling how fast the upscale suburbs of Marin County give way to wild forest as you climb toward the crest of the peninsula. Live oak, evergreens, and eucalyptus trees shade the highway. You can smell the pungent scent of eucalyptus in the air. Expect the climate to be much cooler and breezier on the ocean side of the peninsula than on the bay side. It's common for the ocean side to be fogged in while the bay side enjoys blue skies, and sometimes the fog hangs so low that it seems to spill westward over the ridgeline.

On your descent to the Pacific shore, you'll pass a discreetly marked turnoff leading down to **Green Gulch Farm**, a 115-acre Zen retreat tucked away in a serene coastal valley just above Muir Beach. Soon you'll glimpse the center's orchards and gardens below on your left. Residents follow a rigorous program of work and meditation. There is a temple on the grounds and guests are welcome to tour the organic farm. Sunday is the best day to visit since a special meditation program and speaker is offered then. Closed January. ~ 1601 Shoreline Highway, near Muir Beach; 415-383-3134; www.sfzzc.org, e-mail ggfzc@earthlink.net.

BACK FROM THE BRINK

West Marin County's land conservation policies, dating back to 1907 when a local landowner donated the first 300 acres of Muir Woods to the federal government, have set the standard for forest, wetland, and seacoast preservation. Activists have consistently blocked plans for timber clearcuts, housing tracts, shopping malls, and even a six-lane freeway. Thanks to these efforts, it was announced in 2000 that Marin County is home to America's greatest concentration of northern spotted owls. Ironically, forest product companies quickly used this good news to petition to have the owl removed from the endangered species list—a move that, if successful, would take away one of environmentalists' strongest tools for saving ancient forests.

At the bottom of the hill lies **Muir Beach**, a crescent-shaped cove with a sandy beach; swimming is not advised. Because of its proximity to San Francisco, this semicircular cove is a favorite among city folks as well as local people. It's a good spot for picnicking. The beach is located just off Route 1 on Pacific Way, about 16 miles north of San Francisco; a short drive along a creek brings you to the rather small parking area. It's adequate for weekdays, but on sunny weekends you may find cars parked along the highway for a mile or more beyond the beach road. ~ 415-388-2596, fax 415-389-6957; www. nps.gov/muwo. 🚶 🚲 🐎 🏊 🚣 🎣

Past the Muir Beach turnoff, the highway winds around a high point of land topped by expensive homes with fantastic views and architecture to match. About a mile farther up the road, follow the "vista point" sign to **Muir Beach Overlook**. Here you can walk out along a narrow ridge for a view extending from Bolinas to the coastline south of San Francisco. It's an outstanding place for whale watching in winter. As a matter of fact, this lookout is so well placed it became a site for World War II gun batteries, whose rusty skeletons remain. There are also picnic tables, and this is a popular spot for kite flying.

You have entered a realm that might well be called the Land of a Thousand Views. Until the road descends to the flat expanse of Stinson Beach, it follows a tortuous route poised on the edge of oblivion. Below, precipitous cliffs dive to the sea, while above the road, rock walls edge upward toward Mt. Tamalpais. Around every curve another scene opens to view. Before you, Bolinas is a sweep of land, an arm extended seaward. Behind, the San Francisco skyline falls away into the past. If God built highways, they'd look like this. Watch for wildlife on the rocks offshore, especially the white ones. It's too far away to identify with the naked eye, but binoculars reveal that the rocks are home to colonies of pelicans and other seabirds—which also explains the white coloration.

On a well-marked paved road off Route 1 about one mile south of Stinson Beach is **Steep Ravine Environmental Camp**, a facility designed for nature study. Set on a shelf above the ocean, the camp is bounded on the other side by sharp slopes. Contained within Mt. Tamalpais State Park, it features a small beach and dramatic sea vista. There are six walk-in tent sites ($7 per night) and ten rustic cabins ($34.50 per night).

Reservations required seven months in advance for cabins; 800-444-7275. ▲

On the opposite side of the highway is the parking lot for **Red Rock Beach**, one of the area's most popular nude beaches. Well protected along its flank by steep hillsides, the pocket beach at the foot of the steep trail is wall to wall with sun worshippers on clear weekends. There are no facilities here.

EATING LOCAL AT STINSON BEACH

Stinson Beach sports several restaurants; our favorite is the **Sand Dollar Restaurant**, with facilities for dining indoors or out on the patio. At lunch this informal eatery serves hamburgers and sandwiches. At dinner there are fried prawns, scallops, fresh fish, and pasta; they also serve meat dishes like chicken parmesan and steak. Soup or salad is included, as is homemade garlic bread. With a fireplace and random artwork on the wall, it is a cozy local gathering point. ~ 3458 Route 1, Stinson Beach; 415-868-0434, fax 415-868-8988. MODERATE.

Twenty-three miles north of San Francisco (or 11 miles from the start of Route 1) are the small town of **Stinson Beach** and **Stinson Beach Park**. That broad sandy hook at the bottom of the mountain is one of Northern California's finest strands. Anglers haunt the rocks along one end in pursuit of blenny and lingcod, while birdwatchers are on the lookout for sandpipers, shearwaters, and swallows. Everyone else comes for sand, surf, and sun. Backdropped by rolling hills, this broad, sandy corridor curves for three miles and borders beautiful Bolinas Lagoon. To escape the crowds that congregate here on weekends, stroll up to the north end of the beach. You'll find a narrow sandspit looking out on Bolinas. You still won't have the beach entirely to yourself, but a place this beautiful is worth sharing. There are picnic areas, a

THE COUNTRY INN AT MUIR BEACH

Most folks grumble when the fog sits heavy along the coast. At the **Pelican Inn**, located at the turnoff to Muir Beach, guests consider fog part of the ambience. Damp air and chill winds add a final element to the Old English atmosphere at this seven-chamber bed and breakfast. Set in a Tudor-style building near Muir Beach, the Pelican Inn re-creates 16th-century England. There's a pub downstairs with a dart board on one wall and a fox-hunting scene on another. The dining room serves country fare like meat pies, prime rib, and bangers. Upstairs the period-print bedrooms contain time-honored antique furnishings including canopied beds. Reserve well in advance. ~ Route 1, Muir Beach; 415-383-6000, fax 415-383-3424; www.pelicaninn.com, e-mail innkeeper@pelicaninn.com. DELUXE.

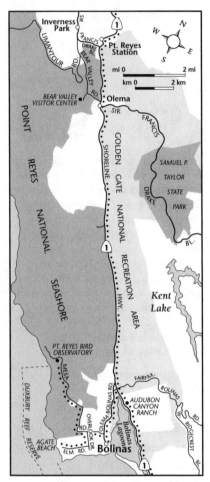

Bolinas to Point Reyes Station

snack bar, and restrooms; life-guards in summer. Because of currents from Bolinas Lagoon, the water here is a little warmer than elsewhere along the Northern California coast (but it's still brisk by Atlantic Coast standards). If you dare swim anywhere along the North Coast, it might as well be here. You'll notice that surfers here wear wet suits, even in midsummer, for protection from the chilly water.

The town of Stinson Beach has a little over 700 residents, but custom homes extend from the central part of the beach up the forested hillside. The small commercial zone along the highway has motels and surfboard rentals. The town looks larger from a distance than it does as you drive through it, and you're out of it before you realize it.

Birdwatchers flock to **Audubon Canyon Ranch**, located astride Route 1 on Bolinas Lagoon. Open on weekends and holidays from mid-March to July (or by appointment), Audubon Canyon Ranch includes four canyons, one of which is famed as a rookery for egrets and herons. From the hiking trails here you can see up to 90 bird species as well as gray fox, deer, badgers, and bobcats. Even driving along this stretch of road with your window open, you can hear a symphony of songbirds in the meadows. ~ Route 1; 415-868-9244, fax 415-868-1699; www.egret.org, e-mail acr@egret.org.

A little farther on, the tidal flats located at the south end of **Bolinas Lagoon** are also a bird sanctuary. Great egrets, ducks, and great blue herons make this one of their migratory stops. A colony of harbor seals lives here permanently and is joined in summer by migrating seals from San Francisco.

Beginning near Bolinas Lagoon and curving around the town perimeter, salt-and-pepper **Bolinas Beach** provides ample opportunity for walking. A steep bluff borders the beach. In the narrow mouth of the lagoon you can often see harbor seals and waterfowl. There are no facilities but the town of Bolinas is within walking distance. ~ Located at the end of Wharf Road in Bolinas. 🏃 🚴 🏊 🚣 ⛵

To reach the next point of interest you'll have to pay close attention. That's because you're approaching the town of **Bolinas**. To get there from Route 1, watch for the crossroad at the foot of the lagoon; go left, then quickly left again and follow the road along the other side of the lagoon; take another left at the end of the road.

There should be signs to direct you—but there probably won't be. Not because the state neglected them or highway workers forgot to put them up. It seems that local residents subscribe to the self-serving philosophy that since Bolinas is beautiful and they got there first, they should keep everyone else out. They tear down road signs and discourage visitors. The rest of Northern California is fair game, they seem to say, as long as Bolinas is left as some sort of human preserve.

The place they are attempting to hide is a delightful little town that rises from an S-shaped beach to form a lofty mesa. There are country roads along the bluff that overhangs the beach. Whether you stroll the beach or hike the highlands, you'll discover in the houses here a wild architectural array. There are domes, glass boxes, curved-roof creations, huts, ranch houses, and stately brown-shingle designs.

SURFING

Surfing is not exactly epic at Stinson: The beach is shallow and the waves are slow, "closing out" potential boarders. Nevertheless, **Live Water Surf Shop** rents all kinds of boards and wet suits. Your best bet is to get your gear here and drive the five miles to Bolinas (which lacks its own surf shop). Here the channel mouth creates more consistent waves, so you can put your board to better use. ~ 3448 Shoreline Highway (Route 1), Stinson Beach; 415-868-0333.

Abutting the Point Reyes National Seashore, Bolinas is also a gateway to the natural world. Follow Mesa Road for several miles outside town and you'll encounter the **Point Reyes Bird Observatory**, where scientists at a research station study a bird population of over 200 species.

WEST MARIN'S HIDDEN MUSEUM

The only manmade visitor attraction in Bolinas, the award-winning **Bolinas Museum** features exhibits on the history of the Marin coast, including displays of Miwok Indian artifacts as well as Living Artist Project shows presenting the work of Marin County painters and sculptors. The normally shy little community welcomes sightseers from mid-April to early June for the museum's biggest annual event, a series of guided tours of the public and private gardens of Bolinas. Open Friday through Sunday and by appointment. Admission. ~ 48 Wharf Road, Bolinas; 415-868-2006; www.bolinasmuseum.org, e-mail info@bolinasmuseum.org.

On the way back to town take a right on Overlook Drive, then a right on Elm Road; follow it to the parking lot at road's end. Hiking trails lead down a sharp 160-foot cliff to **Duxbury Reef**, a mile-long shale reef. Tidepool-watching is great sport here at low tide: starfish, periwinkles, abalone, limpets, and a host of other clinging creatures inhabit the marine preserve. Back in 1971 a huge oil spill endangered this spectacular area, but volunteers from all around the state worked day and night to save the reef and its tenacious inhabitants.

Just north of this rocky preserve is a parking lot from which a path leads down to **Agate Beach**, an ideal spot to find agates, driftwood, and glass balls (however, no collecting is permitted). There are no facilities.

Favored by swimmers and nude sunbathers, **Hagmaier Pond**, three and a half miles north of the Bolinas turnoff (at the foot of Bolinas Lagoon), offers a variation from nearby ocean beaches. It's fringed with grassland and bounded by forest, making it an idyllic spot within easy reach of the highway. A dirt road leads uphill several hundred yards to the lake; take the first left fork. There are no facilities.

Back on Route 1, continue north through Olema Valley, a peaceful, forest-fringed region of family farms and pastures where horses and dairy cattle graze, while overhead, vultures hang motionless on the sea breeze. Peaceful, that is, until you realize that the **San Andreas Fault**, the global suture that shook San Francisco back in 1906, cuts through the valley. As a matter of fact, Route 1 parallels the fault line. See for yourself at Point Reyes National

Seashore's **Bear Valley Visitors Center**, a quarter mile west of Olema on Bear Valley Road. There, a short nature trail follows a crevasse formed along the fault during the 1906 San Francisco Earthquake, whose epicenter was the Olema Valley. The center will provide you with maps, information, and camping permits. ~ 415-464-5100.

Despite being a gateway for Point Reyes National Seashore, the village of **Olema** (the name means "coyote" in the Miwok Indian language) has largely escaped the trendy commercial redevelopment that has transformed other small coastal towns. This is because much of the town and its surroundings are owned by the **Vedanta Center of Northern California**, whose monks wield considerable influence in local politics. The group's 2000-acre meditation retreat at Olema is open to visitors of all religious faiths; overnight and longer stays require approval from the group's swami in San Francisco. ~ Contact the Vedanta Society of Northern California, 2323 Vallejo Street, San Francisco; 415-992-2323, fax 415-992-1476; www.sfvedanta.org, e-mail temple@ sfvedanta.org.

Point Reyes Station, two miles north of Olema, is the largest community along this stretch of Route 1, with a

HORSEBACK RIDING

For horseback riding in one of the most beautiful and accessible areas in Marin County, stop at the **Five Brooks Trailhead** just south of Olema. Among the several paths that originate here is the 5.2-mile Olema Valley Trail, which parallels Route 1 as it tracks a course along the infamous San Andreas Fault. It alternates between glades and forest while beating a level path to the village of Woodville (better known by its former name, Dogtown). You'll find horses for rent, as well as guided tours, a short distance from the trailhead at **Five Brooks Stables**. Reservations recommended. ~ 8001 Route 1, Olema; 415-663-1570; e-mail cowboys@five brooks.com.

CAMP UNDER THE REDWOODS

To discover one of the most attractive camping areas on the Marin Peninsula, turn east at Olema on Sir Francis Drake Boulevard and follow it inland for six miles. The battered two-lane asphalt "boulevard" climbs among bald-domed hills and isolated farms. Then grassland gives way to dense forest as you approach **Samuel P. Taylor State Park**, an expanse of 2900 acres densely forested with redwoods. Originally the site of Camp Taylor Resort, San Francisco's turn-of-the-20th-century elite came here by narrow-gauge railroad to spend the summer surrounded by forest shade at the posh Hotel Azalea. The resort buildings have long since been removed, but gentle hiking trails remain, and the park has picnic areas, restrooms, showers, and 60 campsites ($11 a night). Reservations required Memorial Day through Labor Day. Day-use fee, $4. ~ 415-488-9897, fax 415-488-4315.

year-round population of 350. As the name suggests, the town got its start in 1875 as a narrow-gauge railroad terminal serving the dairy ranches of the Point Reyes Peninsula. Besides linking Point Reyes with the ferry to San Francisco, trains continued north to the redwood forests of the Russian River and beyond to pick up logs and lumber and haul them back to the city. Most of the railroad bed north of Point Reyes Station was later paved to become an automobile highway—Route 1. The last train pulled out in 1933, and the town's population drifted away until President Kennedy created Point Reyes National Seashore in 1962, giving the ghost town a surge of tourism to rekindle its economy. Today, many of Point Reyes Station's 19th-century Italianate and railroad commercial-style buildings have received a fresh coat of paint and a new lease on life as cute cafés and artists' studio-

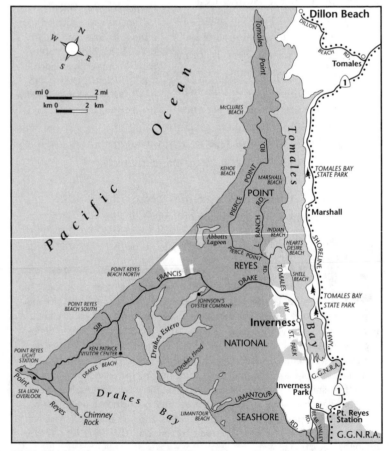

Point Reyes Station to Dillon Beach

sidetrips

INVERNESS—HIDDEN HOSPITALITY

Some of the best food and lodging choices in the Point Reyes area are off the main highway in the little vacation-home village of **Inverness**, located along the segment of Sir Francis Drake Boulevard that parallels Route 1 between Olema and Point Reyes Station.

Top of the line is the **Blackthorne Inn**, an architectural extravaganza set in a forest of oak, bay trees, and Douglas fir. The four-level house is expressive of the flamboyant "woodbutcher's art" building style popular in the 1970s. Using recycled materials and heavy doses of imagination, the builders created a maze of skylights, bay windows, and French doors, capped by an octagonal tower. A spiral staircase corkscrews up through this multitiered affair to the top deck, where an outdoor hot tub overlooks the canyon. There are four bedrooms, all with private baths. Each room has been personalized; the most outstanding is the "Eagle's Nest," which occupies the glass-encircled octagon at the very top of this Aquarian wedding cake. ~ 266 Vallejo Avenue, Inverness Park; 415-663-8621, fax 415-663-8635; www.blackthorneinn.com, e-mail susan@blackthorneinn.com. ULTRA-DELUXE.

Among the area's most unusual restaurants is **Vladimir's Czechoslovakian Restaurant**, operated at this location by a Czech refugee family for more than 40 years. Though, admittedly, sweet stewed red cabbage is an acquired taste, the menu also includes chicken paprikash, goulash, klobasa sausage, and roast duckling. The Old-World atmosphere—walls and ceiling painted deep red, accented with dark wood and decorated with hunting trophies and family heirlooms, with maudlin Czechoslovakian ballads emanating from the sound system—is at least as memorable as the food. Closed Monday. ~ Inverness; 415-669-1021. DELUXE.

galleries. Some of the town's biggest buildings stand empty, such as the Grand Building (c. 1915) on A Street, which once housed a grand hotel, ballroom, and general store.

From Point Reyes Station, Route 1 continues north through rolling golden pasturage before rounding a curve and reaching the east shore of Tomales Bay, a lovely fjord-shaped inlet. As you continue north, salt marshes teeming with egrets, herons, and other wading birds stretch along one side of the road; on the other are rumpled hills tufted with grass.

The waterfront village of **Marshall** consists of fishing boats moored offshore and woodframe houses anchored firmly onshore. Then the road turns inland to

CROSSING THE FAULT LINE

by the way...

If you turn off Route 1 and follow Sir Francis Drake Boulevard onto the Point Reyes Peninsula, you'll cross from the North American Plate, one of the six tectonic plates on which the entire earth's surface rides, to the Pacific Plate, which extends across the ocean. It is the pressure formed by the collision of these two great land masses that causes earthquakes. No sign will notify you as you cross this troubled geologic border, no guide will direct you along the rift zone. Yet the San Andreas Fault runs along the floor of Tomales Bay, separating the triangular peninsula from the mainland.

POINT REYES NATIONAL SEASHORE

sidetrips   From Point Reyes Station on Route 1, you can explore Point Reyes National Seashore, one of the world's finest seaside parks, on a sidetrip of roughly 20 miles each way. One hundred forty miles of hiking trails invite you to explore this realm of sand dunes and endless beaches, Scottish moors and grassy hillsides, salt marshes and pine forests. Bobcats, mountain lions, fox, and elk inhabit its wrinkled terrain, while harbor seals and gray whales cruise its ragged shoreline. More than 45 percent of North American bird species have been spotted here.

Stop first at the **Bear Valley Visitors Center** for maps, information, and permits for the national seashore's four small hike-in campgrounds ($12 per night, four-night limit; for reservations call 415-663-8054). A short hike from the center will lead you to a Miwok Indian Village, where the round-domed shelters and other structures of the area's early inhabitants have been re-created. ~ 415-663-1092, fax 415-663-8132.

The main road out to Point Reyes is Sir Francis Drake Boulevard, which rolls for miles through the park. It takes you past the tiny town of Inverness, then out along the west side of Tomales Bay, a drowned river valley. The road veers inland and then splits in two. The right fork, Pierce Point Road, takes you to **Tomales Bay State Park**, across the bay from Route 1. The bay provides a warm, sunny alternative to Point Reyes' frequent fog. The water, too, is warmer, making it a great place for swimming as well as fishing and boating. Check out the virgin grove of Bishop pine and the self-guided nature trail describing how American Indians used local plants.

Rimming the park are several sandy coves; most accessible of these is **Heart's Desire Beach**, flanked by bluffs and featuring nearby picnic areas. From here a self-guided nature trail goes northwest to **Indian Beach**, a long stretch of white sand fringed by trees. Hiking trails around the park lead to other secluded beaches, excellent for picnics and day hikes. Secluded **Marshall Beach**, a lengthy strip of white sand bordered by cypress trees, is a wonderful place to swim and sunbathe, often in complete privacy. Camping is allowed on the beach; be sure to pack out everything you packed in. No dogs are allowed on any of these beaches. ~ Pierce Point Road; 415-663-8054.

Because of its rich waterfowl population and beautiful surrounding dunes, **Abbotts Lagoon** is a favorite place among hikers. The trailhead is located along Pierce Point Road, two miles past the turnoff for Tomales Bay State Park; follow the trail one mile to the lagoon. From the lagoon it's an easy jaunt over the dunes to Point Reyes Beach. Two miles farther on is the trailhead for **Kehoe Beach**—actually the northern end of ten-mile-long Point Reyes Beach. Bounded by cliffs, it's a lovely place, covered with wildflowers in spring and boasting a seasonal lagoon. The isolation makes it a great spot for explorers.

Sir Francis Drake Boulevard continues over folded hills that fall away to reveal sharp bluffs. Farm animals graze through fields smothered in wildflowers on historic dairy ranches named by letters from "A" (nearest the lighthouse) to "Z." Because of the cool, damp climate, the Point Reyes Peninsula provided ideal pasturage to supply the booming city to the south with milk, cheese, and butter.

Between the ranches, ocean vistas stretch along miles of headland. A turnoff to the south leads to **Drakes Beach**, where you can picnic, beachcomb, or gaze at the surrounding cliffs and wonder whether they truly resemble the White Cliffs of Dover. The well-protected beach is also a good swimming spot. Legend says that in 1579 the English explorer Sir Francis Drake anchored here in Drakes Bay. (Others argue that his anchorage

was actually Bolinas Lagoon or even San Francisco Bay.) Facilities include picnic areas, restrooms, a visitors center, and a snack bar. The **Ken Patrick Visitor Center**, open Saturday and Sunday only, features an aquarium and interactive computer displays.

It will become wonderfully evident why **Point Reyes Beach** is nicknamed "Ten Mile Beach" when you cast eyes on this endless sand swath. A wonderful place for whale watching, beachcombing, and fishing, this is *not* the spot for swimming. Sharks, riptides, and unusual wave patterns make even wading inadvisable. Also the heavy winds along this coastline would chill any swimmer's plans. But that does not detract from the wild beauty of the place, or the fact you can jog for miles along this strand (turnoffs are marked "North Beach" and "South Beach"). From Point Reyes Beach, it's not far to the end of Point Reyes' hammerhead peninsula. At one tip is **Chimney Rock**, a sea stack formed when the ocean eroded away the intervening land mass, leaving this islet just offshore. On the way to Chimney Rock you'll pass an overlook that's ideal for watching sea lions; then from Chimney Rock, if the day is clear, you'll see all the way to San Francisco.

At the other tip is **Point Reyes Lighthouse**, an 1870-era beacon located at the foggiest point on the

A side road turns south off Sir Francis Drake Boulevard to **Johnson's Oyster Company**, where workers harvest the rich beds of an estuary. The farm is a conglomeration of slapdash buildings, house trailers, and rusty machines. The shoreline is heaped over with oyster shells and the air is filled with pungent odors. Raw oysters are for sale. ~ 17171 Sir Francis Drake Boulevard, Inverness; 415-669-1149, fax 415-669-1262.

sights

entire Pacific coast. The treacherous waters offshore have witnessed numerous shipwrecks, the first occurring way back in 1595. The original lighthouse, constructed to prevent these calamities, incorporated over a thousand pieces of crystal in its intricate lens. A modern beacon eventually replaced this multifaceted instrument, but the old lighthouse and an accompanying information center are still open to the public Thursday through Monday. ~ 415-669-1534.

RAW OYSTERS AND HOME COOKING

The **Station House Café** comes highly recommended by local residents. There is a down-home feel to this wood-paneled restaurant. Maybe it's the artwork along the walls or the garden patio. Regardless, it's really the food that draws folks from the surrounding countryside. The dinner menu includes fresh oysters plus chicken, steak, and fish. There are also daily chef's specials such as salmon with a dill-smoked salmon sauce. Dinners are served with soup or salad, and a basket of cornbread and piping hot popovers. The Station House also features a complete breakfast menu; at lunch there are light crêpe, pasta, and seafood dishes, plus sandwiches and salads. Closed Wednesday. ~ 11180 Main Street, Point Reyes Station; 415-663-1515, fax 415-663-9443; www.stationhouse cafe.com. MODERATE.

Tomales, another falsefront old railroad town with a clapboard church and country homes.

Here, Dillon Beach Road turns off to the left and runs four miles to the ocean at **Dillon Beach**. Located at the mouth of Tomales Bay, this beach is popular with boaters and clammers. The surrounding hills are covered with resort cottages, but there are open areas and dunes to explore. There are picnic areas, restrooms, groceries, boat rentals, and fishing charters. Day-use fee, $5.

Route 1 continues inland past paint-peeled barns and open pastureland ablaze with wildflowers in spring and summer. It crosses Americano Creek, which marks the boundary between Marin and Sonoma counties, before turning seaward toward Bodega Bay.

Tomales Bay's Gourmet Oysters

Shacks and storefronts along Tomales Bay sell fresh local oysters, barbecued or on the half-shell. Most oysters in the Point Reyes area are Pacific oysters, imported from Japan in the 1930s to replace local oysters that had disappeared from San Francisco Bay because of pollution. Tomales Bay is one of the few areas where the smaller, sweeter Olympia oyster native to the Bay Area is still harvested. Gourmands consider Olympic oysters a special delicacy.

Just north of Marin County lies the Sonoma coastline, a beautiful and still lightly developed area. Placid rangeland extends inward while along the shoreline, surf boils against angular cliffs. Far below are pocket beaches and coves; offshore rise dozens of tiny rock islands, or sea stacks. The entire coast teems with fish—salmon and steelhead—as well as crabs, clams, and abalone. Rip currents, sneaker waves, and the coldest waters this side of the Arctic make swimming inadvisable. But the landscape, enchanting and exotic, is wide open for exploration.

Film buffs may find the fishing village of **Bodega Bay** hauntingly familiar, for it was the setting of Alfred Hitchcock's eerie film *The Birds*. It's questionable whether any cast members remain among the population of snowy egrets, but the Bay still supports a variety of winged creatures. Conservation efforts have encouraged a comeback among the endangered brown pelicans and blue herons. Serious Hitchcock fans in search of familiar structures from the movie can take a short sidetrip inland along the Bay Highway to the town of **Bodega**. Here they'll find the old Potter schoolhouse and the church from the film.

In Bodega Bay, at **Lucas Wharf**, and elsewhere along this working waterfront, you can watch fishermen setting off into the fog every morning and haul-

by the way...

Thanks to the political clout of Sonoma County's sheep ranchers, who view dogs as a threat to their livestock, the county has one of the strictest leash laws in the United States—and enforces it zealously. Dogs must be on leash at all times except when they are in a fenced yard, and fines are stiff. Dogs are also banned from all beaches in Sonoma County, and any dog trespassing on land used for livestock grazing can be shot on sight. The only exercise option for those with canine traveling companions is to walk them around Route 1's scenic vista points—with a "pooper scooper."

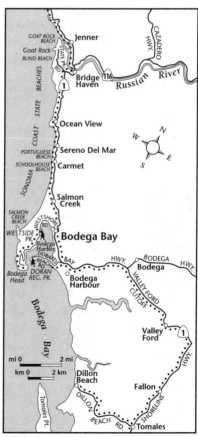

Dillon Beach to Jenner

A PASTORAL B & B

For a rustic detour, follow Coleman Valley Road when it departs from Route 1 north of Bodega Bay. It weaves through farmland and offers fabulous views of ocean and mountains, and leads to the forest-rimmed village of Occidental. Here you'll find the **Inn at Occidental**, a charming Victorian homestead encircled by a wide porch bedecked with potted plants and white wicker rockers. The 16 guest rooms feature fireplaces, spa tubs, antiques, and original artwork. There is also a separate cottage with a full kitchen and two master suites. A full breakfast is included, as is afternoon wine and cheese. ~ 3657 Church Street, Occidental; 707-874-1047, 800-522-6324, fax 707-874-1078; www.innatoccidental.com, e-mail innkeeper@innatoccidental.com. ULTRA-DELUXE.

ing in their catch later in the day. ~ Route 1 and Smith Brothers Lane, Bodega Bay.

One and a half miles north of Bodega Bay on the seaward side of Route 1 stands a strange monument—the **Children's Bell Tower**. The simple framework of poles hung with 130 bells was created in 1994 by Bay Area artist Bruce Hasson in memory of seven-year-old Bodega Bay resident Nicholas Green, who was killed in a shooting incident while visiting Italy. The school bells, church bells, ship's bells, and even cowbells were donated by individual Italians; the large centerpiece bell was made by the same foundry that made the bells of the Vatican and was blessed by Pope John Paul II. It contains the names of seven Italian children whose lives were saved by the donation of Nicholas' organs.

Doran Regional Park is situated on a sandspit between Bodega Harbor and Bodega Bay. With a broad sand beach and good facilities, it's an excellent spot for daytrippers and campers alike. You can explore the tidal flats or fish up on the jetty. There are picnic areas, restrooms, showers and a 134-site campground ($16 a

THE NAME SAYS IT ALL— ALMOST

The **Bodega Bay Seafood, Art and Wine Festival** in late August features live music, seafood from a dozen area caterers, 100 art and craft exhibitors, wine and beer, kids' art activities, and horseback riding. It takes place at Chanslor Ranch, a combination horse ranch/B&B located one mile north of town on Route 1. Admission. For information, call 707-875-3490.

Saving Bodega Bay

Admiring the magnificent seascape of Bodega Bay, it's hard to believe that in 1962 Pacific Gas & Electric started building the Bodega Bay Atomic Park, designed to be the largest nuclear power plant in America. Despite vocal opposition, the utility company excavated a gigantic hole for the plant's foundation on the bay side of Bodega Head. Protests, petitions, and lawsuits failed to thwart construction. PG&E tried to counter the bad publicity by temporarily opening its "park" to visitors but succeeded only in inspiring writers, artists, and even a jazz musician to extoll Bodega Head's pristine beauty. Finally a naturalist from the Pacific Marine Station at Dillon Beach pointed out that an earthquake fault ran right through the proposed site. The Atomic Energy Commission ordered the project shut down, and the huge excavation was filled with sea water to become what locals call "the world's most expensive duck pond." The former Atomic Park, now called Bodega Head Park, is now one of the most popular whale-watching sites on the California coast.

night, no hookups). Day-use fee, $3. ~ Off Route 1 in Bodega Bay; 707-875-3540, fax 707-879-8247; e-mail groupwise@sonoma-county.org. 🚶🚴🐎🏊🛶 🛥️🚤🎣

At **Bodega Head**, pocket beaches are dramatically backdropped by granite cliffs. A good place to picnic and explore, this is also a favored whale-watching site. There are restrooms and showers located in nearby Westside Park (707-875-3540, fax 707-879-8247), which also has 47 tent/RV sites (no hookups); $14 per night for Sonoma County residents and $16 for nonresidents. ~ Off Route 1 in Bodega Bay along Bay Flat Road.

Magnificent **Sonoma Coast State Beach** extends for 13 miles between Bodega Head and the Vista Trail. It consists of a number of beaches separated by steep headlands; all are within easy hiking distance of Route 1. The park headquarters and information center is at **Salmon Creek Beach**, where endless sand dunes backdrop a broad beach. Other beaches up the way range from sweeping strands to pocket coves and abound with waterfowl and shorebirds, clams, and abalone. Some pocket beaches reached by a steep trail down from the

highway, such as **Miwok Beach**, are treacherous enough to merit signs warning that they are not swimming beaches, that there are dangerous undertows and "sleepers"—sudden large waves that have been known to wash far up on the beach and carry unwary beachcombers out to sea.

Schoolhouse Beach is a particularly pretty pocket cove bounded by rocky cliffs; **Portuguese Beach** boasts a wide swath of sand with strange and fanciful rock formations at the north end and bird colonies on the rocks offshore; **Blind Beach** is rather secluded with a sea arch offshore; and **Goat Rock Beach** faces the town of Jenner and is decorated with offshore rocks.

Pick your poison—hiking, tidepooling, birdwatching, whale watching, camping, picnicking, fishing—and you'll find it waiting along this rugged and hauntingly beautiful coastline. Bodega Dunes, Salmon Creek Beach, Schoolhouse Beach, Goat Rock, Portuguese Beach, and Wrights Beach have restrooms; Bodega Dunes and Wrights Beach also feature picnic areas. ▲ 🏃 🚲 🐎 🏊 🎣 🚣

PITCH YOUR TENT AT THE BEACH

Sonoma Coast State Beach is one of the best areas on the Northern California coast for camping just a short walk from the surf. At **Bodega Dunes**, there are 98 tent/RV sites (no hookups); $14 a night. At **Wrights Beach**, there are 27 tent/RV sites (no hookups); $14 a night. Reservations are required; call 800-444-7275. At **Pono Canyon** and **Willow Creek** there are 31 walk-in primitive sites; $7 per night. Day-use fee for developed campgrounds, $4. Closed December through March. ~ 707-865-2391, fax 707-865-2046.

With posted advisory speeds as low as 20 mph, rollercoaster Route 1 weaves in and out of gulches where creeks plunge down to the sea. Finally it reaches the woodframe town of **Jenner** (population 200, elevation 19), where the broad Russian River meets the ocean.

Set on a hillside high above the mouth of the Russian River, sheltered by rock promontories that rise on both sides of the dunes and long sand bar where the river's current meets the ocean's surf, Jenner is the showpiece among the small towns along this stretch of coastline. The large country inns overlook a river bar. Thousands of ducks and pelicans congregate and sea lions bask on their own private beach. (You can take Route 116 up the river valley to the fabled Russian River resort area and the town of Guerneville. See Chapter 6.)

Penny Island, the island in the middle of the river's estuary, was once the home of Elijah Jenner, for whom the town was named decades later. It was taken over in 1965 by a construction company planning to mine the island for gravel, but local conservationists stopped the operation in its tracks. Since that success, Jennerites have taken the lead in most environmental crusades to protect the Sonoma coast. The island is now a wildlife refuge inhabited by seals and sea lions.

As soon as you cross the Russian River, you'll find your-

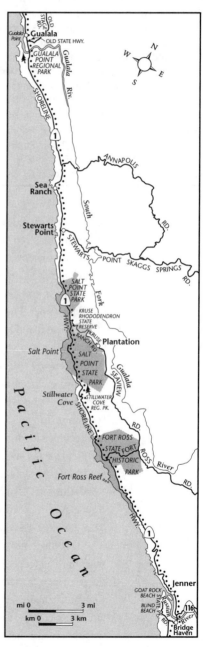

Jenner to Gualala

COMMUNING
WITH WILDLIFE

At the mouth of the Russian River, the water "breathes," pulling salt water and sea life into the river with rising tides and spilling oxygen-rich fresh water into the ocean with falling tides, attracting a remarkable abundance and diversity of fish. Taking advantage of this phenomenon, a colony of sea lions inhabits the tip of the spit that runs between the river and the ocean, along with thousands of pelicans, gulls, ducks, and other water birds.

You can walk out the spit to see them, at **River's End Restaurant**, a white-tablecloths-and-candlelight establishment on the hillside overlooking the river mouth with big picture windows. Dishes range from *médallions* of venison to racklettes of elk to coconut-fried shrimp. Closed Tuesday and Wednesday in summer; Monday through Thursday in winter. ~ 11048 Route 1, Jenner; 707-865-2484, fax 707-865-9621; www.rivers-end.com. MODERATE TO DELUXE.

self on a dizzying, don't-look-down stretch of highway that grips the steep slopes above sheer cliffs that plunge down into the crashing surf as much as 600 feet below, then descends again toward Fort Ross.

Set in a canyon surrounded by bluffs 12 miles north of Jenner, **Fort Ross Reef Campground** is beautifully located and features a redwood grove, wild raspberry bushes, sea vistas, and a hike-in surfers' beach. Divers don wet suits to hunt beneath the surface of the chilly water for abalone, found in abundance around Fort Ross. At one time this was a private park, but the state took it over. The result is a public facility with spectacular surroundings and gorgeous views. There are picnic areas and restrooms. Day-use fee, $4. There are 19 tent/RV sites (no hookups); $10 per night. Open April through October. Depending on the weather, fires may not be allowed. ~ 19005 Route 1; 707-847-3708, fax 707-847-3601. ▲ 🚶 🚵 🦞 🏊 ⛏

The 19th-century Russian stronghold of **Fort Ross**, 13 miles north of Jenner, is today a state historic park. Touring the reconstructed fort you'll encounter a museum, an old Russian Orthodox chapel, a cemetery filled with Russian Orthodox crosses, a stockade built of hand-tooled redwood, barracks and officers' houses, and a seven-sided blockhouse. Together they provide an insight into an unusual chapter in California history. Admission. ~ 707-847-3286, fax 707-847-3601; e-mail frinterp@mcn.org.

Beyond Fort Ross, pine forest creeps down to meet the sea, and you'll find yourself driving through an evergreen forest with intermittent sea vistas. Route 1 winds high above the coast and every curve exposes another awesome view of adze-like cliffs slicing into the sea. Driving this corkscrew route can jangle the nerves, but the vistas are soothing to the soul. With the exception of scattered villages, the coastline remains undeveloped.

Situated amid pine trees on a hillside above the ocean, **Stillwater Cove Regional Park** is a small park with access to a beach. The canyon trail leads up to the restored (but closed) Fort Ross Schoolhouse. There are picnic

Russia's California Beach Fortress

The Russian River is named for a Russian-American Fur Company cadre of Russian explorers and Aleut hunters who in 1808 sailed down the Pacific coast from Alaska, which was part of the Russian Empire at that time. Joining a small band of outlaw Russian hunters who had already established a crude village on the coast, the expedition spent eight months plundering the abundance of sea otters along the coast before returning and obtaining the Russian czar's permission to establish a permanent colony centered around Fort Rossiya, a wooden fortress they built overlooking the sea and named after their homeland. Founded in 1812, the colony lasted for 29 years and grew to include Russian farms and ranches as far away as Freestone, Jenner, and Bodega Bay. The southernmost Russian colony on the American coast, the fort (which never saw combat) bolstered the czar's territorial claim to the entire Pacific Northwest.

When they had killed all the sea otters along the Sonoma coast, Russia withdrew her colonists from the area and proposed to sell the land, including Fort Ross, to Mexico; but after General Vallejo, governor of Sonoma, declined the offer, the fort was instead sold to local real estate baron John A. Sutter, who had recently become a Mexican citizen and one of California's first emigrants from the U.S. Sutter, who would later become famous as the owner of the mill where the California Gold Rush began, purchased all the Russian holdings for $30,000—a small fortune at the time. It was Sutter who Americanized the fort's name by abbreviating it to Fort Ross.

areas, restrooms, and showers. Day-use fee, $3. There are 23 tent/RV sites (no hookups); $16 a night. Reservations must be made at least ten days in advance (707-565-2267). ~ Located on Route 1, about 16 miles north of Jenner; 707-847-3245, fax 707-879-8247. ▲ 🏃 🛶 🎣

Extending from the ocean to over 1000 feet elevation, 6000-acre **Salt Point State Park** includes coastline, forests, and open range land. Along the shore are weird honeycomb formations called tafoni, caused by sea erosion on coastal sandstone. Up amid the stands of Douglas fir and Bishop pine there's a pygmy forest, where unfavorable soil conditions have caused fully mature redwoods to reach only about 20 feet in height. Blacktail deer, black bear, mountain lions, and bobcats roam the area. Miles of hiking trails lace the park, including one through a rhododendron reserve.

Rhododendrons, those tall bushes that burst out in white, pink, or purple flowers from May to early July, thrive in the damp climate of the Northern California coast. Besides the native California rhododendron and its cousin, the western azalea, several Asian and European strains have run rampant along the coast. You'll

Battle for the Beach

Soon after construction began at Sea Ranch in the 1960s, its ten miles of secluded beach became the subject of the longest and most costly litigation in the history of the Northern California coast when the state's voters passed Proposition 20. The law established the Coastal Commission, which was charged with protecting public access to all California beaches. The commission refused to issue permits for continued development at Sea Ranch unless trail easements were set aside to guarantee that the public could use the beach. Lawyers representing Sea Ranch homeowners filed suit, arguing that it had been a private beach before the commission was created and should remain so. After a decade of litigation, the federal district court ruled that Sea Ranch must allow the public to use the beach. Today, seven marked public trails lead to the beach, segments of which are called Blackpoint Beach, Pebble Beach, Pocket Beaches, Shell Beach, and Walk-On Beach. The southernmost trailhead is between the lodge and mile marker 51; the northernmost starts from Gualala Point Regional Park.

A HISTORIC HIDEAWAY

Built in 1903, the **Gualala Hotel** is a massive two-story structure. It's an old clapboard affair, fully refurbished, that includes a bar and dining room. The 19 rooms upstairs are small, but the wallpaper, decor, and old-time flourishes give the place a comfy traditional feel, making it a rare find on the North Coast. Because of the downstairs restaurant/bar, it can get noisy at times. ~ 39301 Route 1, Gualala; 707-884-3441. BUDGET.

see them along the roadside, but for the ultimate visual treat, try a springtime visit to the 317-acre **Kruse Rhododendron State Reserve**, where they reach heights of 20 to 30 feet. There are picnic areas and restrooms. To get there, turn right on Kruse Ranch Road, two and a half miles past the main entrance to Salt Point State Park, and drive inland for about a mile. ~ 707-847-3221. Camping is not allowed at Kruse, but you'll find two campgrounds at nearby Salt Point State Park. There are over 100 tent/RV sites (no hookups); $12 per night. Reservations are required on weekends and from April through September; call PARKNET at 800-444-7275. ~ Located on Route 1 about 20 miles north of Jenner; 707-847-3221, fax 707-847-3843. ▲ 🚶 🚴 ⛵ 🛶 ⚓

ARTS IN THE REDWOODS

For over 40 years running, Gualala Arts has sponsored **Art in the Redwoods**. On the third weekend in August, locals and out-of-staters alike descend on Gualala for the three-day festival of art, food, crafts, and live music. ~ Gualala Arts, 46501 Gualala Road, Gualala; 707-884-1138; www.gualalaarts.org, e-mail ginfo@gualalaarts.org.

You'll pass sunbleached wooden buildings in the old town of Stewarts Point. Then the road courses through **Sea Ranch**—an enclave including lodging, a restaurant, a store, and big, grayish, contemporary vacation homes along the perimeter of the Sea Ranch Golf Links. This grand-scale development, bitterly opposed by environmentalists, nevertheless displays imaginative resort design atop white cliffs overlooking a stark sea.

The Gualala River marks the boundary between Sonoma and Mendocino counties. On the south shore where the river meets the ocean, charming **Gualala Point Regional Park** has everything from a sandy beach to redwood groves. Across the river, there are kayak and canoe rentals. There are picnic areas, restrooms, and an information center. Day-use fee, $3. There are 25 tent/RV sites (no hookups), 1 hiker/biker site, and 6 walk-in sites; $16 per night. Call for reservations (707-565-2267). ~ Located along Route 1 due south of Gualala; 707-785-2377, fax 707-785-3741. ▲ 🏃 ⚓️

S ituated on the north bank of the Gualala River, the town of **Gualala** (pronounced "Wallala," a Spanish spelling of the original Pomo Indian name for the spot where the river meets the sea) is a quiet little former sawmill town turned artists' community. It is best known for the Arts in the Redwoods festival, one of the largest arts events in Northern California, which has been held in late August each year since 1962.

Heading north from Gualala, Route 1 offers peeka-boo sea views through the trees; some of the finest views have been appropriated by inns and vacation homes whose privacy fences block the line of sight from the highway. After passing through **Anchor Bay** (pop. 170), with its restaurant, general store, real estate offices, and acupuncture clinic, the road continues through a diverse forest of ponderosa, madrone, fir and spruce to the picturesque little beach town of **Point Arena**, with its long-established shops and Victorian houses.

The pride of the town of Point Arena is its public fishing pier, a $2.2-million structure that extends 330 feet out into the cove and stands 25 feet above the water.

TRANQUILITY ON THE REDWOOD COAST

The New England–style farmhouse that has become **Glendeven** dates to 1867. The theme is country living, with a meadow out back and dramatic headlands nearby. The sitting room is an intimate affair with comfortable armchairs set before a brick fireplace. In the rooms you're apt to find a bed with wooden headboard, an antique wardrobe, and colorful orchids. Glendeven is as charming and intimate as a country inn can be. A full breakfast is brought to your room on a tray. There's also a two-bedroom rental house available, which is just as beautiful as the rest of the property. ~ 8205 North Route 1, Little River; 707-937-0083, 800-822-4536, fax 707-937-6108; www.glendeven.com, e-mail innkeeper@glendeven.com. DELUXE TO ULTRA-DELUXE.

MENDOCINO COAST
FARMERS' MARKETS

Every Friday from mid-May to late October, Howard Street in central Mendocino is blocked off to vehicles as area growers assemble for the **Mendocino Farmers' Market**. Early in the season, the market showcases magnificent floral displays, while organic and specialty produce takes center stage later in the summer and fall. It lasts for only two hours, from noon to 2 p.m. ~ 707-937-3632.

Many of the same growers also display their bounty at other open-air markets along the coast on other days of the week, including the **Gualala Farmers' Market** (Community Center, Saturday, 10 a.m. to 12:30 p.m.; 707-882-2474) and the **Fort Bragg Farmer's Market** (Laurel and Franklin streets, Wednesday, 3:30 to 6 p.m.; 707-937-4330).

Besides serving as a landing for commercial and sport-fishing boats, the pier is open to all anglers—and no fishing license is required. Offshore, scuba divers can explore the **Arena Rock Underwater Preserve** with its abundant sea life and sunken freighter wreck. The harbor at Point Arena also offers some of the best surfing in Northern California.

Just north of Point Arena, a side road lined with windswept and weirdly misshapen pines leads out to **Point Arena Lighthouse**. The original lighthouse, built in 1870, was destroyed in the 1906 San Francisco earthquake, which struck Point Arena even more fiercely than the bay city. The present beacon, rebuilt shortly afterwards, rises 115 feet from a narrow peninsula. The lighthouse is open for tours. The views, by definition, are outstanding. Open from 10 a.m. to 4:30 p.m. Memorial Day to Labor Day and from 10 a.m. to 3:30 p.m. the rest of the year. Admission. ~ 707-882-2777; e-mail palight@mcn.org.

The highway cuts inland among dairy farms and green irrigated pastures before returning to the sea at **Manchester** (pop. 462), a village of weatherbeaten old cabins as well as a few decrepit former mansions, with surrealistic topiary in front of the fire station.

Nearby, wild and windswept **Manchester State Beach** extends for miles along the Mendocino Coast. Piled deep with driftwood, it's excellent for beachcombing and hiking. There are picnic areas, restrooms, and an information center. There are 46 tent/RV sites (no hookups) and 10 primitive, hike-in environmental sites; $11 per night; first-come, first-served. ~ Located along Route 1 about eight miles north of Point Arena; 707-937-5804, fax 707-937-2953. ▲ 🏃 ⛷ 🛶

Continuing up the Mendocino Coast, the highway passes through tiny seaside villages. The coastline is an intaglio of river valleys, pocket beaches, and narrow coves. Forested ridges, soft and green in appearance, fall away into dizzying cliffs. Wild raspberries grow in brambly thickets along the roadside, and deer abound. Midway between Elk and Albion, the **Navarro River** slices a gorge down to the sea. As it crosses the river, Route 1 intersects scenic Route 128, which climbs the coastal mountains through the giant redwoods of Hendy Woods State Park en route to the Anderson Valley wine country (see Chapter 7).

The village of **Albion** stands on Albion Head—a near-island of rock that rises hundreds of feet above the ocean, separating the Albion River on its south side from the **Little River** on the north. The highway crosses a

Gualala to Mendocino

deep gorge to reach the town and another, equally spectacular gorge to leave it.

Four miles farther north, the village of Little River is the gateway to **Van Damme State Park.** Extending from the beach to an interior forest, the 2069-acre park has several interesting features: a "pygmy forest" where poor soil results in fully mature pine trees reaching heights of only six inches to eight feet; a "fern canyon" smothered in different species of ferns; and a "cabbage patch" filled with that fetid critter with elephant ear leaves—skunk cabbage. This park is also laced with hiking trails and offers excellent beachcombing opportunities. Facilities include a visitors center, picnic areas, restrooms, and showers. Day-use fee, $4 for the fern canyon. There are 74 tent/RV sites (no hookups); $16 per night. The upper campground is closed in winter. For reservations call PARKNET at 800-444-7275. ~ Route 1 about 30 miles north of Point Arena, or three miles south of Mendocino; 707-937-5804, fax 707-937-2953. ▲ 🏃 🚲 🚣 🎣

Just past Van Damme State Park comes the first view of the red-roofed, white and pastel green houses of **Mendocino.** The adjoining **Mendocino Headlands** and **Big**

SPENDING THE NIGHT IN MENDOCINO

Set in a falsefront building that dates to 1878, the 51-room **Mendocino Hotel** is a wonderful place—larger than other nearby country inns—with a wood-paneled lobby, full dining room, and living quarters adorned with antiques. There are rooms in the hotel with both private and shared baths as well as accommodations in the garden cottages out back. ~ 45080 Main Street, Mendocino; 707-937-0511, 800-548-0513, fax 707-937-0513; www.mendocinohotel.com, e-mail reservations@mendocinohotel.com. MODERATE TO ULTRA-DELUXE.

The queen of Mendocino is the **MacCallum House Inn**, a Gingerbread Victorian built in 1882. The place is a treasure trove of antique furnishings, knick-knacks, and other memorabilia. Many of the rooms are individually decorated with rocking chairs, quilts, and wood stoves. Positively everything—the carriage house, barn, greenhouse, gazebo, even the water tower—has been converted into a guest room. ~ 45020 Albion Street, Mendocino; 707-937-0289, 800-609-0492, fax 707-937-2243; www.maccallumhouse.com, e-mail machouse@mcn.org. MODERATE TO ULTRA-DELUXE.

River Beach state parks form the town's seaside border—and quite a border it is. The white-sand beaches are only part of the natural splendor. There are also wave tunnels, tidepools, sea arches, lagoons, and 360-degree vistas that sweep from the surf-trimmed shore to the prim villagescape of Mendocino. From Mendocino Headlands State Park, high atop a sea cliff, you get unmatched views of the town's tumultuous shoreline as you gaze down at placid tidepools and wave-carved grottoes. The only facilities are restrooms; private canoe rentals are nearby. Adjacent to Mendocino Headlands State Park is the historic **Ford House**, an 1854 home with a small museum, which also serves as a visitors center for the park. ~ Main Street, Mendocino; 707-937-5397, fax 707-937-3845.

IT ALL HAPPENS IN MENDOCINO

Mendocino hosts some of the most popular special events of any town on Route 1 North. The biggest of all is the **Mendocino Music Festival**, a 12-day tent show by the seashore that mixes orchestral and chamber music concerts, opera, jazz, and world music. It takes place in mid-July. ~ 707-937-4041.

Coinciding with the first weekend of the festival, the Mendocino Art Center sponsors the **Mendocino Summer Arts & Crafts Fair**. ~ 707-937-5818. In the spring, the big draw is the **Mendocino Whale Festival**, held in March (first and third weeks) at the peak of the California gray whales' annual migration from Baja to Alaska. ~ 707-961-6300.

Perched on a headland above the sea, Mendocino is New England incarnate, with houses that resemble Maine saltboxes and Cape Cod cottages. Settled in 1852, the town was built largely by Yankees who decorated their village with wooden towers, Victorian homes, and a Gothic Revival Presbyterian church. The town, originally a vital lumber port, has become an artists' colony. With a shoreline honeycombed by beaches, Mendocino is a mighty pretty corner of the continent.

A LOCAL CAFÉ

A morning ritual for locals and visitors alike is to climb the rough-hewn stairs to the loft-like **Bay View Café** for coffee, French toast, or fluffy omelettes. On sunny afternoons, the deck overlooking Main Street and the coastal headlands makes an ideal lunch spot, especially for fish and chips or a jalapeño chile burger. ~ 45040 Main Street, Mendocino; 707-937-4197, fax 707-937-5300. BUDGET.

A well-marked left turn off the highway takes you right into the center of town with its quaint architecture, bed and breakfasts, art galleries, gift shops, real estate offices, and traffic congestion. Shiny new luxury cars parked in front of even the more modest residences hint at the extraordinarily high cost of living here.

The best way to experience this antique town is by stopping at the **Kelly House Museum**. Set in a vintage home dating from 1861, the museum serves as a historical research center (open Tuesday through Friday from 9 a.m. to 4 p.m.) and unofficial chamber of commerce. The museum is open daily from 1 to 4 p.m. from June through August, and Friday through Sunday from September through May. Admission. ~ 45007 Albion Street, Mendocino; 707-937-5791, fax 707-937-2156; e-mail kellyhs@ mcn.org.

Among Mendocino's intriguing locales are the **Chinese Temple**, a 19th-century religious shrine located on Albion Street (open by appointment only); the **Presbyterian Church**, a National Historic Landmark right on Main Street; and the **MacCallum House**, a Gingerbread Victorian on Albion Street, which has been reborn as an inn and restaurant. Another building of note is the **Masonic Hall**, an 1865 structure adorned with a hand-crafted redwood statue on the roof. ~ Ukiah Street.

After meandering the side streets, stop at the **Mendocino Art Center**. Here exhibits by painters, potters, photographers, textile workers, and others will give an idea of the tremendous talent contained in tiny Mendocino. There's a pretty garden and a gift shop, and the complex also houses a local theater company. ~ 45200 Little Lake Street, Mendocino; 707-937-5818, fax 707-937-1764; www.mendocinoart center.org, e-mail mendoart@mcn.org.

FORT BRAGG SPORTFISHING

Whatever your sportfishing tastes, **Anchor Charter and the Lady Irma II** aim to please. Besides the usual rockfish, tuna, salmon, and whale-watching excursions, they'll also take you shark fishing, on extended trips, or out for a funeral. ~ North Harbor Drive, Wharf Restaurant, Fort Bragg; 707-964-4550; www.anchorcharterboats.com.

As you continue north from Mendocino on Route 1, the traffic becomes heavier than any you're likely to have encountered elsewhere on Route 1. Together, Mendocino and Fort Bragg, the larger town ten miles to the north, account for more of the coast's population than all the other towns along Route 1 combined, and bumper-to-bumper car and truck traffic is not uncommon. Still, there are a few coastal gems just off the highway.

Two miles north of Mendocino, in a narrow valley with a well-protected beach, **Russian Gulch State Park** has marvelous views from the craggy headlands, a water-

SIMPLY DELICIOUS

Fort Bragg's favorite dining spot is easy to remember—**The Restaurant**. Despite the name, this is no generic eating place but a creative kitchen serving excellent dinners. It's decorated with dozens of paintings by local contemporary artists, lending a sense of the avant garde to this informal establishment. The Restaurant's menu offers seasonal entrées like sautéed prawns, salmon, rockfish, and vegetarian selections. Choose from a selection of house-made desserts, including ice creams and sorbets. Dinner only except for Sunday brunch. Closed Wednesday. ~ 418 North Main Street, Fort Bragg; 707-964-9800; www.therestaurantfortbragg.com, e-mail info@therestaurantfortbragg.com. MODERATE TO DELUXE.

fall, and a blowhole that rarely blows. Rainbow and steelhead trout inhabit the creek while hawks and ravens circle the forest. There are picnic areas, restrooms, and showers. Day-use fee, $4. There are 30 tent/RV sites (no hookups); $15 per night. Reservations can be made by calling PARKNET at 800-444-7275. ~ 707-937-5804, fax 707-937-2953.

At **Jug Handle State Reserve**, about one mile north of Caspar, you can climb an ecological stairway that ascends a series of marine terraces. On the various levels you'll encounter the varied coast, dune, and ridge environments that form the area's diverse ecosystem. ~ Along Route 1; 707-937-5804, fax 707-937-2953.

Approaching **Fort Bragg**, you'll pass mobile home parks, strip malls, convenience stores, mom-and-pop motels, and other trappings of this workingman's town where the lumber mills and fishing fleet remain the biggest industries. Still, the town offers an array of visitor attractions, the lowest lodging rates on Route 1, and plenty of sportfishing charters.

On the outskirts of Fort Bragg, two miles from the town center, meander through the **Mendocino Coast Botanical Gardens** for a thoroughly delightful stroll to the sea. This 47-acre coastal preserve, with three miles of luxuriant pathways, is "a garden for all seasons" with something always in bloom. The unique Northern California coastal climate is conducive to heathers, perennials, succulents, and rhododendrons, which grow in colorful profusion here. Trails lead past gardens of ivy, ferns, and dwarf conifers to a coastal bluff with vistas up and down the rugged shoreline. Admission. ~ 18220 North Route 1, Fort Bragg; 707-964-4352, fax 707-964-3114; e-mail mcbg@mcn.org.

Near the center of Fort Bragg you can board the **Skunk train** for a half- or full-day ride aboard a steam engine or a diesel-powered railcar. Dating from 1885, the Skunk was originally a logging train; today it also carries passengers along a 40-mile route through mountains and redwoods to the inland town of Willits and back. For information, contact California Western Railroad. Reservations recommended. ~ Fort Bragg; 707-964-6371, 800-777-5865, fax 707-964-6754; www.skunktrain.com, e-mail skunk@mcn.org.

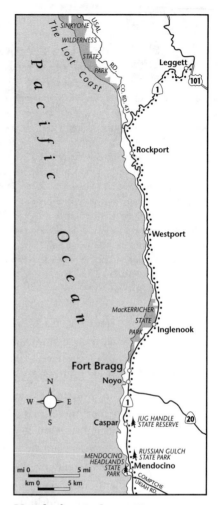

Mendocino to Leggett

Leaving Fort Bragg on Route 1, you'll soon come to the turn-off for **MacKerricher State Park**. Another of the region's outstanding parks, it features a crescent of sandy beach, dunes, headlands, a lake, a forest, and wetlands. Harbor seals inhabit the rocks offshore and over 90 bird species frequent the area. The park has picnic areas, restrooms, and showers. There are 140 tent/RV sites (no hookups), 10 walk-in sites, and 3 hike-and-bike sites ($2 per night, per person); $16 per night. Reservations can be made through PARKNET at 800-444-7275. ~ Along Route 1 about three miles north of Fort Bragg; 707-937-5804, fax 707-937-2953.

Route 1 continues along the coast for almost 30 miles north of Fort Bragg, passing miles of sand dunes and sev-

THE "LOST COAST" BEYOND ROUTE 1

The reason Route 1 comes to an abrupt end near Leggett is the mysterious Lost Coast of California. Due north, where no highway could possibly run, the King Range vaults out of the sea, rising over 4000 feet in less than three miles. It is a wilderness inhabited by black bears and bald eagles, with an abandoned lighthouse and a solitary beach piled with ancient Indian shellmounds. One of the wettest areas along California's Pacific Coast, these lush mountains receive about 100 inches of rain a year. Most of the region is now protected as the King Range National Conservation Area.

From the point 50 miles north of Fort Bragg where Route 1 veers away from the coast, you can see a sample of the Lost Coast by continuing north on unpaved County Road 431 to **Sinkyone Wilderness State Park**, a 7500-acre former ranch with ancient redwood groves and awe-inspiring bluffs. Trailers and RVs are discouraged from taking the narrow, steep, winding road into the park. There are 35 drive-in campsites (no hookups) and 17 hike-in tent sites; $7 per night. ~ Phone/fax 707-986-7711.

eral small villages. Then, after having followed the coast all the way from Southern California, it abruptly turns inland to traverse the dramatic redwood-clad ridges of the Coast Range. With sharper curves and steeper climbs and descents than any other stretch of Route 1, you can expect this last 20 miles to take an hour to drive. Realizing that this wild road is the easiest route through the rugged mountain, you can readily imagine why road-builders did not attempt to extend the coastal highway any farther north.

At its anticlimactic endpoint, Route 1 merges with busy Route 101 near the nondescript town of Leggett. From here you can head south, making the 198-mile trip down the freeway and back to San Francisco in three to four hours. Or, if your tour of Northern California is just beginning, you can continue north along the Avenue of the Giants, the scenic old highway that parallels today's Route 101, north to Eureka/Arcata, the starting point for a completely different hidden highway—Route 299. (See Chapter 8 for details.)

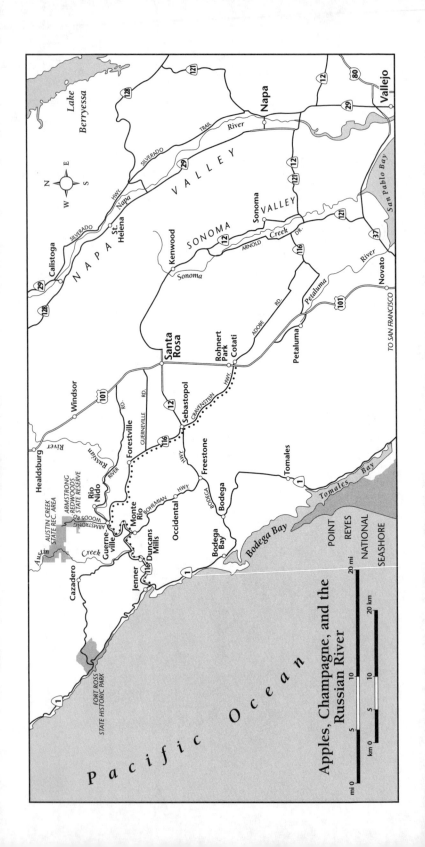

Apples, Champagne, and the Russian River

6 APPLES, CHAMPAGNE, AND THE RUSSIAN RIVER

Route 116 to the Coast

Route 116 is the shortest hidden highway in this book. It runs a mere 36 miles from Route 101 to the Pacific Ocean and takes only about an hour to drive nonstop. And what a trip. Into that short distance the route packs fruit orchards, champagne cellars, redwood groves, the magic-kingdom river resort town of Guerneville, the wild and scenic Russian River, and a spectacular seashore teeming with wildlife. There's another good reason to know about Route 116: it provides the perfect shortcut from the freeway to the spectacular Sonoma coast, bringing its uncrowded beaches and dramatic sea cliffs within daytrip distance of San Francisco and the Bay Area.

To get to Route 116, follow Route 101 north from San Francisco for 50 fast miles to the Cotati exit. (If you should happen to miss Cotati, a barely noticeable town whose biggest claim to fame is the annual accordion festival held there near the end of August, you can as easily stay on the freeway for a few more miles, take the Route 12 exit and drive six miles west to join Route 116 at Sebastopol.)

The Edison of Fruits and Vegetables

Young Luther Burbank arrived in California in 1875 with nothing but ten potatoes from his family's Massachusetts farm and a fascination with Charles Darwin's new theory of evolution. After getting his start with a nursery business in Santa Rosa and achieving his first financial success by importing Japanese plums and selling the seedlings to local farmers, he established an experimental farm in Sebastopol. There, his experiments in cross-breeding plants produced more than 250 hybrid species of fruit, including 113 kinds of plums and ten kinds of berries, as well as new species of corn, peas, tomatoes, flowers, and the russet potato, the most commonly grown potato in the United States today.

You see Burbank's greatest legacy whenever you drive past a California vineyard. Around 1890, California's wine industry was threatened by *Phylloxera vastatrix*, a root louse that destroys grapevines. Racing against time, Burbank worked with the University of California at Berkeley and the State Board of Viticulture to save the grape crop by developing parasite-resistant strains. The effort was successful. Ironically, at the same time it was being conquered in California, the *Phylloxera* spread to Europe, where it quickly destroyed the vineyards of France. Today, to the chagrin of francophiles everywhere, virtually all French wine grapes are descended from cuttings imported from California around the beginning of the 20th century.

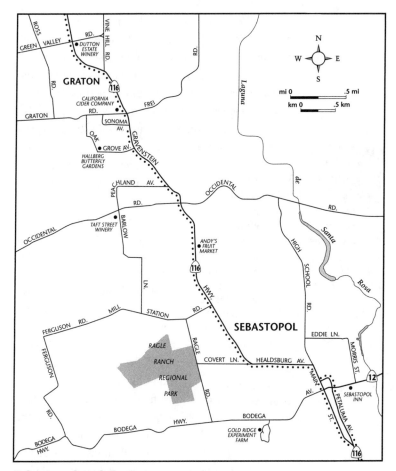

Sebastopol and Graton

*T*hrough the pretty fruit-growing center of **Sebastopol**, Route 116 is called the Gravenstein Highway after the varietal apples grown here to make applesauce, the town's main commercial product. So much civic pride surrounds these apples that you might think they were among the hundreds of hybrid plant strains developed by the town's local hero, Luther Burbank. In fact, however, Gravenstein apples were brought to California as early as 1820 by Russian colonists. The apples are the subject of not one but two annual celebrations—the Apple Blossom Festival, Parade, and Art Show in April and the Gravenstein Apple Fair in mid-August.

Surrounded by miles of modern commercial and residential development, the historic district features about a block of well-preserved red-brick Victorian buildings and Old West–style wooden facade storefronts. There are countless orchards around Sebastopol. Known as the Gold Ridge region, it is California's premier apple-producing area. Many farms allow visitors to wander the orchards and pick apples, pears, berries, cherries, peaches, and vegetables.

A portion of Luther Burbank's **Gold Ridge Experiment Farm** is preserved as a National Historic Landmark. Docent-guided group tours are available by appointment from April to mid-October, and the farm is open for self-guided tours year-round. ~ 7781 Bodega Avenue, Sebastopol; 707-829-6711, fax 707-829-7041.

Burbank buffs may also wish to visit the **Luther Burbank Home & Gardens**, six miles east in Santa Rosa. The Greek Revival cottage, where Burbank's young widow lived for 50 years after his death, is set in more than an acre of gardens. Different parts of the property show off the horticulturist's contributions in medicinal herbs, roses, ornamental grasses, and animal habitats. The former greenhouse contains changing exhibits and a reconstruction of Burbank's office. ~ Santa Rosa and Sonoma avenues, Santa Rosa; 707-524-5445.

North of Sebastopol Route 116 passes Christmas tree farms and fruit orchards, scattered tall coniferous trees, and an occasional incongruous palm tree or century

CULTIVATING BUTTERFLIES

Well hidden just off Route 116 north of Sebastopol, the **Hallberg Butterfly Gardens** is one of the oldest such gardens in the United States. This is not one of those "butterfly world" attractions where a net dome keeps the colorful insects captive. Instead, since 1920 the Hallberg women have focused on plants that attract butterflies and provide food for caterpillars. The gardens provide a sanctuary for thousands of pipevine swallowtails and monarchs, among many other species. Open to the public by appointment from Wednesday through Sunday, April through October. ~ 8687 Oak Grove Avenue, Sebastopol; 707-823-3420.

BED AND BREAKFAST IN FARM COUNTRY

For bed-and-breakfast comfort at more affordable rates than you're likely to find elsewhere in the Russian River Valley, try the **Sebastopol Inn**, a big pink house designed in 19th-century railroad style and located behind the historic Gravenstein Depot downtown. Ground-floor rooms open onto a garden courtyard with a fountain, while upstairs rooms have private balconies overlooking the courtyard or the adjacent wetlands preserve. Rooms have contemporary country-style furnishings and amenities ranging from hair dryers to data ports; balcony rooms also have microwaves and refrigerators. There's an outdoor pool and jacuzzi. ~ 6751 Sebastopol Avenue, Sebastopol; 707-829-2500, fax 707-823-1535; www.sebastopolinn.com. DELUXE.

plant. As you leave town, watch on your left for **Andy's Fruit Market**, a big roadside stand that sells produce grown at several local farms—apricots, bing cherries, carrots, whatever's in season— as well as Russian River Valley wines and microbrews. ~ 1691 Gravenstein Highway North, Sebastopol; 707-823-8661.

The Russian River wine country is famous for gewurz-traminer, a semi-sweet, lightly spicy white wine, and for champagne-process sparkling wines. Other wines commonly made here are chardonnay, California's most popular white wine, and pinot noir. **Taft Street Winery**, is open for winetasting weekdays from 11 a.m. to 4 p.m., and until 4:30 p.m. on weekends. The winery has one of the largest cellars in the valley—25,000 cases of cabernet sauvignon, chardonnay, merlot, zinfandel, and pinot noir. Tours by appointment. ~ 2030 Barlow Lane, Sebastopol; 707-823-2049.

On the same side of the highway is the **California Cider Company**, the state's oldest cider mill, where premium hard (alcoholic) apple cider is made. The company's Ace-in-the-Hole Pub claims to be America's first cider pub. ~ 3100 Gravenstein Highway North, Se-

DOWN ON THE FARM

Kozlowski Farms grows organic apples and sells an assortment of homemade gourmet food and gift items such as all-fruit, sugar-free preserves, apple cider blends, and a variety of baked goods. Other condiments include mustards, salad dressings, salsas, and teriyaki sauces. The farm has a picnic area, a deli, a bakery, and an espresso bar. ~ 5566 Gravenstein Highway, Forestville; 707-887-1587; www.kozlowskifarms.com, e-mail koz@kozlowskifarms.com.

God Goes to Court

Morning Star Ranch, located midway between Sebastopol and Forestville, became the subject of one of California's strangest litigations in 1969, when the former Dominican retreat's owner, folk singer Lou Gottlieb, had a religious experience that inspired him to reject the concept of private property and deed the ranch to God. In the flurry of publicity surrounding the action, a Sonoma County woman filed a lawsuit claiming the ranch as damages because God had caused her house to be struck by lightning nine years earlier. A San Quentin inmate also sued for the ranch—on the ground that he *was* God. The courts resolved both disputes by ruling that God was not a person or legal entity and therefore could not own real estate in Sonoma County.

**A TASTE
OF PARIS**

The **K & L Bistro** is the kind of neighborhood place that quickly
attracts regulars with its atmosphere and housemade foods. The
husband-and-wife team of Karen and Lucas Martin established this eatery in
2001 in downtown Sebastopol. The setting—brick walls and pictures of Paris
at night—is as French as the menu, which rotates classics like bouillabaisse, sardines, duck dishes and terrine. In no time, the place became a neighborhood
hangout for locals who appreciate a chef who makes everything, including veal
stock and boudin blanc, from scratch. Closed Sunday and Monday. ~ 119 South
Main Street, Sebastopol; 707-823-6614, fax 707-823-6743. MODERATE TO DELUXE.

bastopol; 707-829-1101, fax 707-829-1157; www.ace
cider.com, e-mail calcid@aol.com.

You'll find more wine at **Dutton Estate Winery**,
home of Sebastopol Vineyards. Here you can sample
the winery's pinot noir and chardonnay, then picnic
among the grape vines. Open weekends only, 11 a.m.
to 4 p.m. ~ 8757 Green Valley Road, Sebastopol; 707-
829-9463; www.sebastopolvineyards.com.

With all the rolling farm fields in the area, you just
might want to get out and do some fruit picking of
your own. The **Sebastopol Chamber of Commerce** offers a free farm trails map, which highlights the region's
"you pick" establishments. ~ 265 South
Main Street, Sebastopol; 707-823-3032,
877-828-4748; www.sebastopol.org.

**PADDLING
ADVENTURES**

The Russian River is *the* place to
explore in a canoe or kayak.
The river is a Class I from April
to October, and during that
time canoe and kayak rentals
are plentiful. Several outfits offer
everything from one-day excursions to five-day expeditions.
Contact **Burke's Canoe Trips**.
They offer a ten-mile day trip to
Guerneville and outfit you with
a canoe, a lifejacket, and pad-
dles before sending you on a
self-guided ride through the
redwoods. Reservations required. ~ At the north end of
Mirabel Road at River Road,
Forestville; 707-887-1222.

Around **Forestville**, an all-American
small town set in the midst of deep forest
and rhododendron bushes, various farms
welcome visitors and, in some cases, offer
tours—a pleasant nonalcoholic alternative to winery-hopping.

A left turn off Route 116 takes you to
Green Valley Blueberry Farm, a leading
producer of blueberries since 1940. Here
you can buy blueberry plants from
February to April and blueberries, pies,
muffins, and jam from mid-June through
July. ~ 9345 Ross Station Road, Forestville; 707-887-7496, fax 707-887-7499;
www.greenvalleyberryfarm.com, e-mail
info@greenvalleyberryfarm.com.

Leone Farm raises pigs for shows and breeding. This is the place to buy a live piglet, sow, or hog if you're so inclined. Open to the public daily from 8 a.m. to 7 p.m. ~ 4301 Gravenstein Highway North, Forestville; 707-823-6097; e-mail durocpigs003@yahoo.com

Without doubt, one of the prettiest vineyard settings in all California belongs to **Iron Horse Vineyards**. The driveway snaking into this hidden spot is bordered with flowers, olive trees, and palm trees. Hills roll away in every direction, revealing a line of distant mountains. The winery buildings, painted barn-red, follow the classic architecture of American farms. Laid out around them in graceful checkerboard patterns are fields of pinot noir and chardonnay grapes. At harvest time these will be handpicked and then barrel-aged, for the emphasis at this elegant little winery is on personal attention. The outdoor tasting area boasts a view of green valley and is open seven days a week by appointment. ~ 9786 Ross Station Road; 707-887-1507, fax 707-887-1337; www.ironhorsevineyards.com.

Also near Forestville are the **Topolos at Russian River Vineyards**, producing pinot noir and zinfandel as well as more unusual varietals like sauvignon blanc and petite sirah. Open for tasting from 11 a.m. to 5:30

CONCERTS BY THE RIVER

Johnson's Beach in Guerneville hosts the **Russian River Blues Festival**, an all-weekend event in June that has featured such acts as Etta James, Los Lobos, and Average White Band. The beach is also the site of the **Russian River Jazz Festival** in early September, with performers like the Chick Corea Trio, Flora Purim, and the Omega Aires Gospel Singers. ~ 707-869-3940.

GAY NIGHTS IN GUERNEVILLE

Resting on 15 waterfront acres on the edge of downtown Guerneville, **Fifes Resort** is the Russian River's largest gay resort. In addition to a restaurant and a bar, Fifes offers such facilities as a beach, a pool, and volleyball courts, as well as a disco, gym and massage services. Accommodations are as varied as the sports activities. There are 100 budget-priced campsites as well as moderate-to-deluxe-priced individual cabins that were built in the 1920s and haven't changed much since then. Each is simply furnished with a queen-size bed and without television or telephone. Some two-room cabins have a woodburning stove and a futon bed in one room. ~ 16467 River Road, Guerneville; 707-869-0656, 800-734-3371, fax 707-869-0658; www.fifes.com, e-mail info@fifes.com. BUDGET TO ULTRA-DELUXE.

p.m. daily, Topolos also has a full restaurant open for brunch, lunch, and dinner. ~ 5700 Gravenstein Highway North, Forestville; 707-887-1575.

Turning westward, Route 116 follows a narrow valley of horse pastures along the roadside. There's little commercialization along this lazy country road until it crosses the Russian River as it enters Guerneville.

The area around **Guerneville**, where the Russian River begins its headlong rush to the Pacific, has enjoyed a rebirth as a gay resort area. Earlier a family vacation spot, the Guerneville–Forestville–Monte Rio area became a raffish home to bikers and hippies during the '50s and '60s. Then in the '70s, gay vacationers from San Francisco began frequenting the region. Today, the Russian River is San Francisco's answer to Fire Island. There are many gay resorts in and around Guerneville, and almost without exception every establishment in town welcomes gay visitors. In the past few years, Guerneville has begun to project a more inclusive image with its slogan, "Discover the diversity." You're likely to see a fair number of traditional families sharing the local beach with same-sex couples, while grandparents paddle canoes on the placid river. Local resorts are happy to accommodate straight guests (discrimination based on sexual orientation violates a local ordinance), though many will not accept children.

As you arrive in downtown Guerneville you will come to a traffic signal at the intersection of Armstrong Woods Road. Turning north will take you to **Armstrong Redwoods State Reserve**, where you undoubtedly will mar-

sidetrips

CHAMPAGNE-AND-BEER

Founded in 1882 by three brothers, **Korbel Champagne Cellars** produces today's most popular sparkling wines. On any day of the week you may take a short drive north of Guerneville to taste these award-winning bubblies and sample their still wines and brandies. The tasting room and attached gift shop offer nine different champagnes, some of which are available nowhere else; also on the premises is a gourmet delicatessen. While daily guided tours are offered throughout the year, we recommend visiting during spring and summer, when the winery's century-old garden, which you can tour separately, is alive with roses, tulips, and daffodils. No garden tours on Monday. ~ 13250 River Road, Guerneville; 707-824-7000, fax 707-869-2506; www.korbel.com, e-mail info@korbel.com.

vel at the grove of ancient redwoods. Adjacent is **Austin Creek State Recreation Area**. These two parks, lying side by side, are a study in contrasts. Armstrong features a deep, cool forest of redwood trees measuring over 300 feet high and dating back 1400 years. Rare redwood orchids blossom here in spring and there is a 1200-seat amphitheater that was once used for

Guerneville

summer concerts. Austin Creek offers sunny meadows and oak forests. Fox, bobcats, deer, wild pigs, and raccoons inhabit the region, and a nearby shallow bullfrog pond is stocked with sunfish and bass. A four-mile hike takes you to a few swimming holes that offer relief from the sun. There are 22 miles of trails threading the park. Facilities include picnic areas, restrooms, and a visitors center. Day-use fee, $4. Camping is permitted in Austin Creek and Bullfrog Pond Campground, which has 24 sites ($12 per night); there are also three hike-in sites ($7 per night); for restrictions and permit information call 707-869-2015. ~ 17000 Armstrong Woods Road, Guerneville; 707-869-2015, fax 707-869-5629. ▲ 🏃 🚲 🐎 🏊 ⛵

Of course, Guerneville would never have developed into a resort destination had it not been for the waters of the Russian River. The most popular spot around Guerneville to plunge in for a swim or launch a canoe is **Johnson's Beach**. Located two blocks from the heart of downtown, this sunny waterfront strip is also home to many summer events, including the renowned Russian River Jazz Festival. ~ South end of Church Street, Guerneville.

Just upriver from Johnson's Beach is the historic **Guerneville Bridge**, a 948-foot three-truss steel bridge built in 1922. The bridge was scheduled for demolition in the 1980s, but the community protested and, after three years, succeeded in having it placed on the National Register of Historic Places. Route 116 now crosses the river on a new bridge upstream, but the California Department of Transportation has upgraded the original as a pedestrian bridge that offers one of the best views anywhere along the course of the Russian River.

Route 116 hugs the north bank of the Russian River as it winds for three miles through a forest dotted with vacation homes and past the nine-hole Northwood Golf Course (19400 Route 116; 707-865-1116) to **Monte Rio**. This pretty little woodland town sports restaurants, lodgings, kayak and bicycle rentals, a graphic design studio, and a movie theater in a long, corrugated-steel quonset hut with a spectacular mural on the outside depicting a wide-angle view that traces the course of the Russian River from the mountains to the sea. Monte Rio has a public "family-oriented" river beach and park with fishing access. This stretch of the river offers prime fishing and canoeing opportunities.

THE BOHEMIAN HIGHWAY

To extend your trip through the coastal forest, turn south (left) at Monte Rio and follow the **Bohemian Highway** (named for Bohemian Grove, the big redwoods at its north end) for about ten miles through deep forest, where giant branches darken the roadway as only scattered laserlike rays of sunlight penetrate the canopy to flash momentary sparkles on your windshield.

You'll pass through **Occidental**, a contemporary village of faux Old West architecture, site of the Bohemian Cafe, the Union Hotel (c. 1879), and a lost-in-the-woods pizzeria, and drive by a series of church retreat camps before reaching Route 12 and the historic district of **Freestone**, where new development is prohibited and the buildings look much as they must have in the 1880s—fresh paint and all. Their functions have evolved, though. The old Freestone Store now serves as the local post office, deli, and video rental shop. You can get an espresso next door in the converted storage shed that is now Java the Hut.

Across the road is the town's biggest business— **Osmosis Enzyme Bath & Massage**. While hot-spring soaks and mud baths are possible at countless locations, Osmosis claims to be the only place in North America offering Japanese enzyme baths, composed of cedar fiber, rice bran, and more than 600 active enzymes. ~ 209 Bohemian Highway, Freestone; 707-823-8231, fax 707-874-3788; www.osmosis.com.

From Freestone, Route 12 goes west for three miles to join Route 1 at Bodega, 17 miles south of Jenner, where the Russian River flows into the ocean and Route 116 meets Route 1 (see Chapter 5).

WHERE TO DREAM OF A WHITE CHRISTMAS

Monte Rio's historic **Village Inn**, a river resort dating back to 1908, was the location for Bing Crosby's 1942 film classic, *Holiday Inn*. Refurbished, this cozy country inn set amid redwood trees has a comfortable feel. You'll also find a good second-floor restaurant and bar with river views. All rooms come with private bath and begin in the moderate range; a deluxe price includes river views and a deck. They're trim little units: clean and carpeted. ~ 20822 River Boulevard, Monte Rio; 707-865-2304, 800-303-2303, fax 707-865-2332; www.villageinn-ca.com, e-mail village@sonic.net. MODERATE TO DELUXE.

Below Monte Rio, the best river access is not from the highway but from **Moscow Road**, which follows the south shore. As the river rumbles downslope, it provides miles of scenic runs past overhanging forests. Black bass, steelhead, bluegill, and silver salmon swim these waters, and there are numerous beaches for swimming and sunbathing.

From Monte Rio, Route 116 traverses steep slopes for nine miles as it makes its way to the mouth of the Russian River at Jenner. Lofty lodgepole pines tower high above the forest's spirelike Douglas fir trees, while breaks in the trees offer peekaboo glimpses of the river far below, flowing between steep, impossibly green forested slopes.

Six miles west of Monte Rio, **Duncans Mills** (pop. 85) is a former sawmill town dating back to 1877. Historic buildings have been restored and now house wine and cheese showrooms and espresso bars. The main point of interest, a one-room **railroad depot museum,** tells the story of the North Pacific Gauge Railroad, which carried Russian River lumber south to build San Francisco. The museum has no official hours; you can peek in the windows if it's closed.

Route 116 descends through a mixed evergreen and broadleaf forest that arches completely over the highway. A few miles south of Jenner, the highway returns to river level as it joins Route 1. The forest gives way to grassy hills. Soon the ocean comes into view, and the highway brings you to the town of Jenner at the river's mouth, leaving you with a choice: take Route 1 (see Chapter 5) north along dramatic sea cliffs to Sea Ranch, Gualala, and Mendocino, or south along the beautiful strands of Sonoma Coast State Beach to Bodega Bay and the wild west coast of Marin County.

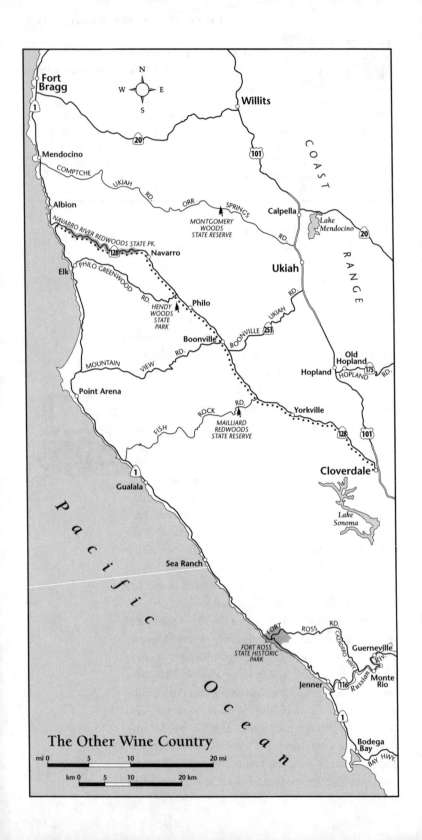

The Other Wine Country

mi 0   5   10   20 mi

km 0   5   10   20 km

7 THE OTHER WINE COUNTRY

Route 128 to the Coast

Route 128 leads northwest from Cloverdale through piedmont country. En route, the two-lane road meanders like an old river, bending back upon itself to reveal sloping meadows and tree-tufted glades. It's a beautiful country drive through rolling ranch land. Sheep graze the hills and an occasional farmhouse stands along the roadside, its windows blinking sunlight at solitary cars.

This drive offers a shortcut to Route 1 that brings the Mendocino Coast within range of an easy two-day excursion or a long day trip from the Bay Area. The scenery is varied and gentle.

The feel of the place is pastoral and idyllic. Along the way you can stop for tasting at a number of hidden wineries or blow the foam off a glass of beer handmade in Boonville. You can buy fresh fruit right at the orchard where it was just picked, then wind your way through one of the most beautiful redwood forests in the coastal mountains. By the time the Pacific Ocean comes into view, the city will seem half a world away.

*E*xiting Route 101 at **Cloverdale**, 89 miles north of San Francisco and 39 miles north of the exit to Sebastopol (see Chapter 6), take the business route through town and turn left onto Route 128 just before it rejoins Route 101. The road begins to climb, passing grape vineyards and entering a forest of shade trees. A sign at the beginning of the climb warns 18-wheelers or semi trucks not to use the route for the next 56 miles. Motorhomes can negotiate it if they have low gears and strong cooling systems, not to mention drivers with nerves of steel. Another sign reminds motorists that slower vehicles must pull over to permit passing.

The road grows steeper and the curves wind tighter; houses and driveways become few and far between as we switchback up out of the Alexander Valley, the headwaters of the Russian River. Cresting a ridge, Route 128 crosses from Sonoma County into Mendocino County and then meanders between hills, gradually working its way to higher altitudes where a

BED, BREAKFAST AND WINE

What more perfect start for a Wine Country excursion than to spend the night surrounded by vineyards at the **Mountain House Winery and Lodge**? The inn has four suites, two with gas-light fireplaces. Opt for winetasting or unwinding beside the waterlily–filled pond, or simply wander through the vineyards of this 41-acre property. Rates include a lavish full breakfast. ~ 33710 Route 128, Cloverdale; 707-894-5683. DELUXE TO ULTRA-DELUXE.

"Boontling"

Boonville has long been known for its local lingo, or intentionally created dialect, "Boontling" (a contraction of "Boonville lingo"). Although most widely spoken between 1880 and 1920, when this was a very isolated community, Boontling was made known to the outside world by linguist Charles C. Adams, who preserved it for posterity in a scholarly book he wrote in 1971. Boontling, his studies found, was made up of at least 3000 specialized names, over 1000 unique words and phrases, and an unusual syntax. Some words derived from the Scottish dialect spoken by many early settlers in the valley; others refer to local characters and events; and still others are contractions. More than 200 Boontling words fall into the category of "nonch harpin's"—objectionable talk—involving subjects that were taboo in the 1880s to 1920s, such as sexuality and bodily functions.

A photo became a "Charlie Walker" after the Mendocino fellow who took portraits. Because of his handlebar whiskers, "Tom Bacon" lent his name to the moustache. Rail fences were "relfs," heavy storms became "trashmovers," and pastors (those heavenly skypilots) were "skipes." Vestiges of the old lingo remain—restaurants, for instance, still boast of their "bahl gorms," or good food.

Stop by for a "horn of zeese."

Translation: Stop by for a cup of coffee.

After 50 years of exposure to television, Boonville residents would have forgotten about Boontling by now if it weren't for the steady stream of visitors curious about this novel, uniquely Californian phenomenon. The best place to hear snatches of it is the longtime local café, the **Horn of Zeese Cafe**. Breakfast and lunch only. Closed Thursday from October through June. ~ 14025 Route 128, Boonville; 707-895-3525. The folks at the **Anderson Valley Brewing Company**, one of several Boonville microbreweries, can introduce you to dozens of Boontling terms that relate to beer. ~ 17700 Route 253, Boonville; 707-895-2337.

For more information, refer to *Boontling: An American Lingo* (Mountain House Publishing: Philo, CA). It's out of print, but you can look for a copy in a used bookstore.

forest of ponderosa pines, firs, and unusually large junipers flanks the highway. This is wild natural country with only an occasional mailbox. There's very little traffic even on weekends.

FAIRGROUND FUN

Boonville is the site of the Mendocino County Fairgrounds. Held in mid-September, the **Mendocino County Fair and Apple Show** includes a carnival, a rodeo, sheep dog trials, square dancing, crafts booths, and a parade. Admission.

The county fair is just one of the events that keep Boonville lively. The fairground is also the site of the **Spring Wildflower Show** in late April and the **Wild Iris Folk Festival** in early June. One of the most unusual annual events is the **Woolgrowers' Barbecue and Sheep Dog Trials** in mid-July. The canine sheepherding competition starts early on Saturday and is followed by a barbecue and a full day of fun activities. ~ For information on all events, call 707-895-3011.

As you reach the little village of **Yorkville** (population 50, elevation 950), fruit orchards come into view, with cattle grazing in their midst. Four miles farther on, Fish Rock Road turns off to the left and goes for about a mile to **Mailliard Redwoods State Reserve**, a 242-acre redwood grove.

The road tops another crest and starts down an eight-percent grade for two miles into the town of **Boonville**, which marks the upper end of the Anderson Valley, 16 miles long and from one-half to one-and-a-half miles wide.

The largest town in the valley with a population ranging from 700 in the winter to 900 in harvest season, Boonville has long been a sheep-ranching community with a heritage rooted in 19th-century Scotland. This little town, with its scattering of modest homes and its two-block main street of cafés and microbreweries, is also the center of the valley's fruit orchard industry.

UPSCALE IN BOONVILLE

Situated in the center of Boonville, the **Boonville Hotel** dates back to 1862. It has eight comfortable upstairs rooms and two more units behind the main building. Guest rooms, ranging from a small, simple double room with sundeck to family-size suites, feature furnishings and decor by local craftsmen—and no phones or TV sets. The hotel's restaurant has long been known for its outstanding California cuisine and rotating gourmet menu, and may feature rib-eye steak with white-bean-and-roasted-vegetable ragout; pork chop with olive tapenade and polenta; and swordfish steak. There are also daily specials as well as your choice of Anderson Valley wines to complete the meal. Dinner only, Thursday through Monday. Closed January. ~ Route 128, Boonville; 707-895-2210, fax 707-895-2243; www.boonvillehotel.com. MODERATE TO ULTRA-DELUXE.

For a closer look at the valley's farms, turn off to the left just west of town on **Anderson Valley Way**, a frontage road that parallels Route 128 and rejoins it several miles farther west. Apple and nectarine orchards, vineyards, barracks-style housing, and modest apartment buildings for seasonal migrant workers line the left side of the road. Returning to the main highway, you soon cross Indian Creek, with its county park campground and lumber mill, and enter the town of Philo.

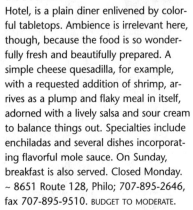

Libby's, owned by a former cook at the Boonville Hotel, is a plain diner enlivened by colorful tabletops. Ambience is irrelevant here, though, because the food is so wonderfully fresh and beautifully prepared. A simple cheese quesadilla, for example, with a requested addition of shrimp, arrives as a plump and flaky meal in itself, adorned with a lively salsa and sour cream to balance things out. Specialties include enchiladas and several dishes incorporating flavorful mole sauce. On Sunday, breakfast is also served. Closed Monday. ~ 8651 Route 128, Philo; 707-895-2646, fax 707-895-9510. BUDGET TO MODERATE.

*P*hilo marks the eastern end of the Anderson Valley wine region. A relatively young wine-producing area, the valley boasts about two dozen vineyards, wineries, and cellars. They run the gamut from mom-and-pop "microwineries," which strut their stuff by competing in county fairs and only selling their wine directly to visitors, to the American division of one of the world's most prestigious champagne cellars. Listed below are those that have public tasting rooms along Route 128.

Pacific Echo Cellars, located on the right side of the road as you drive west through Philo, is the trade name for Scharffenberger Vineyards, which became the valley's first producer of champagne-process sparkling wines in 1981. The quality of their brut, brut rosé, blanc de blancs, and cremant wines inspired the famed French champagne maker Roederer to locate its American outpost in the Anderson Valley. Tasting daily, tours by appointment. ~ 8501 Route 128, Philo; 800-824-7754; www.pacific-echo.com.

ORCHARD-FRESH FRUIT

Stop for just-picked produce, as well as ice-cold homemade cider, at **Gowan's Oak Tree**, a fruit stand with a picnic area in an orchard setting west of Philo. Depending on the season, you may find apricots, cherries, plums, berries, nectarines, any of eight varieties of pears, 36 kinds of peaches, and 60 types of apples for sale. The Gowan orchards were established in 1880, and the fruit stand dates back to the 1930s. It also has a packing and shipping facility and can send crates of fruit to your home anywhere in the United States. Tours by appointment. ~ 6600 Route 128, Philo; 707-895-3353.

Birth of a Wine Valley

Winemaking got off to a slow start in the Anderson Valley. A handful of self-reliant Italian and Swiss settlers brought grape cuttings to the valley in the mid-1800s and made their own wine. In 1855 there was even a distillery near Philo that converted grape skins and pulp into a local brandy called Cream of Science. But it was not until Prohibition that wine became a moneymaking industry here. Secluded deep in the mountains with only a long, narrow dirt road in and out, the Anderson Valley made a prime location for illicit wineries, in much the same way that the mountains of Mendocino County are said to shelter secret sinsemilla-growing operations today.

In 1964, Dr. Donald Edmeades planted 24 acres of vineyards. Experimenting with several varietal grapes, he and other newcomers found that the valley's cool climate was ideal for gewürztraminer. They later discovered that chardonnay, pinot noir, and white riesling also grew well here—and sold better. Through the 1970s more vineyards were started, and by 1982 the results were impressive enough to inspire Roederer, the French champagne makers, to choose the Anderson Valley rather than the Napa or Sonoma valleys as the location for their new American vineyards.

On the other side of the highway, **Brutocao Cellars**, one of the Anderson Valley's small, family-run wineries, specializes in barrel-fermented and sur lie–aged white wines and unfined, unfiltered reds, fermented in small lots to intensify fruit flavors. They make a wider range of wines than other microwineries in the area be-

A LITTLE BIT
OF HEAVEN

Off the road linking Philo and the coast and just a stone's throw from the entrance to Hendy Woods State Park is a private road leading up—way up—to the wonderful **Highland Ranch**. The setting is glorious, a highlands vale surrounded by forests intersected with hiking and horseback riding trails for the lucky guests of this hideaway. The ranch has eight cottages sparingly but attractively furnished, each with a fireplace and a small front porch. At breakfast and dinner everyone gathers in the century-old farmhouse; lunch can also be arranged. Amenities include horseback riding, swimming, fishing in a big (stocked) pond, hiking, mountain biking and wall-to-wall peace and quiet. Everything's included at this casual but extremely well-run retreat. ~ On a private road off Philo-Greenwood Road just west of Hendy Woods State Park, Philo; 707-895-3600, fax 707-895-3702; www. highlandranch.com. ULTRA-DELUXE.

cause the family also has a warm-season vineyard, growing different grape varietals, east of the mountains in Hopland. Tasting daily, tours of the Hopland winery by appointment. ~ 7000 Route 128, Philo; 707-895-2152; www.brutocaocellars.com.

On your right is **Navarro Vineyards**, another small family business that sells most of its wine directly to visitors. In addition to wines, the Navarro tasting room sells nonalcoholic chardonnay, pinot noir, and gewürztraminer juices. Tasting daily, tours are by appointment. ~ 5601 Route 128, Philo; 800-537-9463; www.navarrowine.com.

Just past Navarro Vineyards is the tasting room for **Greenwood Ridge Vineyards**, unique among those around Philo because it is not officially an Anderson Valley vineyard. Its ridgetop location places it within the Mendocino Ridge appellation, the only noncontiguous wine region in America. On the ridge, the vineyards are above the reach of fog and frost and can grow premium white riesling, cabernet sauvignon, and merlot grapes in addition to pinot noir. Three Greenwood Ridge wines have been included in *Wine Spectator*'s list of the Top 100 Wines of the World, and the vineyard has won Best of Show awards at the New World International Wine Competition, the Pacific Rim International Wine Competition, and the Los Angeles County Fair. Tasting daily, tours by appointment. ~ 5501 Route 128, Philo; 707-895-2002,

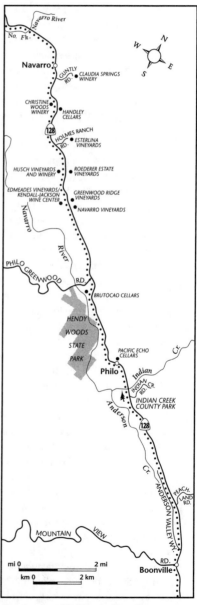

Anderson Valley wineries

California Winetasting

The Greeks had it all wrong. They fervently believed that the gods drank nectar. Anyone who has explored California's vineyards knows that wine, not sweet ambrosia, is the drink of the gods.

In order to find that ultimate wine, keep in mind a few principles. The best season to visit the vineyards is during the harvest in late September and early October. The scent of freshly fermenting wine fills the air and the vineyards are colored brilliant red and gold. Winter is the rainy season and a fallow period. It's also less crowded than the rest of the year and allows opportunities for more relaxed and personalized tours, particularly at small wineries. The growing season begins in March when buds appear on previously bare, gnarled vines. By early summer, the buds are miniature grape clusters that ripen during the torrid months of midsummer.

Once the grapes are picked in autumn, the activity shifts from the vineyard to the winery. The berries are crushed; white wines are then filtered or clarified and fermented in temperature-controlled tanks. Red wines are fermented, together with their skins and seeds, at higher temperatures (70° to 90°). Later the wines are racked, or stored, in wooden barrels to add flavor, and then bottled.

There are two basic types of California wine: *varietals*, made primarily from a particular type of grape such as cabernet sauvignon or zinfandel, and lower-quality *generics*, generally blended from several different grapes and often named for a European wine region like Burgundy.

The true test, of course, is in the tasting. Unfortunately, winetasting can make folks unversed in the liturgy and lexicon of wine sampling feel mighty uncomfortable. Adding to their consternation are the region's self-styled wine connoisseurs. Not to worry. It really only requires a sensitive nose, tongue, and eye to master the art of tasting.

Just remember a few simple criteria. The appearance is important: wine should be clear and brilliant, not cloudy, in the glass. Consider the smell or *nose* of the vintage: this includes *aroma*, or scent of the grapes themselves, and *bouquet*, the smell from fermentation and aging. Of final importance is the taste. Take a little wine onto your tongue and see if the flavor reminds you of anything; then decide if the wine feels light-bodied (watery) or full-bodied, rough or mellow.

In the Anderson Valley, most winetasting rooms open daily at 10 or 11 a.m. and close at 6 p.m. in summer, or 5 p.m. in winter. Despite the trend in other parts of California's Wine Country to charge for samples, tastings at most Anderson Valley vineyards are complimentary. If you want to put your winetasting talent to the test, enter the Wine Tasting Championships held at Greenwood Ridge Vineyards on the last weekend of July each year. Besides competitions in both novice and expert categories, the event features food, wine, and live music. Admission. ~ 5501 Route 128, Philo; 707-895-2002, fax 707-895-2001; www.greenwoodridge.com, e-mail everybody@greenwoodridge.com.

fax 707-895-2001; www.greenwoodridge.com, e-mail everybody@greenwoodridge.com.

Edmeades Vineyards, on the left, is credited with being the oldest varietal vineyard still operating in the Anderson Valley. Grapes were planted here first, in 1964, though a rival vineyard was the first to release a wine vintage. Today it is one of the larger wine producers in the valley, making 18,000 cases a year, mostly pinot noir and zinfandel. Edmeades Vineyards are not open for tours, but you can taste their wines at the **Kendall-Jackson Wine Center** at the entrance to the vineyards. Kendall-Jackson represents an international group of affiliated wineries, which includes Edmeades, and their tasting room shows off wines from various parts of the California Wine Country. ~ 5500 Route 128, Philo; winery: 707-895-3232; tasting room: 707-571-8100.

HISTORY LESSON

A little old red schoolhouse just west of Boonville houses the **Anderson Valley Historical Society Museum**. It displays photographs and artifacts that recount the rich history of the valley, from the culture of the Pomo Indians who originally lived here through the arrival in 1852 of Walter Anderson, the first white homesteader, to the life of the community during its years of isolation from the outside world. Open Friday, Saturday, and Sunday. ~ 12340 Route 128, Boonville; 707-895-3207.

The big kahuna of Anderson Valley wine producers is **Roederer Estate Vineyards**, located on the right across from Edmeades Vineyards. Opened in 1982, this is the American branch of Champagne Louis Roederer, the prestigious French champagne cellars founded in 1776. The French company is most famous for its Cristal champagne, originally made for Napoleon Bonaparte and still the champagne of choice for ostentatious hosts everywhere. The Roederer Estate's Anderson Valley Brut can't call itself champagne because the grapes weren't grown in the Champagne district of France—instead, it's simply termed sparkling wine—but it's made using proprietary techniques centuries old. Utilizing exclusively estate-grown chardonnay blended with small amounts of special oak-aged reserve pinot noir, Anderson Valley Brut could pass anywhere for fine French champagne. Tasting daily, tours by appointment. ~ 4501 Route 128, Philo; 707-895-2288.

Across the highway from Roederer, **Husch Vineyards and Winery** lays claim to being the oldest winery (though not the oldest vineyard) in the Anderson

**CAMPING IN
THE REDWOODS**

State and county parks offer a number of wonderful camping options in the forests that flank the Anderson Valley. Just east of Philo, **Indian Creek County Park** has 10 tent and RV sites (no hookups); $10 per night. ~ 707-895-2465. South of Philo, **Hendy Woods State Park** has two campgrounds with a total of 92 tent and RV sites and four cabins (there are showers but no hookups); $14 per night, $27 for cabins. ~ 707-937-5804, 800-444-7275. In **Navarro River Redwoods State Park** is the Paul M. Dimmick Wayside Campground—an ideal location for swimming, fishing, canoeing, and kayaking—with 28 tent and RV campsites along the river (no hookups); $11 per night. In the same park, at the mouth of the river, reached by an access road from the Navarro River Bridge, is Navarro River Beach Campground, with ten primitive campsites and no hookups or drinking water; $5 per night. ~ 707-937-5804.

Valley. Founded in 1971, it began with eight acres of grapes on an apple farm. Today there are 6000 acres of pinot noir, chardonnay, and gewürztraminer under cultivation. It's worth a visit just to see the tasting room, in a rustic old building that was originally used to store grain and animal feed. Tasting daily, tours by appointment. ~ 4400 Route 28, Philo; 800-554-8824, fax 707-895-2066; www.huschvineyards.com.

On a side road that turns off to the right just past the Roederer property, **Esterlina Vineyards** is a small family operation with just ten acres under cultivation. One of the older vineyards in the valley, it dates back to 1974, when it gained national media coverage because the owner was blind. After his death, it was bought by the parents of an employee at nearby Lazy Creek Vineyards, and eventually sold to the Sterling family in 1999. One of the few minority growers in the business, the Sterlings also own three other vineyards in Northern California. They have continued the tradition of making handcrafted single-vineyard wines on a small scale, using traditional, labor-intensive methods. Tours and tasting by appointment. ~ 1200 Holmes Ranch Road, Philo; phone/fax 707-895-2920; www.esterlinavineyards.com.

A visit to **Handley Cellars** is a must, if only to see their tasting room, strikingly decorated with folk art from Africa, India, Indonesia, Asia, and Latin America, with a patio surrounded by lovely formal gardens. The Handley family also has a smaller, warm-season vineyard in Sonoma County's Dry Creek Valley. Both specialize in chardonnay. Taste and compare to see what a difference climate makes. ~ 3151 Route 128, Philo; 707-895-3876, 800-733-3151, fax 707-885-2603; www.handleycellars.com.

Just past Handley Cellars is the **Christine Woods Winery** tasting room. This small winery was named after the first white child born in the Anderson Valley back in 1857. Her parents founded a village on this site with a general store, a post office, a lumber mill, a grist mill, and a brewery—and named it Christine. A few traces of the old settlement still remain on the property. The winery was started in 1975, when amateur winemaker Vernon Rose decided to plant cabernet sauvignon and gamay beaujolais grapes at the family vacation home. Ten years later, when the Rose family released their first wines to the public, they won top awards at the Mendocino County and San Francisco fairs. ~ 3155 Route 128, Philo; 707-895-2115, fax 707-895-2748; www.christinewoods.com.

HOME IN THE REDWOODS

For nearly two decades, a mysterious local character known only as the Boonville Hermit lived in a huge hollowed-out redwood stump in the middle of what is now **Hendy Woods State Park.** The hermit is gone now, but the stump still stands in this 690-acre preserve, which contains two primeval stands of impressively large redwoods—rare examples of what the entire forest looked like before the first loggers arrived. The park is across the river from the highway on Greenwood Road, which turns off Route 128 just west of Philo. The park headquarters here also administers Navarro River Redwoods State Park. Day-use fee, $4. ~ 707-937-5804.

Last but not least is **Claudia Springs Winery**, located on a side road that turns off to the right. This small boutique winery offers a change of taste from most others in the Anderson Valley. Using both grapes from their own vineyard and those bought from growers in other parts of Mendocino County, they make a range of wines including award-winning Mendocino zinfandel and viognier. ~ 2160 Guntly Road, Philo; phone/fax 707-895-3926; www.claudiasprings.com, e-mail info@claudiasprings.com.

As you leave the wine-growing area, the descent steepens as it plunges into a 12-mile stretch of redwood forest. Secluded deep among the trees is the only sign of habitation in these woods—the village of **Navarro** (pop. 67), with a rustic old store and not much else. Once you leave the Boonville–Philo area, there's hardly any traffic on the road.

Crossing the North Fork of the Navarro River, Route 128 enters **Navarro River Redwoods State Park** and makes a slow curving descent through a sun-dappled redwood forest. Most of the trees are second-growth redwoods, grown to maturity since the heavy logging days of the late 19th century, but this "tunnel through the redwoods" nonetheless makes for an awe-inspiring drive as the road flickers its way through sunbeams and shadows. Moss grows thick on old redwood stumps the size of automobiles, mute evidence of the much larger trees that grew here before lumberjacks arrived. Giant ferns line the roadside, creating an atmosphere that suggests a lost world where it wouldn't seem too surprising to see a dinosaur pop out of the woods (though you're much more likely to encounter deer). ~ 707-937-5804.

Suddenly the highway breaks out of the forest onto grassy hillsides high above the river. Ocean fog most likely hangs in the air ahead. The temperature drops, and the scent of sea breeze hits your face like a wet rag. Route 128 descends to river level, where it merges into Route 1. As we climb up over a headland, the river widens into a sandy delta, bringing us out at Albion, just seven miles south of the charming village of Mendocino (see Chapter 5).

From here, you can explore the Mendocino coast on Route 1, return the same way you came, or head down the coast to Jenner and return to Route 101 by way of Route 116 through Guerneville and Sebastopol for one of the most spectacular loop trips Northern California has to offer.

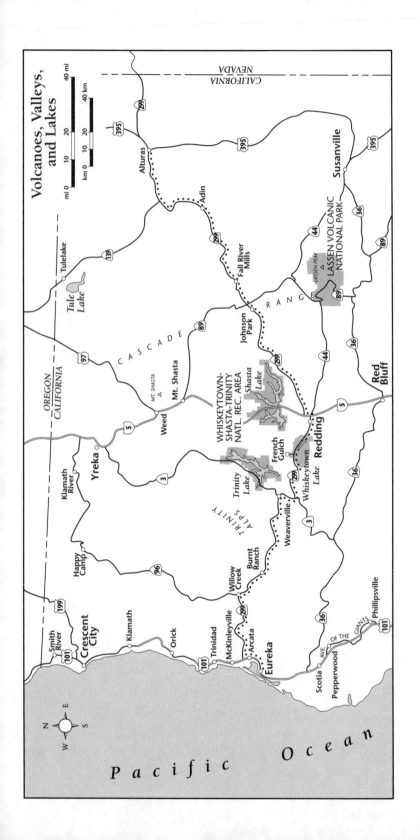

Volcanoes, Valleys, and Lakes

8 VOLCANOES, VALLEYS, AND LAKES

Route 299 through California's Northeast Corner

Route 299 takes you across the strange land that Californians often call "the Far North"—the part of the state that's too distant from any of the state's major population centers to be transformed by weekend tourist hordes. Spilling down from the southern end of the Cascade Range, this region has as much in common with the Pacific Northwest as with the rest of California. This is the land of mountain lakes, volcanoes, tall forests, and Bigfoot.

This 297-mile route can be enjoyed in two easy days of auto touring. But if you're coming from the Bay Area, you'll want to allow at least a third day because this drive starts in Eureka, more than 280 miles north of San Francisco, and ends in Alturas, 189 miles from Burns, Oregon, and not on the way to much of anything else.

That makes this beautiful highway a real find for those of us who enjoy long open-road trips because it means little traffic on the eastern segment of the route. Instead of driving back the same way you came, you can detour on another highway to see Lassen Volcanic National Park, then catch Interstate 5 at Redding, which will take you back to the Bay Area in about four hours.

*E*ureka's 28,600 inhabitants make it the largest town on the Northern California coast. It is the largest of the area's "Tri-Cities," which also include nearby Arcata (pop. 14,000) and the much smaller town of Blue Lake. Visitor accommodations are plentiful and affordable, making Eureka the place to spend the night before setting off to explore Route 299.

Founded in 1850, the town's first industry was mining; the name "Eureka!" came from an old gold mining

sidetrips

DRIVE THROUGH A TREE?

If you're driving north to Eureka on Route 101 with time to spare, hop off the freeway at Phillipsville and cruise along the 31-mile **Avenue of the Giants**. This shady two-lane road was the original Route 101; it could not be widened without harming protected redwood stands, so the highway was rerouted, leaving this scenic drive that combines nature's magnificence with a parade of minor attractions left over from the early days of car tourism.

Here you'll find such oddities as the **Shrine Drive-Thru Tree**, the **Chimney Tree**, the **One-Log House** (carved from a single 40-ton redwood log), and the **Eternal Tree House** (with a 20-foot room inside a living tree). The Avenue of the Giants rejoins Route 101 at Pepperwood, about 35 miles south of Eureka.

MUSIC, FLOWERS AND TRAINS

The cultural center of California's far north coast, Eureka hosts more community events than all the other towns in the area combined. The happening that draws the biggest crowds is the annual **Redwood Coast Dixieland Jazz Festival**, which lasts for three days in late March and features more than a dozen nationally known groups as well as local bands. The event opens with "A Taste of Main Street," an Old Town celebration that allows participants to sample specialties offered by many restaurants and bakeries. In mid-July, Eureka's waterfront is the scene of the two-day **Blues by the Bay** festival, featuring top national acts. Music in the streets is also a highlight of Eureka's spectacular **Fourth of July** celebration. ~ For more information, contact the Chamber of Commerce: 707-445-3378.

Eureka's oldest annual event, the **Rhododendron Festival** features a parade of floats covered with rhododendron blooms, as well as a dance, a golf tournament, and an art show. ~ 707-442-3738.

Old-time steam trains and "donkeys," steam engines that were used to haul logs out of the forest, are stoked up at several celebrations held at Fort Humboldt, located at the southern end of Eureka. **Donkey Days** takes place in late April, and **Steaming Up** happens on the third Saturday of each summer month. ~ 707-445-6567.

---

exclamation meaning "I found it." Today fishing and lumbering have replaced more romantic occupations, but much of the region's history is captured in over 100 glorious Victorian homes ranging from understated designs to the outlandish **Carson Mansion**, a multilayered confection that makes other Gothic Revival architecture seem tame. It was built in the 1880s by William Carson, a wealthy lumber merchant with the same need for os-

SLEEPING VICTORIAN

Ideally located in Old Town, the **Eagle House Victorian Inn** dates to the 1880s and sweeps you back in time to the same era with its outlandish Victorian architecture, combining Eastlake, Queen Anne, and Second Empire revival styles to create an effect that's absolutely over the top. Dozens of colorful flags flutter from the mansard roof to heighten the ostentation even more. There are more than 1000 pieces of antique furniture in the inn's common areas and guest rooms. Each of the 24 rooms is individually decorated in a different color scheme. A typical midrange fourth-floor room has a sweeping view of the bay; peach-tone walls and warm woodwork set off the antique bentwood bed and elaborately carved cabinetry. A woodburning fireplace is built into one corner. Continental breakfast is included in the room rates, which are so affordable you'll find it hard to believe you're in California. ~ 139 2nd Street, Eureka; 707-444-3344. MODERATE TO DELUXE.

tentation that afflicted the robber barons on San Francisco's Nob Hill. The Carson Mansion is a private club, but you can drive by and view its distinctive architecture. ~ 2nd and M streets, Eureka.

Of a more subdued nature are the **covered bridges** on the southern outskirts of town. To reach them from Route 101, take Elk River Road two miles to Berta Road or three miles to Janes Road (there is a wooden span covering both). You'll enter a picture of red barns and green pasture framed by cool, lofty forest. The bridges, crossing a small river, evoke Vermont winters and New Hampshire sleigh rides.

TOURING EUREKA

At the foot of C Street in Old Town, where the bowery meets the bay, the **1910 Madaket** departs. For several well-invested dollars, you'll sail past an egret rookery, oyster beds, pelican roosts, ugly pulp mills, and the town's flashy marina. The cruises operate May through September. No cruises Monday. ~ Eureka; 707-445-1910; e-mail madaket 1910@aol.com.

If you're a landlubber, however, and prefer a shoreside tour of Eureka, you can always take a horse-and-buggy ride around town. The **Old Town Carriage Company** has a turn-of-the-20th-century reproduction carriage pulled by a massive draft horse. ~ 2nd and F streets at the gazebo, Eureka; 707-445-1610.

Fort Humboldt is also stationed at this end of town. Built in the early 1850s to help settlers war against indigenous tribes of Yurok, Hoopa, Wiyot, and Mattole Indians, it has been partially restored. In addition to re-creating army life (experienced here by a hard-drinking young officer named Ulysses S. Grant), the historic park displays early logging traditions. There's a drafty logger's cabin, a small lumber industry museum, a military museum displaying army artifacts, and a couple of remarkable old steam engines. In the winter, the military museum is open only on weekends. ~ 3431 Fort Avenue, Eureka; 707-445-6567.

Nearby **Sequoia Park** provides a nifty retreat from urban life. Tucked into its 52-acre preserve is a petting

GARDEN TO TABLE DINING

Restaurant 301 in the Hotel Carter offers fresh, inventive gourmet food, with imaginative entrées such as teriyaki-bourbon portobello mushroom and coffee-dusted venison medallions. The menu changes seasonally but usually features fish, meat, and vegetarian dishes. Prix-fixe multicourse meals, complete with wine pairings for each course, are also available. Dinner only. ~ Hotel Carter, 301 L Street, Eureka; 707-444-8062, fax 707-444-8067; www.carter house.com. MODERATE TO DELUXE.

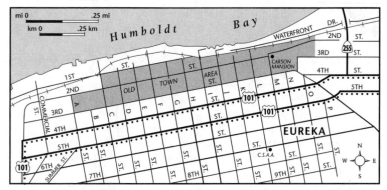

Old Town Eureka

zoo (closed Monday), a picnic area, a playground, and a thick stand of redwoods. ~ W Street between Glatt and Madrone streets, Eureka.

Then head to **Old Town**, Eureka's answer to the nation's gentrification craze. This neighborhood was formerly the local bowery; the term "skid row" reputedly originated right here. It derived from the bums residing beside the nearby "skid roads," along which redwood logs were transported to the waterfront. Now the ghetto is gilded: old Victorians, woodframe warehouses, brick buildings, and clapboard houses have been rebuilt and painted striking colors. Stylish shops have sprung up and restaurants have opened. Old Town is located two blocks north of Route 101.

Route 101 traces the shoreline of Arcata Bay for six miles to the lumber mill town of **Arcata**. Industrial as it looks, Arcata is also a college town, home to Humboldt State University, where the leading fields of study are forestry and natural resource management. For more than a mile you'll drive past an astonishing array of freshly sawed, neatly stacked redwood planks and beams. On the north side of Bay, take the second Arcata exit and you're on Route 299, a divided four-lane highway that crosses the broad, gravelly Mad River, where there are still more lumber mills.

A turnoff on the right goes south for a short distance to **Blue Lake**, a little Victorian town in need of a fresh coat of paint. Chief among its architectural treasures, the Fountain House (c. 1901), with its three-story square tower, greets visitors on their way into town. There is no

Hunting Bigfoot

Bigfoot, or Sasquatch, the legendary forest ape of the Pacific Northwest, appeared in American Indian stories even before 1886, when the first sighting by Anglos occurred on the outskirts of Crescent City, California, on the coast 75 miles north of Eureka. As settlers moved deeper into the Northern California mountains, many reported encounters with the creatures, consistently described as seven to eight feet tall, weighing 300 to 400 pounds, lightly covered with hair, and emitting a terrible body odor. One of the areas where sightings were most common was the forest between Willow Creek and Happy Camp.

Reported sightings stopped soon after the beginning of the 20th century, and for many years local believers theorized that the huge forest apes had become extinct. But in 1935 a set of 18-inch barefoot tracks was found crossing a snowbank on a mountainside north of Willow Creek, rekindling speculation that the deep, wild woods might still harbor mysterious giants.

In 1958, a new rash of sightings began around Willow Creek. Heavy equipment at logging road construction sites was moved, 55-gallon steel drums were thrown around and footprints were everywhere. Over the next 40 years, numerous scientific expeditions were organized to search for Bigfoot, and sightings were reported by more than 50 credible witnesses.

Today, practically everybody in the Willow Creek and Trinity River region has an opinion about whether Bigfoot exists or not. Skeptics point out that no such creature has ever been captured, nor have the remains of a dead one ever been found. Believers answer that the forests of Northern California, Oregon, Washington, and British Columbia are so vast that avoiding human contact would be easy.

lake at Blue Lake. There used to be, but when the Mad River shifted its course in the 1920s, the lake dried up. Today even the resort hotel that used to stand on the lake shore is gone.

The **Blue Lake Museum**, located in the town's old railroad depot, contains historical photographs and displays from the days when the town was the outfitting center for prospectors heading into the Trinity gold country, as well as American Indian artifacts. Hours are limited—open from April to late September on Sunday, Tuesday, and Wednesday afternoons, and the rest of the year by appointment. ~ 330 Railroad Avenue, Blue Lake; 707-668-5576.

CELEBRATING BLUE LAKE'S LEGENDARY LADIES

Normally sleepy little Blue Lake livens up in mid-July, when thousands of people descend on the town for **Annie & Mary Day**, a Sunday celebration that features a fiddle festival, a pancake breakfast, a 4-H petting zoo, a parade, crafts booths, a barbecue and a pageant finale. (Annie Carroll and Mary Buckley were two bookkeepers who worked for the Arcata Mad River Railroad.) ~ 707-668-5655.

*P*ast Blue Lake, Route 299 narrows to become a two-lane blacktop highway. Wildflowers line the roadsides. Tall second-growth forest reveals that this has been a logging area for a long time. Today, you'll encounter logging trucks carrying logs four to six feet in diameter or more. A truck can't carry an entire redwood tree, only three or four lengths of the gigantic logs. Climbing into the mountains, the first scenic vista is **Lord-Ellis Summit**, named for entrepreneurs William Lord and Edward Ellis, who established what is now Route 299 as a pack mule trail in 1895. The vista overlooks steep slopes, most of them densely forested and some completely clear-

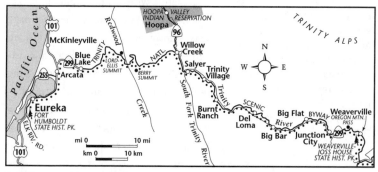

Eureka to Weaverville

cut—reminders of the "cut and run" approach to logging that was practiced in earlier times. Today California has the strictest timber-cutting laws in the nation, and despite what area sawmills and lumberyards might lead you to think, forestry practices on both private and public land have become much more low-impact in recent years.

The highway makes a quick descent to cross Redwood Creek, then soars upward again around sweeping horseshoe curves to another overlook at **Berry Summit**. If it was foggy or overcast when you left Eureka, the ridge crest at the end of this first long climb will probably bring you to sunny blue skies.

From there, it's a ten-mile descent along **Willow Creek** to the town of the same name. Though mainly a logging town, Willow Creek never gives visitors a chance to forget the legend of Bigfoot, the giant, perhaps mythical apelike creature that since 1886 has been reported to roam the forests in these parts. Here you'll find the Bigfoot Rafting Company, the Bigfoot Lumber Company, the Big Foot Golf & Country Club, the Bigfoot Chapter of the Lions Club, and even the Big Foot Podiatry Clinic.

The place to learn more about Bigfoot is the **Willow Creek–China Flat Museum**. You can't miss it. Just watch for the "life-size" eight-foot-tall carved redwood Bigfoot statue with 18-inch-long feet that stands beside the highway. The place used to be a fairly typical local history museum with American Indian artifacts and exhibits about mining, farming, and logging in the Trinity River area. It was transformed in 1998 with the addition of a new wing to house research material donated by the estate of the late Bob Titmus, who spent 40 years making plaster casts of tracks and leading expeditions in search of Bigfoot in the Willow Creek area

RAFTING

The Trinity River between Willow Creek and Weaverville is one of the best whitewater rafting and kayaking areas in the state, especially in late spring. It's a Class I through IV river trip, paralleling Route 299 the whole way. For raft and kayak rentals, shuttle services, or guided river trips, contact **Bigfoot Rafting Company**. ~ Route 299, Willow Creek; 530-629-2263, 800-722-2223; www.bigfootrafting.com. Another company that offers rafting trips and inflatable kayak rentals is **Aurora River Adventures**. They also rent canoes, which can be used on the lower Trinity. ~ P.O. Box 938, Willow Creek, CA 95573; 800-562-8475.

and in British Columbia. Stop in at this free museum, and the collection of footprints and sighting descriptions may make a believer out of you—at least enough to make you want to keep your eyes peeled while exploring this region. Open mid-April through October, Wednesday through Sunday, and the rest of the year by appointment. ~ Route 299, Willow Creek; 530-629-2653.

Willow Creek flows into the Trinity River, which Route 299 follows all the way to Weaverville. **Salyer**, where the South Fork of the Trinity River joins the main river, was the site of the Hupa village of Hlel Den, a major market center where Indians from many tribes came to trade wares such as furs, obsidian, and even redwood canoes. Beyond Salyer, the mountains close in and the canyon deepens and steepens. The road crosses back and forth over the river and through one-store riverbank villages like **Burnt Ranch**. Steep granite cliffs rise along the roadside. The forest is a lush blend of oak, fir, and ponderosa and lodgepole pine.

HOOPA HERITAGE

Twelve miles north of Willow Creek via Route 96, the **Hoopa Tribal Museum** exhibits its collection of Hupa, Yurok, and Karuk artifacts, including basketry, ceremonial clothing, and canoes hewn from redwood logs. The Hoopa Valley Reservation, on which the museum is located, is California's largest and some say, prettiest, Indian reservation, and many of its older inhabitants look striking because of the custom of facial tattoos. The tribal museum also offers guided tours to traditional villages and ceremonial grounds by appointment. Open Tuesday through Saturday. Fee for tours ~ Route 96, Hoopa; 530-625-4110.

The road enters the Forest Service's **Trinity River Recreation Area**, where there's a major river raft pullout point, along with several national forest campgrounds sandwiched between the river and the highway. A scattering of roadside services are available in tiny villages along the way: **Del Loma** (pop. 30) has an RV campground with a few cabins to rent; **Big Bar** (pop. 38) has a restaurant; and **Big Flat** (pop. 200) has river access and many rafting outfitters.

Past Big Flat, the road follows the river northeast for a few miles, offering a good view of the **Trinity Alps** directly ahead. Rising to elevations of more than 8500 feet, the massive cluster of mountains is a designated wilderness area and one of the most popular backpacking areas in California's far north.

DRIFTING TO
SLEEP

An unusual lodging possibility in the Redding area is to rent a houseboat on Shasta Lake or Trinity Lake and pick a secluded cove as your home-away-from-home. On Shasta Lake, you'll find houseboats for rent at **Lakeshore Marina** (20479 Lakeshore Drive, Lakehead; 530-238-2303) and **Shasta Marina** (18390 O'Brien Inlet Road, Lakehead; 530-238-2284, 800-959-3359). On Trinity Lake, houseboat rentals are available at **Trinity Alps Marina** (Lewiston; 530-286-2282, 800-824-0083).

Except for a stone historic marker, scarcely a trace remains of the logging town of **Baghdad**, founded in 1850 and attaining a peak population of 500. That's more than three times the size of nearby **Junction City**—not much of a city, but it does have a bar, a store, and a rifle range.

From the summit of **Oregon Mountain Pass**, elevation 2888 feet, you can see Weaverville below, surrounded by a vast expanse of evergreen forest.

Weaverville, a country-style Victorian town shaded by honey locusts, has small-town charm and a colorful past worth exploring. At the **Jake Jackson Memorial Museum**, displays re-create the tragedy and romance of the Gold Rush days. There's a complete blacksmith's shop, as well as early mining tools (including a stamp mill used for obtaining gold from ore), archaic medical supplies, and a fascinating display of Chinese weapons, gowns, and money.

WEAVERVILLE
DELIGHTS

Tucked away in a woodsy corner, the **Red Hill Motel** delivers comfortable rooms and cabins. Most of the accomodations feature knotty-pine walls and include color cable television, but the best deals are the individual cabins. Some of these include full kitchenettes, afford ample privacy, and cost a few dollars more. They also offer knockout views of the Trinity Alps through the pines. ~ Red Hill Road, Weaverville; 530-623-4331, fax 530-623-4341; www.red hillresorts.com, e-mail redhill@snowcrest.net. BUDGET TO MODERATE.

Located in Weaverville's historic district, **Noelle's Garden Cafe** sits on the upper part of a two-story flat and provides an excellent vantage point for studying the town's street life. Mornings, sample homefries, the breakfast burrito, or an omelette. At lunch, you'll find vegetarian sandwiches, quiche, gourmet salads, and cool fruit smoothies. On warm days, you can eat outdoors on the deck. Dinner Wednesday through Saturday. Call for winter hours. ~ Corner of Routes 299 and 3, Weaverville; 530-623-2058, fax 530-623-1123. BUDGET.

From December through March, it's open only on Tuesday and Saturday afternoons. ~ 508 Main Street, Weaverville; 530-623-5211.

One block away sits **Weaverville Joss House State Historic Park**, known as the "Temple Amongst the Forest Beneath the Clouds." Here Chinese Taoists have worshiped since 1873. Nestled in a grove of trees near a wooden footbridge, this temple is a tribute to the Chinese miners whose hard labor brought them neither riches nor acceptance in the Old West. Closed Monday and Tuesday. Admission. ~ Main and Oregon streets, Weaverville; phone/fax 530-623-5284.

*F*rom Weaverville, Route 299 climbs to an elevation of 3000 feet, then begins its descent following another Willow Creek (no relation to the creek and town we passed earlier) and continues east to one of Northern California's premier recreational destinations. While best known for water sports, this area is also the place to find old mining towns, historic commercial districts, and American Indian landmarks.

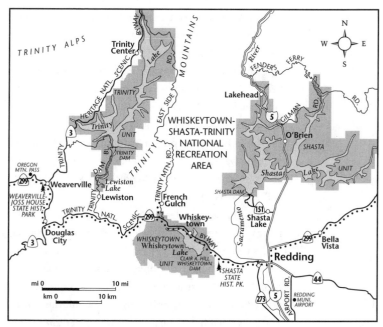

Weaverville to Redding

Three miles north of Route 299 on Trinity Mountain Road, a paved road that turns off to your left is the historic mining town of **French Gulch**, now a National Historic District. Settled in 1849, the town was once an important way station on the Old Oregon Pacific Trail; it's a place where time has refused to budge for the last 100 years. The townsfolk still take family walks down Main Street, paint their picket fences white, and rarely lock their bikes.

Among the municipal heirlooms is **St. Rose's Church**, a picturesque wood-frame structure.

WATERFALL WALK

For a scenic, moderate, two-hour hike, turn off to the right from Route 299 on Crystal Creek Road, about a mile west of the French Gulch turnoff. After a couple of miles the road deteriorates into a washed-out former logging road that is no longer maintained. Follow this road on foot for about two miles to reach **Crystal Creek Falls**, a string of cascades that fall a total of 200 feet, set in a pocket of primeval forest.

Route 299 follows the north shore of **Whiskeytown Lake**, one of California's best boating, fishing, camping, and swimming spots. With 36 miles of shoreline and surrounded by green rolling hills and dense stands of ponderosa pine, the 3220-acre body of water dotted with tiny wooded islands is ideal for swimming, canoeing, and sailing. There are beaches at Brandy Creek and Oak Bottom; the fishing for bass, kokanee salmon, and brown and rainbow trout is good. There are picnic areas, restrooms, a summer hamburger stand at Brandy Creek and Oak Bottom, an information center, and canoe rentals at Oak Bottom. Rangers often lead free educational programs; call for information. For campers, there are 37 free RV sites (no hookups) at Brandy Creek. Reservations are available at Oak Bottom (800-365-2267), which offers 42 RV sites and 100 tent sites; $14 to $18 per night. You'll also find seven primitive campgrounds (permit required). Day-use fee, $5. ~ Located along Route 299 about eight miles west of Redding; 530-246-1225, fax 530-246-5154. **▲**

As soon as you leave the lake behind, Route 299 brings you to the late, great gold mining outpost of **Shasta**. At **Shasta State Historic Park**, you'll find a restored county courthouse, abandoned brick structures along Main Street, American Indian artifacts, antique photos, wanted posters, and paintings by early California artists. The old jail has holograms, and an 1880s mercantile store stands nearby. Closed Monday and Tuesday. Admission. ~ Route 299W, Shasta; 530-243-8194, fax 530-225-2038.

*R*edding, capital of the "Inland Empire," is the closest facsimile around to a buzzing metropolis. This town of 85,000 folks is also the major jumping-off point for sightseers. In 1872, when it was founded as the end-of-the-line terminal for the California and Oregon Railroad, the town was called Poverty Flat, but after

sidetrips

LAND OF LAKES

Whiskeytown-Shasta-Trinity National Recreation Area, established by Congress in 1965, offers numerous recreational activities. With environments that vary from coniferous forest to mountain lake, hiking, horseback riding, swimming, and boating are just a few of the sports available here. Bear, mountain lion, raccoon, and deer are plentiful throughout the area and bald eagles and osprey are often spotted soaring in the sky. The recreation area, jointly administered by the National Park Service and the National Forest Service, consists of three large lakes north of Redding. ~ www.nps.gov/whis.

The name may be a mouthful, but this labyrinth of water, granite, and pines is a wonderland for water sports enthusiasts. Besides Whiskeytown Lake, which lies alongside Route 299, the recreation area includes two other major lakes. **Trinity (Clair Engle) Lake** measures 150 miles of shoreline and sits in the shadow of the Trinity Alps. Popular for swimming, sailing, waterskiing, and houseboating, it's also recommended for trout and smallmouth bass fishing. There are picnic areas and restrooms; restaurants, groceries, boat rentals, and hotel facilities are located near the lake. Some of the ten forest service campgrounds are located on sandy beaches; $6 to $15 per night depending on the site. ~ The lake parallels Route 3 just a few miles north of Weaverville. Another road from Lewiston, several miles east of Weaverville, takes you to smaller Lewiston Lake and the Trinity Lake dam. ~ 530-623-2121, fax 530-623-6010. ▲ ⚲ ⎴ ⚲ ⌐

California's largest artificial lake, **Shasta Lake** boasts 370 miles of shoreline. Its dam is the second-largest and -highest concrete structure in the United States (602 feet high and 3460 feet wide); free guided tours are offered daily. The lake's water temperature in the summer months averages 76°, making it

BOATING

Fun-seekers who prefer to play on water that isn't moving rapidly can head for Whiskeytown Lake. There, nestled in a valley surrounded by trees and water, **Oak Bottom Marina** rents waterskis, innertubes, and several kinds of recreational boats for use on Whiskeytown Lake. For those who like to sail, there are small sailboats. ~ Oak Bottom Marina Northwest, Whiskeytown; 530-359-2269, phone/fax 530-359-2027.

ideal for houseboating, swimming, windsurfing (although winds are tame), and waterskiing. Fishing is excellent year-round, with bass, trout, bluegill, and sturgeon among the most frequent catches. There are restrooms, picnic areas, and boat ramps; restaurants, groceries, boat rentals, and hotel facilities are located near the lake. There are both public and private campgrounds available, including several reached only by boat; free to $26 per night depending on the campsite. ~ The lake is off Route 5 about ten miles north of Redding; 530-275-1587, fax 530-275-1512; www.r5.fs.fed.us/shastatrinity. ▲ ⚲ ⎴ ⚲ ⌐

VICTORIAN LIVING
IN REDDING

In a town where the lodging scene is dominated by chain motels and motor inns, a delightful exception is the **Tiffany House Bed & Breakfast Inn**. This late Victorian home in a residential area with a great view of distant Lassen Peak has two upstairs guest rooms, each with private bath, queen-size bed, and sitting area plus special touches like hand-crocheted bedspreads and embroidered pillowcases. There is also a separate cottage with a seven-foot spa tub and an antique laurel wreath iron bed. The parlor is furnished in Victorian-era antiques and has a fireplace for chilly evenings. There is also a music room with an upright piano and old-time sheet music, while a more contemporary swimming pool is in the backyard. A full gourmet breakfast is served in the dining room or outdoors in the gazebo. ~ 1510 Barbara Road, Redding; 530-244-3225; www.sylvia.com/tiffany.htm, e-mail tiffany hse@aol.com. MODERATE TO DELUXE.

local land promoters objected to the name, claiming that it made it hard to attract new residents, it was renamed Redding in honor of the railroad's land agent.

Following Route 299 through Redding is tricky; as it meets Interstate 5 on the city's eastern edge, it suddenly becomes Route 44 to Lassen Volcanic National Park, but there's not much in the way of signs to apprise motorists of this fact. To continue on Route 299, get on I-5 north-bound and drive about two miles to the next exit, Lake Boulevard/Collyer Drive. Exit here, turn right, and you're on Route 299 again.

All of Redding's major sightseeing attractions are clustered together at the **Turtle Bay Exploration Park** complex, an ongoing $47-million project set on both banks

WATCH THEM
COOK

A special Redding restaurant is the **C. R. Gibbs American Grille**. It's bright, modern, wood-trimmed blue-and-white interior features an open exhibition kitchen that lets you watch as your meal is prepared and a central bar that offers a carefully selected assortment of California wines and microbrews as well as "the biggest selection of martinis around." The menu includes full dinner entrées such as Boston-style Halibut filet and grilled ribeye steak, along with salads, sandwiches, pasta dishes, and a creative array of brick oven–baked pizzas like the California shrimp pizza, made with baby spinach, roasted garlic, Roma tomatoes, and button mushrooms. ~ 2300 Hilltop Drive, Redding; 530-221-2335, fax 530-221-2867; www.crgibbs.com, e-mail info@crgibbs.com. MODERATE TO DELUXE.

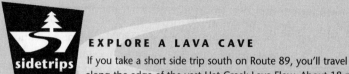

EXPLORE A LAVA CAVE

sidetrips If you take a short side trip south on Route 89, you'll travel along the edge of the vast Hat Creek Lava Flow. About 18 miles south of the Route 299 intersection is **Subway Cave**, a Lassen National Forest scenic area. An easy trail from the parking lot takes you to the lava cave, which was formed 2000 years ago when the surface of the lava flow cooled and hardened while the still-molten rock beneath it flowed away. You can explore the cave on your own; bring a flashlight.

of the Sacramento River, linked by a footbridge. A general admission fee gives you access to all the sites on the grounds. At the heart of the complex is the **Turtle Bay Museum**, which features a multitude of interactive exhibits. Its art gallery has fascinating historical displays recreating local pioneer and American Indian life as well as selected contemporary items. The museum also houses a natural science display. At the hourly animal discovery time, two or three animals are brought out from their indoor cages for a show-and-tell session. Visitors are given an up-close view of these injured animals that cannot be safely returned to their native habitats. Special exhibits cover a wide range of natural science topics, and hands-on exhibits include computers, microscopes, and puzzles. Also check out the river aquarium with underwater fish viewing and the large ever-changing Exploration Hall.

A short jaunt north of the main complex is the **McConnell Arboretum**. Located along the Sacramento River, it provides acres of wildflowers and grass gardens. Visitors can walk or bike the nature trails where turtle ponds allow you to see the indigenous western pond turtles up close. The seasonal wetlands, streams, and oak woodland landscape this 200-acre preserve.

Paul Bunyan's Forest Camp, located just outside the museum, has a woodsy, pseudo-rustic play area for kids along the bank of the Sacramento River, as well as a life-size replica of a logging camp. Exhibits show how to identify trees and make forest crafts. A nature trail presents a cross-section of Northern California forests. Close by is the Butterfly House, which features about 1000 live butterflies inside a greenhouse filled with flowering plants.

The rest of the Turtle Bay Exploration Park is slated for completion sometime in 2004. The new additions will include a sundial foot bridge, a wildlife center, and a nursery. Closed Monday in winter. The Turtle Bay complex is adjacent to the freeway entrance where routes 299 west and 44 east meet Interstate 5. ~ 530-243-8850; www.turtlebay.org, e-mail info@turtlebay.org.

The elaborate footbridge under construction at the Turtle Bay Exploration Park, designed by Spanish architect Santiago Calatrava, will eventually link the north and south grounds of the park and serve as the downtown entrance to the **Sacramento River Trail System**. Visitors should check out this beautiful urban trail which runs through lush riparian woodlands. It meanders for three miles along the south side of the river as a wheelchair-accessible walking and biking trail, then crosses over on a footbridge and continues for five more miles along the

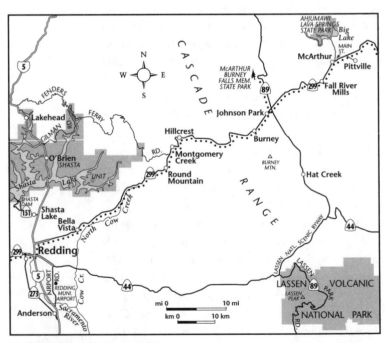

Redding to Fall River Mills

sidetrips

UNDER THE VOLCANO

For a spectacular change of scenery on the return trip from Alturas, or a great loop trip out of Redding, visit **Lassen Volcanic National Park**. From Route 299 between Fall River Mills and Burney, turn south and follow Route 44/89 for 35 miles to the park's north entrance. Located about 50 miles southeast of Redding, Lassen Peak, a 10,457-foot volcano, is the highlight and high point of this extraordinary region. This is the southern tip of the Cascade Range, the same volcanic mountain chain that brought you the Mt. St. Helens catastrophe. Lassen's last eruptions were between 1914 and 1921. Spewing fumes and ash 20,000 feet in the air, one explosion tore away an entire side of the mountain and flicked 20-ton boulders down the hillside. Today it's still a semi-active volcano, and the surrounding area is filled with steam vents, mud pots, and moonscape features.

The Lassen Park Road bisects the park, curving along three sides of the volcano, reaching an elevation of 8512 feet. Along this magnificent roadway are startling views of Lassen Peak, which still reveals scars from its furious eruptions. Also be sure to see **Bumpass Hell**, near the southern park boundary; it's a roaring region of boiling springs, mud pots, and pools colored gold and turquoise.

This area is popular with sightseers, cross-country skiers, and hikers. The finest hike in the park is **Lassen Peak Trail** (2.5 miles). Leading to the summit, it provides 360° views of the surrounding countryside and reveals evidence of recent volcanic activity. Hikers should be in good physical condition, bring water and jackets, and turn back in case of thunderstorms. **Chaos Crags and Crags Lake Trail** (1.8 miles) begins near the Loomis Museum parking lot. Along this relatively easy walk are half a dozen immense crags, as well as wildflowers and a variety of geologic formations. During wet years a small lake forms in a "recently" (300-year-old) collapsed dome at the top of the trail. The best spot for summer wildflowers is **Paradise Meadows Trail** (1.5 miles). Beginning at the Hat Lake parking area, the moderate trail climbs for a mile before reaching the meadows. Beginning at Badger Flat, the Lassen Park section of the **Pacific Crest National Scenic Trail** (17 miles) carries past Soap Lake, Fairfield Peak, Lower Twin Lake, Swan Lake, Pilot Mountain, Boiling Springs Lake, and Red Mountain to Little Willow Lake. In this area, the trail (which in its entirety extends from Canada to Mexico) is fairly level and can be hiked in two days at a comfortable pace.

The park's 50 lakes and numerous streams provide limited catch-and-release flyfishing. Motorized boats are prohibited. The park has picnic areas, restrooms, and a snack bar. Camping is permitted in eight campgrounds; $10 to $16 per night. The Manzanita Lake and Summit Lake campgrounds are the most popular, right off the Lassen Park Road. The park is open year-round, but Lassen Park Road is closed from the end of October to mid-April. ~ 530-595-4444, fax 530-595-3262; www.nps.gov/lavo. 🚶 🏕 🎣 ⛺

When you're ready to leave, Route 44 will take you from the park's north entrance west to Redding, a distance of 48 miles. Or, from the south entrance, Route 36 will return you to Interstate 5 at Red Bluff, 30 miles south of Redding.

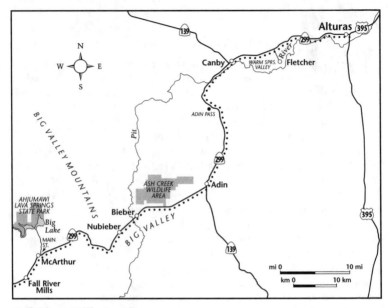

Fall River Mills to Alturas

north bank, with several exits to the city streets. Take Market Street north to Riverside Drive and the trailhead.

East of Redding, Route 299 heads into a landscape of pines and oaks with golden meadows of grass and a scattering of old-fashioned family farms. At an elevation of 1000 feet, Lassen Peak comes into view in the distance. It then follows Little Cow Creek up a canyon with cream-colored limestone walls and slopes scarred by a large forest fire area now partly overgrown with low oaks and three-foot-tall pine trees. At an elevation of 2000 feet is the town of **Round Mountain**, where there's a huge power substation and roadside signs that advertise fresh eggs for sale. At 4000 feet the highway crests Hatchet Mountain Pass, overlooking the Burney Basin and the old-fashioned mountain town of **Burney**. To the east rises the solitary, cone-shaped Burney Mountain; beyond it, a series of vol-

BIRTHPLACE OF RIVERS

North of Route 299 in the Fall River Valley, about 80 miles east of Redding, is **Ahjumawi Lava Springs State Park**. Here a 6000-acre wilderness of pine, juniper, chaparral, and black lava flows honeycombed with tubes surrounds a chain of spring-fed lakes that form one of the largest freshwater spring systems on earth. The lakes form the headwaters of the Tule, Fall, and Pit rivers. Completely undeveloped, the state park can only be reached by boat. If you brought your boat along, follow the unpaved road from the town of McArthur for three and a half miles north to an unimproved launch site on Big Lake; the state park starts on the opposite shore of the lake. ~ 530-335-2777.

canic buttes juts up from the broad black expanse of the
Hat Creek Lava Flow.

Route 299 continues straight across the Burney
Basin. The scent of pine hangs heavy in the air. Four
miles east of Burney, the highway intersects Route
89, which goes south to Lassen Volcanic
National Park. If you take Route 89 for five
miles north of this intersection, you'll find
**McArthur–Burney Falls Memorial State
Park**. It features a spectacular waterfall fed
by springs that cascades over a 129-foot cliff.
Ornamented with rainbows and an emerald
pool, the fall was reputedly deemed the eighth
wonder of the world by President Theodore
Roosevelt—a fitting climax to this long, lonely loop
into California's most secluded realm. The mist that
hangs over the fall makes for a welcome, cool stop on a
hot day. A half-mile trail leads to the top of the fall, and
another one-mile trail leads along the lush floor of the
gorge. The park also has a 128-site tent and RV campground with showers but no hookups; $15 per night.
Reservations required Memorial Day through Labor Day.
Parking fee, $4. ~ 530-335-2777. ▲ 🚶

The Route 89 intersection is the farthest that tourists
ordinarily travel on Route 299. The only sightseeing attraction you can reach by car beyond this point is the
wide open road itself: driving from here all the way to
the highway's end, you may not see another vehicle.

🌙 BED, BOARD, AND BOOZE IN THE WILD WEST

The **Niles Hotel** is a museumlike hotel "where the West still lives."
There's an incredible array of antiques here, including several vintage Wurlitzers,
and hundreds of sepia-toned photographs. It was estab-
lished by J. Eugene Niles, a local entrepreneur who parlayed
the county's only flour mill into ownership of an insurance
company, an electric company, and the first (and only)
movie theater in the valley, as well as the hotel and saloon.
A major restoration was done in the 1980s, returning the
frosted-glass doors, brass lighting fixtures, and hardwood
floors to their original elegance. A Mexican restaurant is located on the first floor. ~ 304 South Main Street, Alturas;
530-233-3261, fax 530-233-3440; www.nileshotel.com.
MODERATE TO DELUXE.

Crossing Hat Creek and the shallow, whitewater Pit River, Route 299 traverses a semi-arid south-facing slope covered with sage and chaparral. Climbing out of the basin, it runs high on the side of a gorge, crossing

slopes of crumbling volcanic lava with chain link fences to keep the rocks from spilling down onto the highway. It passes **Fall River Mills**, a town that seems lost in time, and heads into farm country, the pungent smell of onions filling the air. Climbing again to an elevation of 4000 feet, you re-enter oak and pine forest. Ahead are **Big Valley**, a ranching area, and the towns of Nubeiber, Beiber, and Beiber Station along the banks of the Pit River. Old West architecture is the norm, and nothing in sight seems very modern. To the north is the **Ash Creek Wildlife Area**, which protects the wetlands known as Big Swamp; there's a visitors center. At the east end of Big Valley, with its miles of hay fields, is **Adin** (pop. 500), a

town of little white houses with carefully tended lawns and another turnoff to the wildlife area. Here Route 299 merges briefly with Route 139 to cross 5173-foot **Adin Pass**, the highest point on this trip, and splits off again to descend through semi-arid pine-juniper forest into Warm Springs Valley, where sagebrush desert alternates with irrigated fields. Deer graze on the alfalfa.

Finally, the highway reaches **Alturas**, a ranching center with a population of about 3000, a collection of murals on building exteriors depicting life on the frontier, and its own nine-hole golf course. Built on the site of a prehistoric Achomawe Indian village, it was known until 1874 as Dorris Bridge, named after the valley's first white settler, who built a wooden footbridge across the Pit River here and then built a house nearby so he could charge a toll to cross the bridge.

In Alturas, the **Modoc County Museum** has an extensive collection of Paiute and Pit artifacts and the counter from a turn-of-the-20th-century general store with its inventory of corsets, high button shoes, and other period pieces. There's also an entire wall of weaponry, a rock and gem collection, and an intriguing exhibit on the region's bird life. Another display tells the story of Fort Bidwell, the pioneer military headquarters for this region. Here you'll learn about some of California's last Indian battles. Closed Sunday and Monday, and from November through May. ~ 600 South Main Street, Alturas; 530-233-6328.

Aside from the museum, there's not a lot to do out here except marvel at the feel of what may be the most remote community in California, while the locals wonder what a tourist is doing way out here. Alturas is the end of Route 299. If you continued northwest from here on Route 395, in about 30 miles you'd come to **Goose Lake**, a large, little-used lake that straddles the California–Oregon state line and has a tiny Indian reservation on its west shore.

For most travelers, though, Alturas is the place to turn around and start back. You don't need to retrace your route all the way back to the sea. Midway, at Redding, you can catch Interstate 5 south and be in the Bay Area within about four hours.

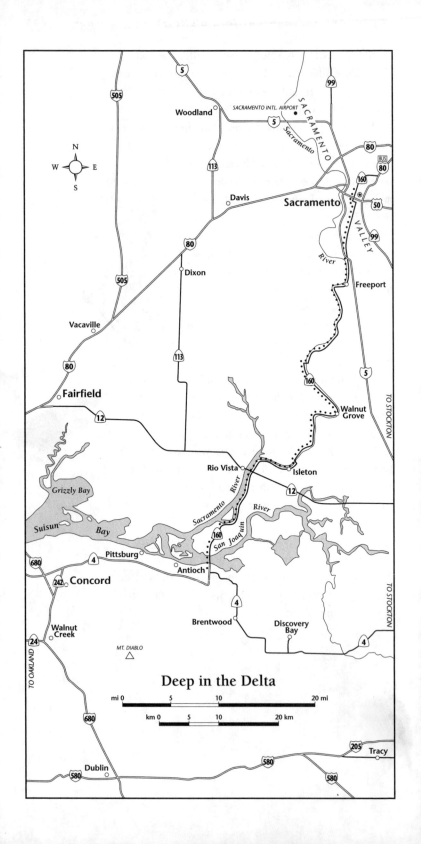

Deep in the Delta

9 DEEP IN THE DELTA

Route 160 to Sacramento

Route 160 slices through the middle of the California Delta, the endless expanse of flatlands and orchards, levees and dikes, wetlands, bogs, and tule grass swamps where the Sacramento, San Joaquin, Mokolumne, Middle, and Old rivers converge in a labyrinth of channels and sloughs meandering across an ancient flood plain to empty into Suisin Bay, the easternmost of a chain of connected bays including San Francisco Bay. A thousand miles of waterways meander through this mazework. Channels bear names like Hog, Whiskey, Disappointment, and Montezuma Slough.

Route 160 starts at Antioch, about 40 miles by free-way from the East Bay cities of Oakland and Berkeley, and traces the banks of the Sacramento River for 66 miles to Sacramento, running along the tops of massive levees that hold the river back from flooding the surrounding farmlands during the spring runoff. The trip takes less than two hours, and it makes for a great start to a longer excursion up the Feather River Canyon (see Chapter 10) or into the heart of the Gold Country (see Chapter 11). Touring the California Delta can also be a weekend getaway in itself if you detour on side roads to explore more of this vast, little-known world of farmlands and wetlands.

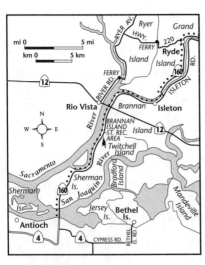

Antioch to Ryde

Along the way, you'll find hideaway hotels, waterfront restaurants that specialize in "mudbugs," and marinas that invite you to indulge in water sports from fishing to windsurfing.

The **Antioch Bridge** marks the southern end of Route 160. To get there from the Bay Area, take Route 580 to Oakland; get off on Route 24 eastbound to Walnut Creek, where the freeway merges into Route 680 north; then follow Route 4 east to Antioch. Passing over the Sacramento River, the freeway ends as you pay a $2 toll and enter Sacramento County. This vertical-lift bridge, with a midsection that rises like an elevator to let large boats pass beneath it, was built in 1927 as the first automobile bridge on the Delta. Previously, the only way onto Sherman Island was on one of the two competing ferry services that operated out of the town of **Antioch**. Founded in 1849, Antioch prospered by mining coal in the hills south of town and hauling it by rail to the waterfront, where it fueled the steam engines of paddlewheeler riverboats.

ANTIOCH'S BIGGEST PARK

Listed on the National Register of Historic Places, the **Black Diamond Mines Regional Preserve**, a 3900-acre park at the foot of Mt. Diablo, features a 19th-century cemetery complete with cracked tombstones engraved in Welsh. Approximately 34 miles of hiking and biking trails traverse the park, which has picnic areas and campsites. Two first-come, first-served underground tours of the mines begin at 12 p.m. and 3 p.m. on the weekend (arrive early to buy tickets). Weekend admission. ~ Somersville Road, three miles south of Route 4, Antioch; 925-757-2620, fax 925-757-0335; www.ebparks.org, e-mail bdvisit@ebparks.org.

BOATERS' PARADISE

sidetrips If you want to explore the watery world of the Delta that lies beyond the highways, head for **Bethel Island**, one of the 55 islands that comprise the Delta. Featuring marinas, motels, restaurants, and boat rentals, it sits about ten miles east of the intersection of Routes 4 and 160. From Antioch, drive east on Route 4 to Bethel Road and turn left; you'll cross Taylor Slough on a low bridge just before reaching the village. Like the rest of the Delta, it is busiest during summer and on weekends. In the winter, many local businesses close for the season, so it's best to check in advance.

'BOARDS AND BEER

Just off Route 160 is one of Sherman Island's few recreation businesses—**Windcraft Sports**. The oldest business of its kind in the area, the funky little shop has everything you might need for fun on the river. It sells ice, beer, sodas, food, fish line, bait and tackle, and wind- and kite-surfing equipment. ~ 17124 East Sherman Island Levee Road, Rio Vista; 916-777-7067.

The Sacramento River is slow-flowing and so broad that even a mild breeze kicks up waves. Crossing it, you enter a landscape of low-lying cornfields with no real sense of being on an island. Sandwiched between the Sacramento and San Joaquin rivers, however, **Sherman Island** is completely surrounded by water, and this highway is the only way on or off it.

To appreciate the character of a Delta island, take a detour along Sherman Island Levee Road, getting you out of traffic (which can be heavy in the Antioch

Transforming the Delta

Settlement of the California Delta began in 1848 with the discovery of gold 75 miles northwest along the American River. The next year, paddle-wheel steamers began carrying fortune-seekers from San Francisco up the Delta's waterways to Sacramento, the jumping-off point for overland treks to the Gold Country. Soon, as many as 300 steamboats were operating on the Delta, many announcing their arrival with music from steam-powered calliopes.

The first settlers to homestead the area in the 1850s reclaimed small tracts of swamp land with the use of crude levees that rarely lasted longer than a single flood season. Around 1870, two events touched off the transformation of the Delta. The completion of the Transcontinental Railroad in 1868 left 12,000 Chinese laborers unemployed in Northern California; meanwhile, the invention of the clamshell dredge made it possible to scoop up muck from the river and slough bottoms and deposit it on the banks to dry and harden into more durable levees. Over the next 60 years, Chinese workers built thousands of miles of such levees, rechanneling the waters of the Delta to create 55 broad, flat manmade islands containing 550,000 acres of the richest farmland in America—most of it below sea level.

With the arrival of automobile roads in the 1920s, 18 ferry lines were established to carry cars and passengers between the islands. Most of these were eventually replaced by bridges. Five ferries still operate and can be ridden for free, and several of the century-old drawbridges that replaced the others still function. The last development in Delta transportation took place in 1963, when the completion of the Sacramento River Deep Water Ship Channel, a straight canal a few miles west of Route 160 and the main river, made it possible for oceangoing freighters to cross the Delta to Sacramento's port facilities.

The Town that Moved Downriver

Rio Vista was founded in 1857, and within four years it had grown into a thriving river town with a hotel, a butcher shop, a blacksmith shop, a livery stable, a general store, and a pharmacy. But in 1861, it rained steadily for 40 days, bringing a flood that carried the town away without a trace. It was rebuilt two miles downriver on higher ground donated by local ranchers.

area) to view the river at your leisure. The road hugs the shoreline all the way around the island, though it's unpaved through the **Lower Sherman Island Wildlife Area** on the western shore.

Route 160 crosses a bridge that looks lower than it is, taking you from Sherman Island over a wide slough to Brannan Island. Just over the bridge lies Windy Cove, part of **Brannan Island State Recreation Area**, with a visitors center and a boat launch.

A turnoff from Route 160 on the west shore of Brannan Island takes you on a historic steel-beam bridge over the Sacramento River to the town of **Rio Vista**. At the turnoff, you can stop to sample some of the succulent fresh fruit for which the Delta is famous at the **Lug Box Fruit Stand**, where you'll find fresh strawberries picked daily as well as peaches in season. Best known for its annual striped bass festival, Rio Vista is really two towns—the old town down at river level, where vintage brick buildings and deteriorating waterfront warehouses invite reflection on the bygone steamboat days, and the motel strip up at bridge level. The town's two levels seem like entirely different worlds.

You can learn more about the town's early days at the **Rio Vista Museum**, open weekend afternoons only. ~ 16 North Front Street, Rio Vista; 707-374-5169; or contact the Chamber of Commerce; 707-

DELTA FISHING

Striped bass may be the preferred catch on the Sacramento River, but the deep, slow waters of the Delta also conceal some more unusual creatures, large and small. This is the place to fish for sturgeon—strange, prehistoric-looking fish that weigh in at 300 to 400 pounds. Under current fishing restrictions, you must throw back any sturgeon under 46 inches long or over six feet. (Legend has it that the largest sturgeon ever caught in the Delta weighed over 1000 pounds and had to be hauled from the water by a mule team.) You can rent motorized and non-motorized aluminum fishing boats at **Herman & Helen's Marina**. ~ Venice Island Ferry, at the end of Eight Mile Road, Stockton; 209-951-4634, 800-676-4841.

374-2700. There's also a public boat ramp in town, with a $5 launch fee.

Back across the bridge, Route 160 runs along the top of the levee on the south bank of the Sacramento River, impressive in size even though much of its water is diverted at the Port of Sacramento into the Sacramento River Deep Water Ship Channel, which bypasses this part of the Delta several miles to the west and rejoins the main river at Rio Vista.

A few miles down the road is **Isleton**, a modest town of 900 residents that dates back to 1874.

A detour off the highway takes you along the main street through the historic part of town, known as Chinatown. The influence of the Chinese workers who built and occupied Isleton from its birth until the 1930s can be seen in the brightly decorated facades of old tin buildings. Historic district status has done little to gentrify this town bypassed by time. Many buildings are

The Delta in the Movies

When you watch a vintage motion picture that takes place on the Mississippi River, chances are it was filmed on the California Delta. Hollywood has used this Bay Area backwater as a lookalike location ever since the 1914 silent film *Cameo Kirby*, remade in 1923 and again in 1929 with different actors and the same scenery. Mickey Rooney rafted through the Delta in the original 1930 film version of *Huckleberry Finn*, as did Eddie Hodges, Jr., in the 1960 version. Broderick Crawford politicked his way among these "bayous" in the Academy Award–winning *All the King's Men* (1946), Sydney Poitier called it Old Man River in *Porgy and Bess* (1959), and Paul Newman fled prison guards and bloodhounds through the Delta's swamps in *Cool Hand Luke* (1967).

Filmmakers have also used the California Delta to double for other rivers around the world. It was the Yukon River for Charlie Chaplin's 1924 masterpiece *The Gold Rush* and the Missouri River in Buster Keaton's 1928 film *Steamboat Bill Jr.* In 1933, a film crew planted palm trees along its banks for *Mandalay*. The Delta appeared as China's Hongshui River in *Blood Alley*, a 1954 adventure starring John Wayne and Lauren Bacall. On the small screen, the Delta represented the Amazon in a 1985 episode of *The A Team*, and a decade later it was the Congo for a *Young Indiana Jones* episode. In none of the more than 100 films and TV shows shot here, however, has the Delta purported to be in California. Nobody would believe it!

BORN-AGAIN SPEAKEASY ▬▬▬▬▬▬▬▬

Hidden away in the tiny riverbank village of Ryde, the peach-tone art-deco **Ryde Hotel** got its start in 1927 as an elegant speakeasy and bordello hidden so deep in the Delta that local authorities could credibly claim they knew nothing about it. Once owned by the family of Lon Chaney, Jr. (a star of early Hollywood horror flicks), it played host to such San Francisco notables as Al Jolsen and Dashiell Hammett. When Prohibition ended, business dried up, and the hotel became a boardinghouse for levee workers.

In 1998, a major renovation of the hotel began. The owners retained the original art-deco design while adding modern amenities such as jacuzzi tubs—some with river views. The 32 guest rooms, individually decorated in turn-of-the-20th-century style, range from simple, budget-priced rooms with shared bath to lavish river-view suites. On the grounds are a nine-hole golf course, a large swimming pool, boat docks, and a pear orchard.

The elegant dining room, reminiscent of a 1930s supper club complete with arched windows, palms, and a grand piano, is open Friday and Saturday from April through November. It's famous for its sumptuous grand hotel–style Sunday brunch. The plush hotel bar, open weekends only, is one of the hottest nightspots in the Delta. ~ 14340 Route 160, Ryde; 916-776-1318, 888-717-7933, fax 916-776-1195; www.rydehotel.com, e-mail rydehotel@hotmail.com. MODERATE TO ULTRA-DELUXE.

boarded up, a few are freshly painted, and others still exist in a state of limbo somewhere between restoration and collapse. Several of the storefronts serve as unmarked artists' studios.

The crossing from Brannan Island to long, narrow **Andrus Island** is barely noticeable, since the slough that separates the two is dissipated into a maze of irrigation ditches. The farms along Route 12 are large, with extensive flat-as-a-flapjack fields and fruit orchards. Here and there, rundown and abandoned houses recall the days of small family farms, before they were swallowed up by larger ones. Their rustic appearance contrasts the large, contemporary waterfront homes across the river with sailboats moored at their docks.

Passing a large grain elevator complex, Route 160 crosses a bridge to Grand Island and continues on the north bank of the Sacramento River. (Actually, almost identical roads run atop the levees on both sides of the river; the Route 160 designation is given to the side with the most substantial towns between any two bridges.)

Here, as on the south side, vast acreages of cornfields lend this route a feeling like Kansas with sailboats. Large, prosperous-looking farmhouses—both vintage rural mansions and modern ranch-style plantation homes—stand alongside the road, many of them landscaped with palm trees that sway high above any other vegetation in sight, visible for miles.

STRANGE DECOR

The Delta's most bizarre restaurant is **Al's Place**, better known as "Al the Wop's." It may be the strangest joint you've ever entered. The bar out front is a saloon with hunting trophies protruding from the walls and a fading mural of a cowboy challenging a bucking bronco. Dinner consists primarily of steak and steak. A stack of sliced bread accompanies your slab of meat. At lunch, every table is set with big jars of peanut butter and marmalade. The idea is to swab the peanut butter on the bread, add a dollop of jelly, and enjoy it with your steak. Sorry you asked? They do, however, have homemade minestrone soup, while Tuesday and Friday are lobster tail nights. The high ceiling is plastered with dollar bills (it'll cost you a buck to find out how they got there). Every February the cash is removed from the ceiling and used to finance a free feast attended by hundreds of Delta locals.
~ 13943 Main Street, Locke; 916-776-1800. MODERATE.

The little town of **Ryde** (pop. 60) is best known for its art deco hotel and its shady past. Here Route 160 meets Route 220, a local highway that offers another interesting detour deep into the Delta. Route 220 heads west, crossing from Grand Island to Ryer Island on the free **Ryer Island Ferry**, to reach the south end of the deep water ship channel. On the opposite side of the river from Route 160 are mobile homes and modest houses with fishing boats at their riverside docks, another odd contrast to the mansions and yachts that dominate other segments of the riverbanks.

Just around the bend is **Walnut Grove**, the only town on the Delta that occupies both banks of the river. Ferries used to carry passengers from one side to the other before construction of the bascule bridge here. ("Bascule" is French for "teeter-totter," and that's pretty much the way the bridge works, raising one end to let boats pass beneath it.)

The high point of any Delta trip is a visit to **Locke** (pop. 75; elevation 13 feet), a creaky community of clapboard houses and falsefront stores. This intriguing town, located around the bend and across the river from Route 160 (use the bridge at Walnut Grove), is the only rural community in the entire country built and occupied by Chinese. Many contemporary residents trace their ancestry back to the pig-tailed Asian immigrants who mined California gold fields and helped build the transcontinental railroad, then moved on to construct the Delta's intricate levee system.

During its heyday in the early 1900s, Locke was a wide-open river town. Chinese and non-Asians alike frequented its gambling parlors, speakeasies, and opium dens. These raffish denizens have long since disappeared, but little else has changed.

Today Locke is like an outdoor museum, an example of what America's small towns would be like if time were measured not in terms of human progress, but in the eternal effects of the elements. You can still stroll along wooden sidewalks, which now slope like the pathways in an amusement park funhouse. Elderly Asians sit in the doorways reading Chinese newspapers.

On either side of the town's block-long Main Street, there are tumble-down two-story buildings with balconies that lean toward the road. Rust streaks the tin roofs, and some structures have sagged so heavily that the doors are rectangular forms collapsing into parallelogram shapes. Some of the outer walls are covered with rose vines; others are buried in an avalanche of honeysuckle. Along the edge of town are the trim orchards and communal gardens that Chinese residents have tended for generations.

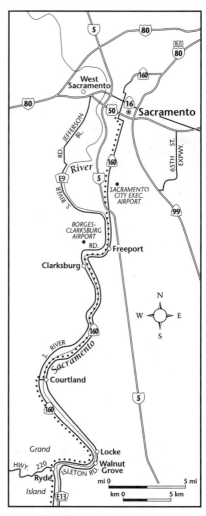

Ryde to Sacramento

Every building has a story to relate. As you wander through town, glance up near the ridgetops of the false-

front buildings. On many you can still discern the outlines of hand-lettered signs proclaiming that once this place was a Chinese "Bakery and Lunch Parlor," the "Star Theatre," or "Waih & Co. Groceries & Dry Goods."

Beyond Locke stand scattered, mansionlike farmhouses of turn-of-the-20th-century vintage with big wraparound verandas, some wildly landscaped with everything from rhododendrons to coconut palms.

Route 160 crosses back to the east side of the river (if you just visited Locke, you're already there) at the tiny hamlet of Painterville to Randall Island, where old trees line both sides of the road, forming a shady canopy as you approach **Courtland**, which modestly bills itself as "The Pear Capital of the Universe." As if to live up to the title, pear orchards soon line both sides of the highway, continuing for several miles to the little town of **Hood** (pop. 246), whose central feature is Robin Hood Park, a small grassy park with pear trees in the middle, dropping overripe fruit at random around the lawn.

As you approach Sacramento, on your right you'll see the **George Hack House**, a two-story Victorian that dates back to 1855. Hack was one of the first farmers on this part of the Sacramento River, a dairy farmer who became known for his apricot orchards. The historic home now serves as the headquarters of the adjacent **Capital City Golf Course**.

The last of the Delta's small river towns, **Freeport** (pop. 125) has a marina, a bed and breakfast, a Montessori school, and three bait-and-tackle shops. A little farther on, Route 160 crosses into the Sacramento city

RIVER ROAD GALLERY

In the Delta, try the antique community of Locke, where you can combine shopping with a search for the town's historic roots. **River Road Art Gallery** is housed in a building that has experienced several incarnations as a grocery, pool hall, and old-style ice cream parlor. Today it contains oil and pastel paintings, ceramics, and silver jewelry, all created by local artists. Closed Monday through Thursday, and January through February. ~ 13944 Main Street, Locke; 916-776-1132, fax 916-331-4398; www.locketown.com.

limits. Why not round out your tour of the California Delta with a look at the historic center of the state's capital city? Route 160 continues north through the city as Freeport Boulevard, leading you through suburbs and straight to the State Capitol.

*F*reeport Boulevard becomes 16th Street as it approaches downtown **Sacramento**, where all north–south streets are numbered and east–west streets are lettered. Continue for one block past Capitol Avenue and turn left on L Street; a block later you'll be driving past **Capitol Park**. Surrounding the State Capitol Building, this urban oasis includes a trout pond, cactus and rose gardens, and a grove of trees transplanted from Southern battlefields to memorialize the Civil War dead.

Set on the west side of this gracefully landscaped park, adorned with statuary and lofty pillars, the **State Capitol Building** is an impressive sight. Like capitols everywhere, the Roman Corinthian structure is capped

LAST OF THE PADDLEWHEELERS

One of the last and most luxurious riverboats to travel the California Delta is now permanently moored on the waterfront in Old Sacramento, where it serves as a fine restaurant, hotel, and theater. The **Delta King** was prefabricated in Scotland and assembled in California, where it carried passengers between San Francisco and Sacramento from 1927 to 1940. During World War II it was pressed into service as a troop transport and barracks for men tending submarine nets under the Golden Gate Bridge. It never operated under its own power again after the war ended.

Four decades later, the decrepit old riverboat was towed to Sacramento, where it underwent a complete renovation. Today its 43 staterooms glow with bright modern rattan furnishings or traditional nautical mahogany. Each stateroom has windows looking out onto the river or Old Sacramento, and each has a private bath, air conditioning, and a queen-size bed. Or you can splurge and opt for the lavish captain's quarters—a two-story suite at the bow of the boat in the original wheelhouse. ~ 1000 Front Street; 916-444-5464, 800-825-5464; www.delta king.com, e-mail dking@deltaking.com. DELUXE.

The *Delta King*'s oak-paneled dining room, the **Pilothouse Restaurant**, serves mainly seafood with an Italian flair. Among the house specialties are pan-roasted halibut with lobster in shiitake mushroom sauce, filet mignon with Sonoma duck foie gras and roasted fingerlings, and seafood paella saffron rice with lobster, prawns, clams, mussels, chicken, and chorizo. ~ 916-441-4440. MODERATE TO DELUXE.

Also on the boat are an intimate cocktail lounge, promenade decks that evoke the elegance of a bygone era, and a 115-seat dinner theater that presents contemporary comedies and dramas in the cargo hold.

with a golden dome and dominated by a grand rotunda. What makes this building different from others is that many rooms have been renovated and are open to the public. The old governor's office has been furnished with period pieces, equipped with a coal-burning, pot-bellied stove, and returned to its 1906 glory. The state treasurer's office has been converted to a historical condominium—half re-creating 1906 and the other half portraying the Depression era. Guided tours are available. Wander up to the third floor when the legislature is in session and you can sit in the gallery and watch the solons battle it out. Both the **Assembly** and **Senate galleries** are often open to visitors. Like the rooms downstairs, they feature antique furnishings and traditional decor, but the chambers also incorporate such newfangled devices as automatic vote counters and electronic sound systems. A museum offers exhibits about California history and government; a film and free guided tours are available. All of the Capitol is wheelchair accessible. ~ 10th Street between L and N streets; 916-324-0333, fax 916-445-3628; www.leg info.ca.gov.

Capitol Mall, a tree-lined boulevard, takes you five blocks west to the waterfront and **Old Sacramento**, a National Historic Landmark that provides a perfect

A STRANGE NIGHTSPOT

Without doubt the weirdest spot in Old Sacramento is **Fanny Ann's Saloon**, a multitiered bar and restaurant. The staircase rises past an endless series of rooms, each decorated in high tack fashion with old boots, wagon wheels, dangling bicycles, and striped barber poles. The main action occurs along the ground-floor bar, where drinkers line up elbow to elbow. ~ 1023 2nd Street; 916-441-0505, fax 916-441-7189.

SWEET DREAMS AT THE CAPITOL

They aren't kidding about the breakfast at the **Capitol Park Bed and Breakfast**. Omelettes, pancakes, french toast, and eggs—it almost makes you forget the beautifully appointed guest rooms and elegant parlor. Each of the four suites are named after a famous 19th-century railroad baron and feature a private bath and antique furnishings (except for the queen- or king-sized beds, which are comfortable contemporary); several have jacuzzis and one unit has a fireplace. Cookies and port are served every evening. ~ 1300 T Street, Sacramento; 916-414-1300, 877-753-9982, fax 916-414-1304; www.capitolparkbnb.com, e-mail info@capitolparkbnb.com. DELUXE TO ULTRA-DELUXE.

lagniappe to a California Delta excursion as well as an introduction to the Gold Country. Lined with wooden sidewalks and heavy-masonry storefronts, its streets date to Sacramento's gilded era. Once considered the city's skid-row section, Old Sacramento today is a 28-acre historic park comprising more than 100 restored and re-created buildings. The neighborhood, situated between the Sacramento River and roaring interstate Route 5, can easily be seen in the course of a short walking tour.

Begin at the **B. F. Hastings Building** located at 2nd and J streets. Behind the iron doors of this 1852 structure is a museum commemorating the western headquarters of the Pony Express.

It's just one block to the **California State Railroad Museum.** The high point of any visit to Old Sacramento, this

Downtown Sacramento

showplace challenges all the senses. The sights, sounds, and smells of the railroads are evocatively displayed here. Trains hoot, station-yard dogs bark, and steam engines hiss as you wander past antique locomotives and narrow-gauge passenger trains. Docents are always on hand to explain the history of railroading. There's also a full-scale diorama illustrating the construction of the transcontinental railroad in the High Sierra during the 1860s. If the re-creation is not enough for you, you can take a six-mile train ride on a historic locomotive from the nearby Central Pacific Depot (every weekend from April through September). Admission. ~ 2nd and I streets; 916-323-9280, 916-

445-6645, fax 916-327-5655; www.csrmf.org, e-mail csrmf@csrmf.org.

A walking tour will also carry you past the **Eagle Theatre**, an 1849 playhouse where Gold Rush–era plays and dramas are occasionally still presented. Free guided tours are available, complete with a video about old Sacramento. ~ 925 Front Street; 916-323-6343.

You'll also pass the **Globe**, a replica of a brig that sailed around Cape Horn in 1849. ~ Foot of K Street. At Front and L streets, the **Old Sacramento Schoolhouse**, with its bolted desks and wood stoves, evokes the days when stern taskmasters wielded cane rods. Then continue past the balconied buildings and brick warehouses that create a sense of nostalgia throughout this antique enclave.

Sacramento is the crossroads of interstate Routes 5 and 80, so you have plenty of choices for planning your route from here. Interstate 80 West can return to the Bay Area in less than two hours. Or, for a more extended road trip, you can take Interstate 5 North to Redding (see Chapter 8) or Interstate 80 East to Auburn, a good place to pick up Route 49 through the Gold Country (see Chapter 11). Or, if you have plenty of time for exploring and an aversion to freeway traffic, take Route 70 (El Centro Avenue) north for 72 miles to Oroville and the start of the Feather River Canyon tour described in Chapter 10.

by the way...

DELTA BOUNTY

Crops grown on the California Delta are corn, varietal wine grapes, potatoes, rice, tomatoes, sunflowers, alfalfa, sugar beets, onions, carrots, and pumpkins. In addition, much of the grass for lawns in the Bay Area is grown on Delta sod farms. Bluegrass sod grown on McDonald Island in the Delta was laid as turf in PacBell Park, the San Francisco Giants' baseball stadium.

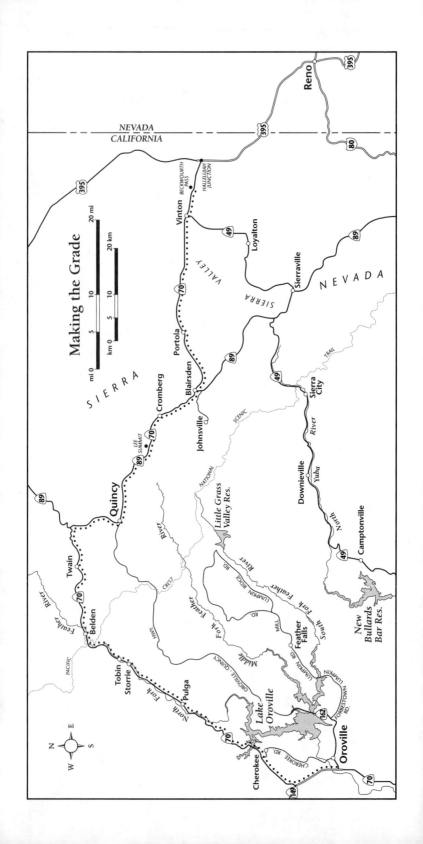

10 MAKING THE GRADE

Route 70 from Oroville to the Nevada Border

R oute 70 begins as a leisurely drive through the oak-covered hills east of Oroville, a little-known historic gem of a Central Valley town, but soon heads into one of Northern California's most spectacular canyons. After climbing continuously for more than 80 miles through Plumas National Forest, it brings you out high and dry on Beckwourth Pass, so far removed from civilization that it's hard to believe it once ranked among the busiest roads on the American frontier.

This 130-mile drive takes you directly to the start of Route 49 (see Chapter 11) and fits neatly into an extended exploration of the Gold Country. It also offers a breathtaking, though much slower, alternative to busy Interstate 80 for travelers headed to the Reno–Lake Tahoe area. Because it's so much faster to take the interstate, and because there are no major population centers on Route 70 east of Oroville, traffic along this highway usually ranges from light to nonexistent, leaving you free to savor the sheer joy of driving one of Northern California's finest scenic routes.

Route 70 starts at an exit from Interstate 5 six miles north of Sacramento. It heads north as a divided four-lane highway, but after another six miles it narrows to two lanes as it continues north for another 60 miles to Oroville, where this tour begins.

The town of **Oroville** may not look like much at first. Approaching from the south on Route 70, you'll see only modern suburbs and highway strip development. Take time to search out Oroville's historic district and discover its distinctive mix of Victorian architecture and Chinese heritage.

The city was founded in 1848 as a supply center for gold prospectors on the Feather River, and it grew so fast that by 1856 it was the fifth-largest city in Cali-

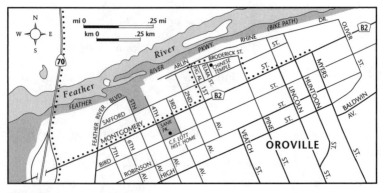

Oroville

fornia. Beginning in 1868, Chinese laborers came to Oroville in such numbers that within two years there were 10,000 Chinese people living in makeshift shacks on the flood plain at the edge of town, many of them employed laying the tracks for railroad lines in the Central Valley.

After the Gold Rush, Oroville's population declined as it evolved into an agriculture and rail shipping center. Oroville resident Freda Ehmann invented the process for preserving ripe olives, built the first olive packing plant here, and in 1919 became Oroville's first woman mayor. Today the area's farmers specialize in olives, figs, nuts, and citrus fruit. The city's entire population is just over 9000 (few of them Chinese).

Yet the memory of Oroville's glory days persists. Geologists have long known that the gravel flats on which Oroville stands contain gold washed down from the hills, and for nearly a century promoters have been scheming to move the town, or even raise it on stilts, in order to dredge out the treasure that lies beneath its streets.

LAKE OROVILLE RECREATION AREA

Lake Oroville Dam has the distinction of being America's tallest earthen dam (770 feet high), blocking a canyon where the North, Middle, and South forks of the Feather River come together. The result is a 16,000-acre reservoir with 167 miles of forested shoreline that stores water for the Bay Area and Southern California and provides a playground for boaters, bass anglers, and hikers. There are 150 tent and RV campsites, all with full hookups, set in an oak forest teeming with deer and wild turkeys. The best hike is the nine-mile roundtrip from the trailhead on Lumpkin Road to **Feather Falls**, a 640-foot cascade that is the sixth-tallest waterfall in the United States. A more accessible attraction is the **Bidwell Bar Suspension Bridge**, built in 1856 and moved to the mouth of Bidwell Canyon when the lake flooded its original location. Admission. ~ Route 162 east of Oroville; 530-538-2200.

To get to Oroville's old town, stay on Route 70 as it briefly becomes a freeway through town, and take the Montgomery Street exit just before the freeway crosses the Feather River. Turn right from the exit ramp and head east down **Montgomery Street**, which takes you through a neighborhood of beautiful Victorian homes. The only one open to the public is the **C. F. Lott Historic Home**, a two-story Gothic Revival Victorian built in 1856 for an early state senator and judge. Inside are furniture, paintings, rugs, and other decorative art objects from the last half of the 19th century. The judge's family lived here for 93 years, and his son-in-law, Jesse Sank, left it to the City of Oroville in his will in 1953.

It's surrounded by **Sank Park**, which contains the remnants of the family orange grove as well as rose gardens, herb gardens, and a gazebo. The house is open Sunday, Monday, and Friday afternoon for tours, admission; the park is open during daylight hours, free. ~ 1067 Montgomery Street; 530-538-2415.

As you're heading east on Montgomery, turn left on 1st Avenue, go two blocks and turn right on Broderick Street to Oroville's brick **Chinese Temple**. Funds to build and furnish it were provided by the emperor of China. It was dedicated in the spring of 1863 and served Oroville's Chinese population for generations. After most Chinese people moved away from Oroville, the temple was given to the city in 1935 and restored in 1949. Set in a grove of ginkgo trees, the temple contains exhibits of Cantonese tapestries, lacquerware, and porcelains. The formal courtyard garden showcases flowers and plants native to China. Open noon

SLEEP BY THE RIVER, EAT BY THE TRACKS

In general, the lodging scene in Oroville is as unexceptional as it is inexpensive. One real find, though, is **Riverside Bed & Breakfast**, a modern redwood lodge set on two wooded acres of Feather River waterfront. Each of the nine guest rooms is individually decorated, with wood paneling and handcrafted furniture; all have private baths and most have private entrances. Pricier rooms have king-size beds plus Franklin fireplaces and jacuzzis. The parlor has a fireplace made of gold-bearing quartz and features Victorian-era entertainment—a Victrola and old books. The riverbank setting is ideal for lounging, fishing, birdwatching, and gold panning. ~ 1142 Middlehoff Lane, Oroville; 530-533-1413; www.riversidebandb.com, e-mail riversidebnb@yahoo.com. MODERATE TO DELUXE.

For fine dining in Oroville, the place to go is **The Depot**, a former Western Pacific Railroad station that was used from 1906 to 1966. Decorated with railroad artifacts, the restaurant offers a range of beef, poultry, and seafood dishes, daily pasta specials, plus burgers and a soup and salad bar. Try the roast duck in black cherry–Grand Marnier sauce. Get there before 5:30 p.m. and try their early arrivals menu for budget meals. No lunch on the weekend. ~ 2191 High Street, Oroville; 530-534-9101. MODERATE TO DELUXE.

to 4 p.m. Thursday through Monday, shorter hours on Tuesday and Wednesday. Admission. ~ 1500 Broderick Street, Oroville; 530-538-2497.

Continuing east on Montgomery will bring you to the foot of **Myers Street**. Most of Oroville's nearly two dozen antique shops cluster around the intersection of Montgomery and Myers. Stroll up Myers Street for a nostalgic touch of Main Street USA. Buildings are decorated with murals recalling Oroville's heritage, including the Gold Rush, a Chinese parade, Ishi, and a stagecoach holdup.

*T*hree miles north of town, the four-lane highway splits, and Route 70 becomes a two-lane road once more as it heads east, crossing an arm of Lake Oroville. From golden grassy meadows, it climbs into foothills

The Brain of "the Last Wild Indian"

Perhaps the most famous event in Oroville's history took place in August 1911, when a 50-year-old Yahi Indian named Ishi was found scavenging for food on the city's outskirts. The last living member of his tribe, the starving Ishi had wandered south from his homeland in the wild Mill Creek area near Mount Lassen. Though free to return to the forest, after his health was restored he chose to stay with Professor Alfred Kroeber at the University of California's Museum of Anthropology in Berkeley, where everything from his language to his physiology was closely studied. Kroeber's wife, Theodora, wrote his biography *Ishi in Two Worlds*, which captured the public imagination, bringing Ishi celebrity as "the last wild Indian"; it's still in print today. In 1916 Ishi died of tuberculosis after catching his first cold. But Ishi's strange saga did not end there.

Kroeber insisted that Ishi's remains not be dissected "in the interest of science," as was common practice at the time, but instead that he be cremated and his ashes buried in his tribal homeland. His brain, however, was secretly removed and preserved. Some 75 years later, it was discovered in a warehouse tank of the Smithsonian Institute in Maryland. A Northern California Indian tribe sued under a new federal law, demanding that Ishi's brain be returned to them; however, they lost the case because they could not prove that they were the closest living relatives of the Yahi people. The controversy was finally laid to rest—literally—when the Smithsonian turned the brain over to the National Park Service to be buried with Ishi's ashes on the slope of Mount Lassen. The **Ishi Monument** can be seen alongside Route 70 several miles east of Oroville.

HIDDEN GHOST TOWN

sidetrips Just before Route 70 crosses the Lake Oroville Bridge north of town, a side road turns off to the right and goes for about a mile to the ghost town of **Cherokee**, which got its start in 1853 when a schoolteacher from the Indian Territory (now Oklahoma) arrived with a group of Cherokee Indian students to hunt for gold. They found a deposit so rich that other miners banded together and ran them off the land. But the usurpers did name the new town that sprung up on the site after the Indian students. Financed by a cartel that included Cornelius Vanderbilt, John D. Rockefeller, and Jay Gould, a gold mining company soon set up the world's largest hydraulic mining operation in Cherokee, blasting away the hillside with high-pressure jets of water 24 hours a day, seven days a week. During its boom days, Cherokee supported 17 saloons, eight hotels, two churches, a school, a racetrack, and a brewery. When hydraulic mining was banned in 1886 because of the damage the runoff caused to farmlands downstream, the town was all but abandoned. Though gold mining was the main order of business in Cherokee, the hydraulic blasting also unearthed more than 200 commercial-quality diamonds.

covered with pines, olive oaks, and manzanita, then descends in serpentine curves to the **North Fork of the Feather River**, wide and still at this point because it is backed up by the reservoir.

From here, Route 70 ascends steadily for the next 80 miles. The impression is of climbing up the side of a plateau—but never reaching the top. Like a flight of stairs, each time the road seems to near the crest, another, higher rim appears ahead. Soon it has gained sufficient elevation so that fir trees and ponderosa appear. At the **Plumas National Forest** boundary, a vista point affords a dramatic view of the river below.

The canyon walls become steeper. At an elevation of 2000 feet the highway traverses granite cliffs, with only occasional glimpses of the river far below in the gorge. The tracks of the Western Pacific Railroad follow the opposite bank of the river, switching sides with the highway at **Pulga Bridge**. Completed in 1932, this steel arch bridge was an engineering marvel in its day, built by workers hanging from the canyon rim on ropes. Two hundred feet above the river and 170 feet above the railroad bridge, Pulga Bridge is unique in that it not only curves as it crosses the river, it is also banked at a five-degree angle.

Soon after crossing the bridge, the river that ran far below in the gorge is suddenly at the same level as the highway. Now wide, deep, and slow, the river is backed up by the **Poe Hydro-electric Dam**, one of a series of hydro-electric dams nicknamed the "Staircase of Power" that provide electricity to the Bay Area. Built in the 1960s, these dams have been the subject of a longstanding environmental controversy. Not only do they make the river unsuitable for recreational activities such as whitewater rafting, they interfere with what used to be the biggest salmon runs in California.

To preserve the salmon run on the lower part of the river, the **Feather River Hatchery** was built below Lake Oroville Dam. Each year up to 20 million salmon eggs are incubated and hatched there. Later, adult salmon instinctively return to the hatchery, rather than the mountain streams upriver, to spawn. You can observe the process through large viewing windows at the hatchery and take a self-guided tour to learn more about the facility. Though there are no more salmon in the Feather River Canyon, anglers can still be seen along the wide

Runaway Railroad Budget

The Western Pacific Railroad through the Feather River Canyon was the most expensive of California's major railroad lines. Its construction through the canyon cost $100,000 per mile. The last spike in the railroad, which ran between San Francisco and Salt Lake City, was driven at Spanish Creek north of Quincy in 1909, but due to huge construction cost overruns and a lack of feeder lines, the railroad was forced into receivership just two years later.

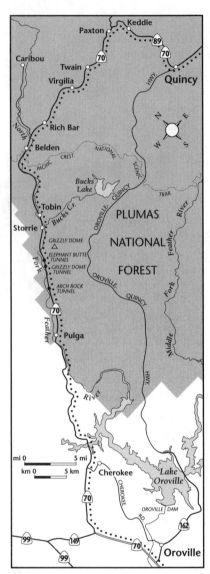

Oroville to Quincy

parts of the river above the power dams, fishing for rainbow and brown trout. Spawning only occurs on certain weekdays, September to mid-November. Call 45 days in advance to arrange guided tours. ~ 5 Table Mountain Boulevard, Oroville; 530-538-2222.

The highway passes through the **Arch Rock Tunnel**, the first of three tunnels in quick succession, as the railroad passes through its own tunnel on the far side of the river. Emerging from the tunnel, the road traverses a steep, sloping sheet of solid granite. Then, crossing the Plumas County line, it enters the **Grizzly Dome Tunnel**, which bores straight through another huge slanted granite slab. Soon after comes **Elephant Butte Tunnel**, which has three "windows" that let light into the curving tunnel and offer motorists quick drive-by glimpses of the cliff and railroad tracks on the far side of the canyon. The tunnels were made by Works Progress Administration (WPA) workers in the 1930s, and the stone removed from them was used to make the low, crenelated guardrails that line the scarier dropoffs along Route 70.

The river widens and deepens again as it backs up behind **Bucks Creek Powerhouse**, built in 1927 as the first of the canyon's seven hydroelectric dams. As the highway crossing another bridge to the north bank of the river, the canyon widens to give motorists a brief view of the **Pacific Crest**, the northern part of the Sierra Nevada. It's hard to believe that the river here is the

**CABINS IN
THE CANYON**

Historic Tobin Resort, several miles up the canyon from the tunnels at the Tobin twin bridges, offers rustic cabins—each different, some with kitchenettes. An exclusive resort dating back to the 1930s, it once boasted a trout pond, a beauty salon, a movie theater, a casino, and "the busiest bar in Northern California." The fancy 50-foot bar is still in operation, as is the resort's restaurant; the rest is gone, leaving the riverbank cabins that are as affordable as they are historic. The cabins are open year-round, while the lodge offers certain rooms and is open during select periods in the summer.~ 6162 Route 70, Tobin; 530-283-2225; www.tobinresort.com. BUDGET.

same one as a few miles back above the power dam. Here tumbled rocks larger than a car make the river bank hard to reach, and the river runs shallow, and in places boulders fill the river bed from bank to bank. There's no whitewater rafting or kayaking on this stretch of river, but on summer weekends you may see sunbathers on top of the big rocks.

Waterfalls spill down the cliff face. The highway and the railroad keep crisscrossing the river, always keeping to opposite banks like mirror images. The railroad was built first, zigzagging back and forth across the river to pick the easier route, leaving no room for a road alongside the tracks. The highway builders were stuck with the task of building Route 70 along the more difficult slopes that the railroad had avoided.

Route 70 crosses the **Pacific Crest National Scenic Trail** at a point where the trail descends steeply to cross the railroad, river, and highway, then climbs up the other side of the canyon and back into the high peaks. Just past the trailhead are Belden Powerhouse and **Belden**, once a busy town with the only stagecoach stop and post office in the canyon, now a low-rent resort with an RV park, a store, a restaurant, a saloon, and a scattering of tin-roofed cottages. Built in

HIKING

If hiking the Pacific Crest National Scenic Trail (or even a few miles of it) sounds a tad ambitious, try the **Yellow Creek Trail** (1.5 miles), a gentle hillside trail above a creek that goes up a box canyon to a modern-day mining camp. The trail takes you through oak groves and Douglas-fir forest and past idyllic pools fed by the creek. The trail starts at the Eby Stamp Mill parking area across the highway from Belden.

1912, the rust-colored bridge to Belden is the oldest bridge in the canyon. Across the river from Belden is the old **Eby Stamp Mill**, a reconstruction that shows how huge iron stamps were used to crush quartz rocks and extract gold from them.

All the gold is not gone from these hills. Thumb-sized nuggets have been found around the Feather River as recently as 1996, and prospecting brings many city folks to the canyon every summer.

Those who want to get serious about gold hunting should contact the **Golden Caribou Mining Club**, operating out of the Caribou Corner Campground and Café. The club owns more than 1500 acres of mining claims in the canyon and is steadily acquiring more. Members share their knowledge of techniques such as sluicing and dredging and get together on weekends to mine the claims and split the proceeds. Free claims tours, including panning lessons and placer mining demonstrations, are offered on the third weekend of each month from June through September. ~ Route 70 at Caribou Road; 530-283-5141; www. golden-caribou.com. On the opposite side of the highway from the Twain Store and RV Park, you can see what little remains of the old railroad town of **Twain**: tin-roofed buildings, some quite large, and the foundations where others once stood. Continuing up the canyon, Route 70 skirts a spectacular cliff of red, black, and white rock as it approaches the **Keddie Y**. Take time for a look at this engineering feat, where the railroad splits as it emerges from a tunnel under the highway. Serious railroad buffs can often be seen along the highway, cameras ready, waiting for a train to come along and complete the picture. They know that this is the only trestle of its kind in the world. A little farther on, the road merges with Route 89 and turns away from the Feather River as it follows Spanish Creek into the American Valley and the town of Quincy.

CELEBRATING QUINCY

The liveliest event in town is the **Plumas–Sierra County Fair**, held at the Quincy Plumas–Sierra County fairgrounds in August. It has the distinction of being the oldest county fair in California. The town stages several other celebrations each year, including the **High Sierra Music Festival** in early July, the **Mountain Harvest Festival** in October, and the **Main Street Sparkle** in December. ~ 530-283-0188.

A NIGHT IN QUINCY

Up at the end of Quincy's old-fashioned Main Street stands a sign that reads, "Hotel Quincy." But you won't find a hotel there. Since 1866, three hotels have stood on the site, and all three burned down—the last one in 1966. There are no plans to erect another hotel on the ill-fated site as it is now Shirley Dane Plaza, a public park. Fortunately for those who wish to steep themselves in downtown Quincy's old-fashioned charm overnight, several residences in the historic district have been converted into bed and breakfasts. Try **The Feather Bed**, a peach-and-teal Queen Anne Victorian built as a family home in 1893 and renovated in 1980. The house has a large yard with shade trees and gardens. The five

upstairs guest rooms and two guest cottages have period furnishings and private baths, some with clawfoot tubs; some rooms have fireplaces. Guests enjoy the free use of bicycles. A full country breakfast starts with a berry smoothie or fresh-picked fruit and features homemade baked goods. ~ 542 Jackson Street, Quincy; 530-283-0102, 800-696-8624; www.featherbed-inn.com, e-mail info@ featherbed-inn.com. MODERATE TO DELUXE.

Quincy, with a population of 4300 and an elevation of 3543 feet, is the county seat and largest town in Plumas County, two-thirds of which is national forest land. An old lumber mill town, Quincy has become a model historic district emulated by preservationists around California. Among its graceful turn-of-the-20th-century buildings are the big, architecturally intricate **Quincy School** (c. 1905), now the Plumas County School District offices, and the four-story Greco-Roman **Plumas County Courthouse**, on two sides of a pretty, green park near the old town center. Peek inside the courthouse for a look at the massive pillars and staircases of pink and blue marble and the one-ton bronze-and-plate-glass chandelier. Built in 1921 at a cost of $350,000, the courthouse touched off a political scandal because of its extravagance.

QUINCY CUISINE

A favorite restaurant in Quincy, **Moon's** was started by a Chinese family in the early years of the 20th century. Although the ownership and menu has changed several times since then, it remains the place to go for fine dining. The fair now focuses on pastas and hand-spun gourmet pizzas, along with selected seafood, beef, and poultry entrées; there's also an extensive California wine list. Dinner only. Closed Monday. ~ 497 Lawrence Street, Quincy; 530-283-0765. MODERATE TO DELUXE.

Behind the courthouse, the **Plumas County Museum** adds to the old-timey atmosphere of the historic district with historical documents and photographs and rooms furnished with period decor. One of the most comprehensive rural museums in California, it also has a large collection of Maidu Indian basketry and artifacts, as well as displays focusing on the roles of Chinese workers, agriculture, mining, logging, and the railroad in local history, plus wildlife displays and local art. Closed Sunday, November through April. Admission. ~ 500 Jackson Street, Quincy; 530-283-6320. Around the corner is the **Coburn-Variel Home**, a three-story late Victorian home with old-fashioned formal gardens furnished from the museum's collection. Open on Saturday and Sunday. ~ 137 Coburn Street, Quincy; 530-283-6320.

Besides its historical appeal, Quincy is still a lumber mill town and ranching center. Its modern business district, called East Quincy, is separated from the historic district by about a mile of forest and meadows full of grazing sheep. The surrounding slopes show the scars of clearcut timbering over the decades.

Leaving Quincy, Route 70 climbs another thousand feet to **Lee Summit**, elevation 4439 feet. After virtually nonstop uphill grades for almost 80 miles, the highway begins a descent through tall pine forest with a view of massive, bare granite mountains directly ahead. Past the tiny village of Cromberg, the climb begins again; traversing a steep hillside at treetop level, it begins to follow the **Middle Fork of the Feather River**. Grizzly Ridge, a mountainous wall patched with snow even in midsummer, rises ahead. On the left side of the highway, the **Feather River Inn** was once an exclusive resort. Today it is a conference center catering to groups, but its nine-hole golf course is open to the public; cart rentals are available. The restaurant is also open to the public for breakfast and dinner. ~ 530-836-2623.

On the opposite side of the highway from Feather River Inn, a side road turns off to **Plumas-Eureka State Park**, one of the best-kept secrets in the state park system. This 6700-acre park surrounds **Johnsville**, a well-preserved 1849 mining town at the base of Eureka Peak (formerly called Gold Mountain), where the Eureka Mine and Mill yielded $17 million in gold to Cornish hard-rock miners. Nearby Jamison Creek won fame as the site where a 52-pound gold nugget was found. The park has an indoor-outdoor museum that includes a restored miner's home, a partially restored stamp mill, and a complete blacksmith shop. During the summer, gold-panning is offered. Get some basic instructions and tips, then try your hand at the sport. Call ahead to sign up. There are also miles of hiking trails, a 67-site

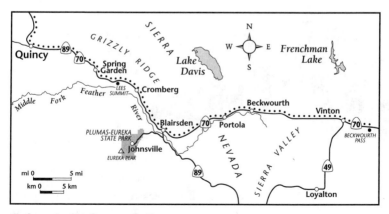

Quincy to Beckwourth Pass

campground (no hookups; $15 per night) beside the creek, and cross-country and occasional downhill skiing in winter. ~ Johnsville Road; 530-836-2380 ▲ 🚶 🏃

The next town of any size is **Portola**. Turn right on Gulling Street to see the historic district located on the other side of the river from the highway. The main attraction is the **Portola Railroad Museum**, created by the Western Pacific and Union Pacific railroads. Considered by train buffs to be one of the West's finest railroad museums, this big old building and railyard exhibits antique railroad cars and engines (including an unusual snowplow engine) plus a matched pair of WWII army tanks. Visitors are welcome to clamber aboard the vintage trains or board a diesel train for a ten-minute loop through the museum grounds. Open Memorial Day through Labor Day. ~ 700 Western Pacific Way; 530-832-4131.

East of Portola, Route 70 finally levels out as it enters the **Sierra Valley**, a broad, green wetland across which many small channels meander before coming together to form the headwaters of the Feather River. On the far side of the valley, the highway reaches the summit of **Beckwourth Pass**, elevation 5221 feet. The highest point on Route 70, it is also the lowest pass over the Sierra Nevada. Its discovery in 1851 caused the rerouting of the Emigrant Trail, used by wagon trains to reach the California gold fields.

Looking east from Beckwourth Pass, you can see Hallelujah Junction, where Route 70 ends at Route 395, a major highway between Susanville, California,

SLAVE, EXPLORER, INDIAN CHIEF

Beckwourth Pass was discovered by James Beckwith, a freed slave who became a Crow Indian war chief and perhaps California's first African American explorer. Changing the spelling of his name for reasons that are lost to history, Beckwourth built a wagon road over the pass, established a trading post, and profited from the waves of pioneers using the new route. In the 1860s, when the rush died down as other routes were developed, Beckwourth left for Montana to spend the remainder of his life among the Crow Indians.

UNION PACIFIC
UP 900002

and Reno, Nevada. To continue exploring the state's hidden highways and gold camp history, we suggest you turn around and return to the town of **Vinton** (pop. 90), a tiny ranch town where cattle graze within the city limits—and the main business in town seems to be a video rental store. Here you can pick up Route 49 and head south through the Sierra Valley to tour the heart of the California Gold Country (see Chapter 11).

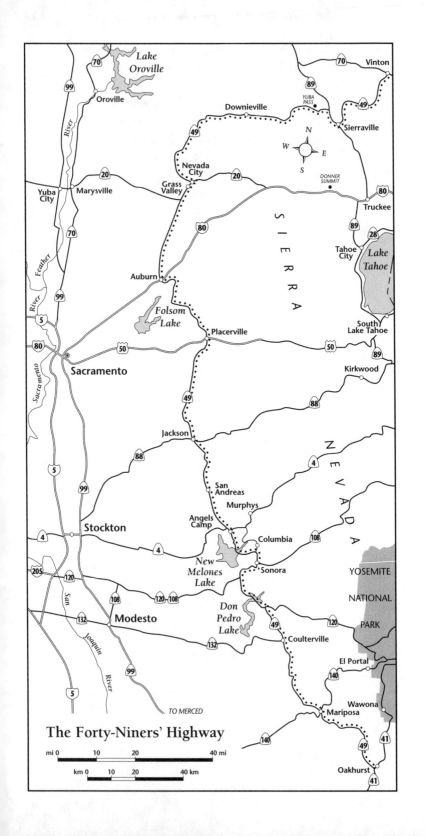

The Forty-Niners' Highway

mi 0   10   20   40 mi

km 0   10   20   40 km

11 THE FORTY-NINERS' HIGHWAY

Route 49 through the Gold Country

Route 49 runs north and south along the foothills of the Sierra Nevada for 298 miles, linking almost all the major mining towns that sprang up during the California Gold Rush. The longest hidden highway in this book, the Forty-Niners' Highway can't be fully explored in a weekend. Fortunately, it's easy to break down into shorter segments. Most gold seekers arrived in California at San Francisco, traveled by boat across the delta to Sacramento or Stockton, and then took their choice of trails into the hills. As a result, Route 49 intersects no less than 11 highways, including two major freeways, that can take you from the Bay Area to any part of the Gold Country and back quickly and easily. The route divides naturally into three segments. Northern Gold Country between Route 70 (see Chapter 10) and Interstate 80, including Downieville, Nevada City, Grass Valley, and Auburn, is a forested region of colorful pinnacles, mining museums, ghost towns, and 19th-century hotels that invite you on a journey back in time. Central Gold Country, from Interstate 80 south to Route 120, taking in Coloma, Placerville, Sutter Creek, and Angels Camp, was the birthplace of the Gold Rush and the stomping grounds of authors Mark Twain and Bret Harte; today it offers American Indian landmarks, giant sequoias, wineries, caves, a famous frog-jumping contest, whitewater rafting, and some favorite hiking trails. Southern Gold Country from Route 120 south to Route 140, including Columbia, Sonora, and Mariposa, is the least developed part of the Mother Lode region, a gently rolling foothill landscape laced by rivers that pour down from the Sierra Nevada; attractions include covered bridges, a steam railroad, and numerous monuments to the region's 19th-century heyday.

Route 49 itself didn't exist as an established road during the Gold Rush days. The winding descents and steep ascents in and out of one river valley after another would have made the route difficult for wagons, as they do today for drivers of large motorhomes or trucks pulling trailers. You'll find plenty of traffic on the highway segments nearest Interstate 80 and Route 50, especially on weekends; as soon as you get past the historic towns closest to these major freeways, you'll find traffic light even on summer weekends.

The northern part of the Gold Country is higher in the mountains than the rest and boasts cool temperatures even in midsummer. In winter, however, Route 49 north from the Sierra Valley to Nevada City can be icy enough to require tire chains, and at some times may be closed by snow.

Route 49 starts at Vinton, just west of Beckwourth Pass (see Chapter 10), and heads south across the **Sierra Valley** with its wetland meadows and sagebrush flats surrounded by rugged mountains. It has been a farming

event

GOLD COUNTRY FESTIVALS

Virtually every surviving Gold Country town has its own annual celebration. In May, Angels Camp's **Calaveras County Fair and Jumping Frog Jubilee**, immortalized by Mark Twain, includes not only jumping-frog contests but also a carnival, a wine show, a rodeo, and a county fair. In July, Plymouth's **Amador County Fair** includes demonstrations of antique farming, mining, and lumbering equipment. August brings the **Nevada County Fair** in Grass Valley, with entertainment, food, music, livestock, living-history displays, and gold panning. The **Mariposa County Fair and Homecoming** takes place in late August and early September, as do Auburn's **Gold Country Fair** and Placerville's **Harvest Fair**. In October, the festivities at **Murphys Gold Rush Street Faire** include grape stomping, a team costume contest, a waiters' race, and belly dancers.

Fortunes Won and Lost

Authorized by a Mexican land grant, using American Indians as serfs, Swiss immigrant John Sutter set out to create an inland empire: New Helvetia. From his armed fortress on the site of present-day Sacramento, his domain spread from Bodega Bay to the Sierra foothills. It was in these hills, in a sluice that powered a sawmill on the American River, Sutter's associate, James Marshall, discovered gold. This event should have secured Sutter's power and Marshall's fortune. Instead, it destroyed them both.

That was January 1848. Word of the find did not get out until May. Californians got a head start in the race for gold claims, since it took almost seven more months for messengers to carry the news around Cape Horn to the East Coast. The next year, machinists and farm hands, scoundrels and preachers, filled with hope and a hunger for gold, began descending in mobs. Those who came by ship using a new overland shortcut through Panama began arriving in February. Travelers who came west on the Oregon and California trails arrived that fall. By the end of 1849, 40,000 miners had come to the gold fields; three years later there were 100,000, as the extent of the Mother Lode, the rich vein of quartz and gold that parallels the Sierra Nevada range for hundreds of miles, became known.

John Sutter's workers were among the first to quit and join the miners, farmland fell fallow, projects went unfinished, buildings were stripped for firewood. By 1852, Sutter was bankrupt; he lived out the rest of his life on a $250-a-month government pension. James Marshall got a $100-a-month pension for a while, but it was eventually cut off, and he died penniless in a cabin within sight of the spot where he'd found the first gold nugget.

The Gold Country became a land of dreams, but its gold fields were often a nightmare. Eventually two *billion* dollars worth of yellow metal was mined, yet for many argonauts (so dubbed by the Eastern press, comparing them to the followers of Jason in his mythical quest for the golden fleece), prospecting meant coming up empty-handed while facing inflated prices for provisions. For ethnic minorities— Chinese, Chileans, Mexicans, Indians, and emancipated Black slaves—it often meant persecution at the hands of vigilante groups. Little wonder most of the towns that mushroomed in the wilderness have long since vanished. The towns that remain—Mariposa, Sonora, Coloma, Nevada City, and dozens of others—still maintain antique buildings and old mining scars, and locals talk of the Gold Rush as if it ended only yesterday.

and ranching valley since the 1850s, when it supplied hay and timber for boom towns like Sierra City and Downieville. It later supplied the same for the towns of the silver boom in Nevada. At an elevation of 5000 feet, approaching the south end of the valley, the road passes through the town of **Loyalton**, which has a sawmill, a cluster of Old West–style buildings, and not many modern ones. Hundreds of cattle graze the green pastures between Loyalton and Sierraville, irrigated by the Sierra Valley Channels, a maze of more than a dozen creeks interconnected by manmade ditches that meander throughout the valley and make up the headwaters of the Feather River. The last of the valley's tiny villages, **Sattley** (pop. 60) has a cash store, a firehouse, and not much else. There are no travelers' services in the valley.

Climbing out of the Sierra Valley, the highway heads into the evergreens of **Tahoe National Forest**. A scenic overlook commands an impressive view of the valley below. The route continues up through a forest of ponderosa, sugar pine, and Douglas fir, passes a sign that announces an elevation of 6000 feet, and keeps climbing. The air temperature drops quickly. The pines grow gargantuan in size. Just over the summit of 6700-foot Yuba Pass, the first of 14 National Forest campgrounds

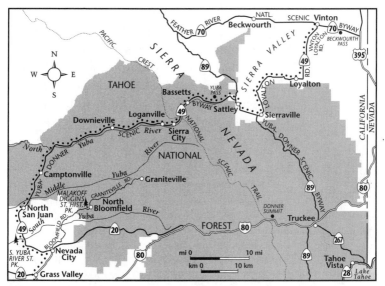

Vinton to Grass Valley

between the Sierra Valley and Downieville appears on the left, as directly ahead the jagged peaks of the Sierra Nevada tower above the forest.

Descending along the North Yuba River, you'll pass a trailhead for the **Pacific Crest National Scenic Trail** and then enter **Sierra City**, an avalanche-plagued town of weatherbeaten, two-story 19th-century buildings in the shadow of the Sierra Buttes. This little "city" is remembered in California history as the birthplace in 1857 of the Ancient Order of E Clampus Vitus, a parody of fraternal orders, whose meetings in the Hall of Comparative Ovations were presided over by their leader, the Noble Grand Humbug. The society spread to many other Gold Rush towns and mixed legitimate charitable activities with its high-spirited irreverence.

The highway streams past fruit orchards, alpine meadows, and wildflower roadsides on its way down the Yuba River, becoming steep as it crosses a rockslide area and suddenly comes out high above the river. Descending to an elevation of less than 3000 feet, it enters Downieville on a one-lane bridge over the confluence of the Downie and Yuba rivers. **Downieville** is an enchanting town cradled in a canyon. The crooked streets, wooden sidewalks, and tin-roof houses of this 1849 settlement are completely encircled by mountains. The town gallows and many picturesque buildings still stand in this natural amphitheater. Once one of the most im-

DOWNIEVILLE MOUNTAIN BIKING

Roads came slowly to the northern Gold Country. Decades after the Gold Rush, many people lived in areas that could only be reached by single-track mountain trails impassable in wagons. Many such trails still exist around Downieville, making the little town a mountain-bike mecca. For bike rentals, trailhead shuttles, and guided tours, contact **Yuba Expeditions**. ~ Route 49, Downieville; 530-289-3010; www.yubaexpeditions.com, e-mail yuba@nccn.net. Another local enterprise that offers rentals, shuttles, and organized group trips is **Downieville Outfitters**. ~ Route 49, Downieville; 530-289-0155.

ROOMS BY THE RIVER

The **Downieville River Inn and Resort** has guest rooms and private cottages, each with a private bath and a porch or balcony, in a riverbank setting framed by pine-clad mountain slopes. The old-fashioned pastel room decor features pile carpeting and white wicker furniture. On the grounds are English gardens, a heated pool, and a picnic area with barbecue grills. Pet-friendly. ~ Route 49, Downieville; 530-289-3308, 800-696-3308, fax 530-289-0310; www.downievilleriverinn.com, e-mail dennis@downievilleriverinn.com. MODERATE TO ULTRA-DELUXE.

CELESTIAL FARE

The inviting **New Moon Cafe** serves up big-city style in a small-town atmosphere. The sophisticated seasonal menu utilizes organic vegetables and natural, free-range meats in entrées such as pork chop with a blackberry barbecue sauce, ginger prawns over udon noodles, and pepper-crusted roasted duck breast. In a nod to the restaurant's name, the dessert menu changes with each new moon. Patrons can dine on an outdoor deck when the weather's nice. There's an extensive wine list. No lunch Saturday and Sunday. Closed Monday. ~ 203 York Street, Nevada City; 530-265-6399; www.thenewmooncafe.com, e-mail mail@thenewmooncafe.com. MODERATE TO DELUXE.

portant Gold Rush towns, with over 5000 residents in 1850 (Los Angeles reached a population of 1600 that year), Downieville has a population of only 350 today. Gold was literally everywhere. One local legend tells of a housewife who found $500 worth of gold while sweeping her floors. Today, Downieville's main industry is whitewater rafting on the Yuba River.

Leaving town, the highway traverses a forested slope about 200 feet above the Yuba River, winding around the contours of slopes covered in tall pines. The river boils its way over rocky rapids and around huge boulders. Farther down the descent, big oak trees arch over the highway and ivy grows rampant over rock cliffs along the road. It's a long 46 miles from Downieville to Nevada City, with almost no services along the way. If you find yourself in need of

BOOKS IN NEVADA CITY

Looking for books about Gold Country history? Nevada City is the place. Independent bookstores seem to thrive here. Within a few blocks of the historic district, you'll find **Harmony Books** (231 Broad Street; 530-265-9564), **Brigadoon Books** (108 North Pine; 530-265-3450), and **Broad Street Books & Espresso Café** (426 Broad Street; 530-265-4204).

gas or refreshments, your best bet is the **Lost Nugget**, a lost-in-the-woods general store. Through the trees you'll catch quick glimpses of a deep canyon on the left, then cross the Middle Fork of the Yuba River into Nevada County.

North San Juan is a settlement of 125 people with decaying old buildings, a park, and a seniors' center; if there was ever a San Juan or South San Juan, no trace of it remains. After careening down a steep, straight slope with a treacherous zigzag curve at the bottom, Route 49 continues on a gentler, winding descent to a bridge

HIDDEN HISTORY AND HIKING

For an adventurous side trip, head to **Malakoff Diggins State Historic Park**. From Nevada City, take Highway 49 north for 11 miles and make a right onto Tyler Foote Crossing Road. Follow the paved road 17 miles to Derbec Road, which leads to the park, where the scenery is startling and the seclusion splendid. The 3000-acre park rests near the Yuba River, where anglers catch rainbow and brook trout; there are also black bass and bluegill in nearby Blair Reservoir. The park's slopes, climbing from 2200 to 4200 feet, are open to hikers. Swimming is good in the reservoir. The park has an information center and museum, picnic areas, and restrooms. While it is a fully developed park, this area is so remote it's a good representation of "hidden California." Camping is permitted in 30 sites, $10 per night. There are also three rustic cabins for rent; $18 per night.

The park includes the rustic town of **North Bloomfield**, built during the 1860s as one of the nation's largest hydraulic mining centers. There's a livery stable filled with wagons, plus a whitewashed church and old general store, all neatly preserved. Tours are available daily during the summer and on the weekend in winter. The immediate area has been heavily eroded by hydraulic mining, which involves washing away hillsides with hoses, then sifting gold from the mud. Bald cliffs and a miniature lake remain as evidence of these destructive techniques. But the rest of the region is wild and untouched, wide open for exploration. Day-use fee, $4. ~ 23579 North Bloomfield–Graniteville Road; phone/fax 530-265-2740.

over the South Yuba River, where **South Yuba River State Park** provides rafting access and a picnic area.

The ascent up the other side of the river valley is a tough climb for large RVs, and there are only a few places to pass. The first tip-off that you're nearing civilization comes as side roads start to appear, leading to houses in the woods, many of them with long-haul truck tractors parked in the yard. This is the outskirts of **Nevada City**. A turn off the main highway on Broad Street takes you there. Nevada City was once the third largest city in California. Still grand by local standards, it nevertheless has a country village charm. The first thing you see is a large **cemetery** with a number of ostentatious monuments. Listed on the National

THE CONCUBINE OF GRASS VALLEY

Grass Valley's most famous resident was Lola Montez, a dancer who had become notorious for her love affairs with European notables such as Alexander Dumas, Czar Nicolas I of Russia, and "Mad" King Ludwig of Bavaria. After a performance tour of Gold Country opera houses, Montez retired to a house in Grass Valley, but scandal pursued her. Though prostitutes worked the streets of this mining town openly, the aging mistress of a foreign king aroused moral indignation. Montez was ultimately forced to flee California after horsewhipping a local newspaper editor who had attacked her in print.

Register of Historic Places, the old town has gaslights, turreted houses, and balconied stores. Much of the Victorian elegance remains amid the widow's walks, church steeples, and gingerbread facades. Searching for a parking space in the historic district, you'll soon discover that the reason there's so little traffic on the highway north of here is that everybody's shopping in gentrified Nevada City, conveniently located 30 miles from Interstate 80 and just over two hours' drive from the Bay Area. A walking map of the town, available from the **Nevada City Chamber of Commerce**, will guide you through the historic heart of town. Closed Sunday. ~ 132 Main Street, Nevada City; 530-265-2692, 800-655-6569, fax 530-265-3892; www.nevadacitychamber.com, e-mail info@nevadacitychamber.com.

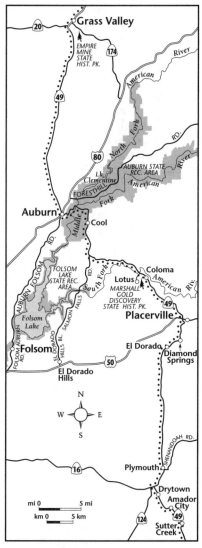

At the south end of Nevada City, Route 49 joins Route 20 to become a wide four-lane freeway for about two miles to **Grass Valley**, a modern town engulfing a historic district, which you can see by taking the Colfax exit. Along Mill and Main streets, the gas lamps, awnings, balconies, and brick facades remain from the gold era. A replica of the Lola Montez House contains the **Nevada County Chamber of Commerce**, where you can obtain brochures and walking maps. Closed Sunday. ~ 248 Mill Street, Grass Valley; 530-273-4667, fax 530-272-5440; www.gvncchamber.org, e-mail info@gvncchamber.org.

The mines around Grass Valley and Nevada City were a far cry from the simple mining

Grass Valley to Sutters Creek

claims that started the Gold Rush. Prominent during the latter half of the 19th century, these big-bucks operations were heavily industrialized. Grass Valley, for instance, has 367 miles of tunnels running beneath its streets. The town's **North Star Mining and Pelton Water Wheel Museum** displays the sophisticated machinery that replaced the gold pan and rocker. Open May to mid-October. ~ End of Mill Street on Allison Ranch Road, Grass Valley; 530-273-4255. At nearby **Empire Mine State Historic Park** you can view the engineering office and machine shops of the richest hardrock gold mine in California. Walk about 50 feet into the black entranceway of a shaft that leads nearly a mile down and wander through the many buildings comprising this multimillion-dollar venture. With its eroded hillsides, the surrounding area presents a graphic illustration of how mining destroyed the landscape. It's ironic that the rich mine owners, whose opulent homes you can view here, chose to build their estates in neighborhoods they were turning to rubble heaps. Admission. ~ 10791 East Empire Street, Grass Valley; 530-273-8522, fax 530-273-0602; www.cal-parks.ca.gov.

WHERE TO CATCH A STURGEON IN GOLD COUNTRY

One of California's most popular parks, **Folsom Lake State Recreation Area** completely encircles the lake's 75-mile shoreline. Visitors come to boat, waterski, ride horseback, picnic, swim, and camp. Anglers try for trout, bass, perch, and sturgeon. There are also 65 miles of hiking trails around the lake. Quite crowded in summer, the park is best visited during the week. Facilities include a water education center at Folsom Dam, an information center, marinas, picnic areas, restrooms, and showers. There are 150 sites in two campgrounds; $15 per night. Day-use fee, $5 per car. ~ Located south of Auburn on Folsom–Auburn Road; 916-988-0205.

Past Grass Valley Routes 49 and 20 separate to become two-lane highways again, still fast, with uphill passing lanes to keep the traffic moving. We enter Placer County and drive past cattle pasturage on our way into Auburn, where Route 49 meets Interstate 80.

Auburn has grown too large to enjoy the rural charm of other Mother Lode communities. Well hidden in a gulch out of sight of the surrounding suburbs and shopping malls, the **Old Town historic district** was built near the American River in the 19th century. Among the sights are a trim three-story firehouse capped with a bell tower, an antique shopping center, and a maze of falsefront streets. The centerpiece is the **Placer County Museum and Courthouse**. One of the showier edifices in the Gold Country, where county seats competed to see who could erect the most extravagant public architecture, the 1894 courthouse contains an extensive collection of American Indian artifacts from around the West and a multimedia presentation about this region's Indian inhabitants, as well as a restored turn-of-the-20th-century sheriff's office; a video shows how the pioneers' Truckee Route, established in 1844, evolved into Interstate 80. Closed Monday. ~ 101 Maple Street, Auburn; 530-889-6500.

EATING CHINESE IN AUBURN

In the Old Town section of Auburn, the **Shanghai Bar & Restaurant** is a Chinese eatery that has been around since 1896, making it the oldest family-owned bar and restaurant in the state. This high-ceilinged establishment features the standard array of Cantonese dishes and live music Thursday through Sunday. Closed Tuesday. ~ 289 Washington Street, Auburn; phone/fax 530-885-1705. MODERATE.

There's an interesting **walking tour** through this brick-and-woodframe neighborhood, which you should take after obtaining an Old Town map from the **Auburn Area Chamber of Commerce**. Closed weekends. ~ 601 Lincoln Way, Auburn; 530-885-5616, fax 530-885-5854; www.auburnarea.com.

Leaving Auburn, Route 49 plunges down a long descent with sweeping curves and a dropoff on the right, descending several hundred feet to the North Fork of the American River and the headquarters of **Auburn State Recreation Area**. This sprawling park covers over 30,000 acres and includes **Lake Clementine**, a small reservoir. Long and narrow in its configuration, the park follows the north and middle American River basin for 30 miles. There are opportunities to hike, swim, and fish in this former mining region. Camping is permitted in 22 primitive sites; $9 per night; boat-in at Lake

Clemetine ($9 to $12 per night; closed October through May). ~ Route 49, about one mile south of Auburn; 530-885-4527. 🚶👣🛶⛵

In the Gold Country, most county lines in the Gold Country follow rivers; crossing the American River, Route 49 enters El Dorado County in a series of tight curves up a steep grade (one of those stretches we wouldn't want to attempt in a large motor home or tractor-trailer truck, though some do it slowly and much to the frustration of drivers behind). At the top of the climb, the road levels out to wind among golden grassy hills with little pockets of modern commercial development such as **Cool**, designed in kitsch frontier style and surrounded by large country homes, most with horse corrals. Soon, however, the route leaves civilization behind as it heads into the oak thickets of the national forest.

Marshall Gold Discovery State Historic Park features the remains of the Gold Rush town of **Coloma**. It also happens to be the place where it all began. Here on January 24, 1848, James Marshall found shining metal in a sawmill owned by John Sutter. "Boys," Marshall exclaimed, "I believe I have found a gold mine." The history of California and the West was changed forever. Within the park, a self-guiding trail leads past a reconstruction of Sutter's mill and to the discovery site on the banks of the American River. With the skeletal-looking mill on one hand and a foaming river on the other, it's an eerie sensation standing on the spot that once lured tens of thousands across a continent. There's also a museum with display cases portraying the days of '49 and a miner's cabin complete with long johns and animal pelts hanging from the rafters. In all, this 285-acre park

RUNNING THE RIVER

The South Fork of the American River is one of the most popular whitewater runs in the United States. More than 30 rafting and kayaking outfitters operate out of the Coloma area from April through September. Among those that offer guided rafting tours is **Beyond Limits Adventures**. Reservations required. ~ Riverbank; 209-869-6060, 800-234-7238; www.rivertrip.com. Another good raft touring company is **Gold Rush Whitewater Rafting**. Reservations required. ~ Lotus; 800-900-7238; www.goldrushriver.com. Kayakers of all skill levels can arrange guided trips on this Class III+ river through **California Canoe & Kayak Rentals**. ~ 409 Water Street, Jack London Square, Oakland; 510-893-7833; www.calkayak.com.

features two dozen points of interest and is second only to Columbia State Historic Park in its ability to evoke California's glittery past. Admission. ~ Route 49, Coloma; 530-622-3470, fax 530-622-3472.

Just past Coloma, the area around the bridge that crosses the South Fork of the American River is jammed with rafters and kayakers on summer weekends.

A few miles farther along Route 49 is **Placerville**, one of the largest towns in the Mother Lode. Located on busy Route 50 from Sacramento, the town has been heavily developed and lacks the charm of neighboring villages. Route 49 runs along the west end of the historic district, which is heavily commercialized with galleries and curio shops and so reverent about the Gold Rush days that even the public restrooms are plaqued as a historic landmark. The most worthwhile sightseeing highlight in town is the **Gold Bug Mine**, where you can step between the timbers and explore a narrow stone tunnel that leads deep into the earth.

SHOPPING MOUNTAIN MAN STYLE

For unique Gold Country mementos, check out the **Two Feathers Trading Post**, where you'll find buckskinning and craft supplies, trade goods, gold-panning kits, and gold samples found near the Sutter's Mill discovery site on the American River. Closed Monday through Thursday. ~ 381 Route 49, Coloma; 530-621-0793.

One of the few mines open to the public, Gold Bug also features a weatherbeaten stamp press mill used to grind gold from bedrock. ~ Gold Bug Lane, off Bedford Avenue, one mile from downtown Placerville.

Old Town Placerville is located in the bottom of a deep ravine, and continuing south means climbing a 17-percent grade, the steepest you'll find on any of the hidden highways in this book. This hill seems to discourage many motorists; south of Placerville, the traf-

FRENCH CUISINE IN PLACERVILLE

Zachary Jacque, a provincial French restaurant, is trimly appointed with paintings and decorative china plates. Wood paneling and a cozy fireplace add to its warm appeal. Though the menu is seasonal, you can always choose from staples like rack of lamb, duck with ginger and lavender, and fresh fish. Dinner only. Closed Monday and Tuesday. ~ 1821 Pleasant Valley Road, Placerville; 530-626-8045. DELUXE TO ULTRA-DELUXE.

PLACERVILLE'S GRAND HOTEL

When it was built in 1857, the three-story **Historic Cary House Hotel** was reputed to be the finest hotel in Gold Country. Its name was changed twice, and in 1915 it was demolished and rebuilt using the same bricks. In 1997, after a complete renovation, the original name was restored. The lobby is richly appointed with deep teal carpeting, dark wood trim, and leather couches. The 37 guest rooms are Victorian in style, decorated in hues of peach and blue. All have private baths and air conditioning, and most have kitchenettes and king- or queen-size beds. ~ 300 Main Street, Placerville; 530-622-4271, 866-245-9439; www.caryhouse.com. DELUXE.

fic thins out dramatically, and even on weekends you may have the road to yourself a good deal of the time. Trees line the highway like deep green walls, with occasional breaks that offer glimpses of endless rolling golden hills half-blanketed with oaks. Three miles down the road, **Diamond Springs** was named for the crystal-clear springs that provided its water supply. One of the richest towns in the Gold Country, Diamond Springs was the discovery site of a 25-pound nugget, one of the largest ever found in the county. It was a leading con-

sidetrips

WINES OF THE GOLD COUNTRY

From Plymouth, take a sidetrip up Shenandoah Road (County Road E16) to the **Shenandoah Valley wine-growing region**. Vineyards have prospered here since Gold Rush days and at present almost two dozen wineries dot the area. Many are clustered along a ten-mile stretch of Shenandoah Road.

Foremost is **Sobon Estate**, which dates from 1856. Enjoy the tasting room or take a self-guided tour through the original cellar. This rock-walled enclosure still contains the old handmade oak casks and hewn wooden beams. Specializing in zinfandel, Sobon also produces French syrah and viognier. While this winery is open daily, others have limited schedules and often require reservations. ~ 14430 Shenandoah Road, Plymouth; 209-245-6554, fax 209-456-5156; www.sobonwine.com, e-mail info@sobonwine.com.

You can pick up a free winetasting brochure from the **El Dorado County Chamber of Commerce**. Closed Saturday and Sunday. ~ 542 Main Street, Placerville; 530-621-5885, fax 530-642-1624; www.visit-eldorado.com, e-mail chamber@eldoradocounty.org.

If visiting between September and December during the apple harvest, ask at the Chamber of Commerce for information about **Apple Hill**. Located on a mountain ridge east of Placerville, this area is crowded with orchards where for a modest fee you can pick your own apples. Many of the orchards lie just off Route 50 on Carson Road.

tender for the El Dorado County seat, but its placer gold deposits dwindled early, and the town was eclipsed by neighboring Placerville. Some 19th-century buildings remain intact, but most of the town's historical-style buildings are of recent vintage.

At the small gold camp town of **El Dorado**, Route 49 takes a left turn and continues south among forested hills, Christmas tree farms, and a scattering of large country homes with broad green lawns along the way. Another steep two-mile descent brings you to the Cosumnes River and the Amador County line. **Plymouth**, with a population of about 500, has little to distinguish it from other towns on the route. A number of its historic buildings stand boarded up. The pleasant residential streets have tin-roofed, Victorian-era cottages mixed in among modern suburban-style homes.

To continue on Route 49, turn off to the left, south of Plymouth. (If you stayed on the same highway instead of turning, you'd find yourself heading for Sacramento on Route 124.) Another steep descent brings you into **Drytown**, made up mainly of antique shops, including

SPEND THE NIGHT IN A GOLD VAULT

Amador City's **Mine House Inn** may be the region's most intriguing hostelry. It's located in the former office building of the Old Keystone Consolidated Mining Company. Millions of dollars worth of gold was assayed and smelted in this century-old building. As a result, the place is built of brick with walls 13 inches thick. Each of the eight guest rooms was once an individual office, so if you check into the "Vault Room" be prepared to share the space with a ceiling-high iron vault. The "Keystone Room" was fashioned from the dumbwaiter shaft used to transport bullion, and the "Retort Room" features a keystone arch built to support the vault. Three luxury suites occupy the former superintendent's quarters, and feature canopy beds, Jacuzzis, and fireplaces. The attached Victorian house contains two ultra-deluxe suites, both almost 500 square feet and one outfitted with authentic Louis XV antiques. An inn since 1957, the Mine House is creatively furnished with period pieces and has a swimming pool and gazebo-enclosed Jacuzzi on the premises. A full breakfast is served. ~ 14125 Route 49, Amador City; 209-267-5900, 800-646-3473; www.minehouseinn.com, e-mail minehse@cdepot.net. MODERATE TO DELUXE.

one with a front yard full of jeeps and antique cannons that specializes in military collectibles and cigars. It was the creek, not the miners, that was dry in Drytown. As a matter of fact, the place contained about 25 saloons during its golden youth. Today there's only one.

Next Route 49 bisects **Amador City**, a town of almost 200 people with more than a dozen antique shops. The focus of a quartz mining operation, this pretty community still contains many of its original brick and woodframe buildings. At one time, the Keystone, Amador's most productive mine, produced about $24 million in gold. It closed in 1942.

Named for the man on whose land gold was first discovered, **Sutter Creek** warrants a walking tour, too. Within a few blocks along Main and Spanish streets are dozens of vintage buildings—most of them now operating as antique shops—and homes rich with history.

Route 49 turns left again, briefly merging with east–west Route 88 from Stockton. A little farther on,

The Chilean War

Chileans were a large and prosperous ethnic subculture in Northern California during the mid-19th century; when ships from Chile carried much of the cargo that reached California during the Mexican era (1821 to 1846). When the Gold Rush came, Chilean businessmen grubstaked sailors from these ships and other Chilean fortune-seekers in prospecting expeditions. First to find the rich placer deposits of Chili Gulch, the Chileans recruited thousands of Chinese laborers in an arrangement that amounted to slavery, and had these workers stake individual claims in the gulch and then transfer them to the bosses. This scheme gave the Chileans control of what other gold hunters considered an unfairly large area, and in 1849 Americans attacked Chili Gulch, driving the Chileans out in what came to be known as the "Chilean War" and touching off attacks against Chileans by vigilante groups throughout the region. As a result, most Chileans soon left Northern California and returned to their homeland.

a scenic vista overlooks the town of **Jackson.** In 1848 Jackson was a village of huts and tents called Botilleas ("Bottles") by the Mexicans because of the accumulation of liquor bottles dis-carded by its transient populace. In 1849 it was renamed for a Colonel Jackson who was an early-day resident. In 1853, Jack-son became the county seat of the newly created Amador County. In addition to a balconied Main Street lined with gift shops and frequented by men in pioneer buckskins, the town features the **Amador County Museum**. One of the region's best mu-seums, it honors the Chinese with displays of abacuses, Chinese drums, and coolie hats. Also here are a Ken-nedy Mine model, geology display cases, and a photo-graph collection featuring the dourest-looking people imaginable. Closed Monday and Tuesday. Closed De-cember. ~ 225 Church Street, Jackson; 209-223-6386, fax 209-267-0774.

Outside of Jackson stand the roofless stone ruins of the **Butte Store**, constructed by Italian stonemasons in 1857. It served early settlers and miners as a post office and gen-eral store and later became known as Ginocchio's.

Just over the Calaveras County line, a country lane be-tween Victorian-style houses with white picket fences leads into the argonaut community of **Mokelumne Hill**, its Main Street lined with old-time buildings, in-cluding an **IOOF hall** that was the Gold Country's first three-story structure. South of town is **Chili Gulch**; the richest placer mining site in Calav-eras County extended for five miles up and down the gulch, which got its name not from chili con carne but from a group of Chilean immigrants who worked the gulch in 1848 and 1849. The world's largest known

by the way...

GOLD COUNTRY WOMEN'S CLUB

Jackson was the birthplace in 1886 of the order of the Native Daughters of the Golden West, a women's historical society that soon spread throughout the Gold Country. The group was a companion or-ganization to the Native Sons of the Golden West, organized in 1875 with a membership limited to white men born in California after it became U.S. territory. Although the Native Sons fell into disre-pute after World War II because of its out-spoken opposition to Japanese Americans in California, both groups are still active in preserving Gold Country history today.

VOLCANO SIDETRIP

Volcano is another well-preserved mining center. Located on Sutter Creek Road about 12 miles east of the town of Sutter Creek, Volcano was a booming town of 5000 back in the days of the argonauts. In addition to a Masonic hall, an express office, and a three-story hotel, the community sports another relic—"Old Abe." According to local folks, this cannon was used during the Civil War to warn off Confederate sympathizers who sought to divert the town's gold to the Rebel cause. The limestone Masonic Caves just south of town were used for secret ceremonies in the 1850s.

On the same road two miles from Volcano is **Indian Grinding Rock State Historic Park.** Here along a limestone outcropping the Miwok Indians gathered to collect acorns and grind seeds, berries, and nuts. Using the limestone bedrock as a natural mortar, they eventually ground over a thousand cavities in the rock. These unusual mortar holes, together with several hundred petroglyphs, can be toured along a self-guided trail. You'll also pass facsimile displays of ceremonial bark houses, granaries, and a Miwok playing field. An on-site museum covers Sierra American Indian tribes. Nearby is an authentic roundhouse, still used by local Miwok. Admission. ~ Pine Grove–Volcano Road; 209-296-7488, fax 209-296-7528.

quartz crystals were found in a mine on the north side of the gulch. A historical monument marks the spot.

The spirit of '49 remains alive and well on Route 49 as it continues south toward Angels Camp. There are buildings of note in **San Andreas**, with its quaint two-block-long historic district set apart from a strip of

modern commercial development along the highway. Housed in the county courthouse, the **Calaveras County Museum and Historical Society** offers some of the best resources for delving deeper into Gold Country history (including an extensive photo collection of mother lode history). Besides the usual Indian artifacts, mining memorabilia, and Victoriana, the museum features a garden of native California trees and plants in the old jail yard. Admission. ~ 30 North Main Street, Angels Camp; 209-754-3918.

An 11-mile drive through gently rolling hills brings you to **Angels Camp**, one of the most famous towns in the Gold Country. The community boasts several antique buildings and a museum, but its chief notoriety is literary. Samuel Langhorne Clemens, a young freelance journalist who reported on the waning days of the gold camps for San Francisco newspapers and literary magazines under the pen name Mark Twain, lived near Angels Camp in 1864 and '65, and it was here that he heard—and wrote— "The Celebrated Jumping Frog of Calaveras County," the story that brought him his first national recognition. The annual jumping-frog contest still takes place every May. Another Gold Country author, Bret Harte, used the mining center as a model in his story, "The Luck of Roaring Camp." Today Mark Twain has a shopping center in

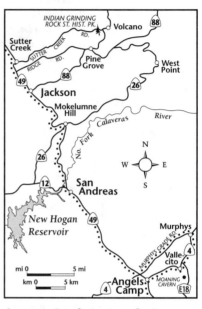

Sutters Creek to Angels Camp

Angels Camp named after him. The local high school is named after Bret Harte, and a motel and other businesses commemorate the famous frog.

From Angels Camp, a short detour along a pastoral back road called Murphys Grade (turn left at the Jumping Frog Motel) takes you to one of the best preserved and most enjoyable Gold Country towns. **Murphys** was established by two enterprising Irishmen in 1848, and it still wears its Irish heritage with pride. Among the historic buildings fronting its tree-lined streets is **Murphys Historic Hotel** (c. 1856), which hosted an impressive assemblage of guests, including Bret Harte, Jacob Astor, Jr., Count Von Rothschild, and Ulysses S. Grant. ~ 457 Main Street, Murphys; 209-728-3444, 800-532-7684; www.murphyshotel.com, e-mail mhotel@caltel.com.

Just east of Murphys, Main Street joins Route 4, returning you to the Angels Camp historic district in nine miles. Along the way is **Moaning Cavern**, one of several

MARK TWAIN SLEPT HERE

If anything, **Murphys Historic Hotel** is historic. The place dates to 1856 and numbers among its previous guests Ulysses S. Grant, Mark Twain, Black Bart, and William Randolph Hearst. Stay here and your dreams might even carry you back to those roughhewn days. The nine rooms are still maintained much as they were back when, with oak wardrobes, antique dressers, and patterned wallpaper. Each room has the name of a famous guest painted on the door, and all rooms share baths. For a historic splurge, book the presidential suite, containing the same bed on which Grant slept. (There's also an adjoining motel with 20 rooms, but staying there contradicts the reason for coming to Murphys.) Though there are antiques dotted about, the hotel's dining room lacks the charm of the hotel. The Continental menu features a full breakfast, lunch, and an array of dinnertime spreads. There's also an old-time miners' saloon with occasional live music. ~ 457 Main Street, Murphys; 209-728-3444, 800-532-7684, fax 209-728-1590; www. murphyshotel.com, e-mail mhotel@ caltel.com. MODERATE TO ULTRA-DELUXE.

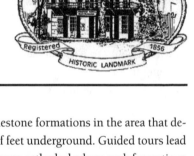

extraordinary limestone formations in the area that descend hundreds of feet underground. Guided tours lead into this subterranean cathedral where rock formations are twisted into bizarre figures. Entering it is like descending into an ice palace filled with sparkling creations. Above ground, you can polish gemstones in a flume system or walk the interpretive nature trail. Despite the tourist trappings, this cavern warrants a visit. Admission. ~ Vallecito; 209-736-2708, fax 209-736-0330; www.caverntours.com, e-mail caverns@caverntours.com.

From Angels Camp, Route 49 runs through beautiful hill country marred only by a strip mining operation at **Carson Hill**, where the whole hillside has been sliced away in terraces—not for gold, but for stone building materials. Soon after, the highway reaches **New Melones Lake**. Set on the lakeshore, Tuttletown Recreation Area and New Melones Lake Gloryhole Recreation Area are popular with boaters and anglers. The entire lake is surrounded by oak trees and rolling hills, making it a pretty place to picnic. It was even more beautiful, conservationists claim, before the reservoir was created by the controversial Melones Dam, which flooded the historic Stanislaus River Valley. The visitor center/

museum addresses this controversy and also features exhibits on Miwok culture, local ecology, and Gold Rush and mining history. There are 144 campsites, including hike-ins, at Gloryhole Campground, and 175 sites, including a few big enough for motorhomes, at Tuttletown Campground (no hookups); $14 per night. ~ 209-536-9094, fax 209-536-9652; www.usbr.gov. ▲ 🏃 🚤 🎣

*T*wo competing ferries used to transport people and livestock across the Stanislaus River during the Gold Rush days. Today a long bridge carries motorists across the lake and into Tuolumne County. A mile or so down the highway at **Jackass Hill**, a side road turns off sharply and steeply to the left and goes up the hill for about a mile to **Mark Twain's Cabin**—or at least the

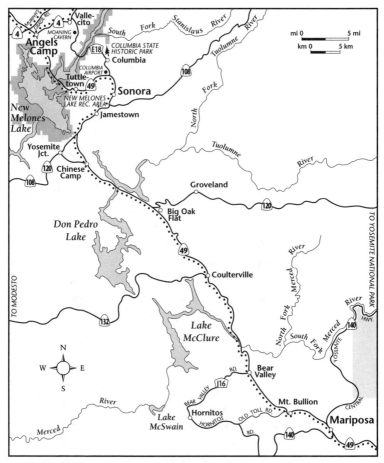

Angels Camp to Mariposa

GHOST TOWN
HOSPITALITY

Staying at the **City Hotel** is almost a civic responsibility. Situated in Columbia State Historic Park, this charming establishment is a non-profit organization and a training ground for hospitality management students from nearby Columbia Junior College. The ten-room hotel, dating from 1856, has been nicely restored and furnished with period pieces. There's a dining room and saloon downstairs. The guest rooms feature rugs across refinished pine floors, patterned wallpaper, and wall sconces. All include half-baths, with shared showers down the hall. "Balcony rooms" include patios overlooking the town's quiet Main Street. ~ Main Street, Columbia; 209-532-1479, 800-532-1479, fax 209-532-7027; www.cityhotel.com, e-mail info@cityhotel.com. MODERATE.

For gourmet dining in a Gold Rush–era atmosphere, the City Hotel's dining room is appointed with brass chandeliers, high-back chairs, and gold-framed oil paintings. Dinner is an extravaganza featuring roasted rack of lamb, pan-seared salmon, and roast breast of pheasant. Sunday champagne brunch is also served. The food is delicious here and highly recommended. Closed Monday and first two weeks in January. ~ DELUXE.

---

original chimney and fireplace, with rebuilt wood walls and roof—where young Mark Twain stayed in 1864 and '65 as he gathered material for his book *Roughing It*. Though reconstructed, the cabin looks decrepit enough to be the original. It stands surrounded by an iron fence in the center of a cul-de-sac of country homes with goats, donkeys, llamas, and emus grazing in their yards.

Route 49 then brings you to the turnoff for **Columbia**. Known in its day as "the gem of the southern mines," Columbia is not to be missed. Gold was discovered here after a rainstorm in 1850, and the population grew to 6000 in six weeks. Much of the old mining center has been preserved as **Columbia State Historic Park**, a window on 19th-century life in the Sierra foothills. The refurbished buildings and rare artifacts create a picture that will help make sense of the random ruins found elsewhere in the Mother Lode. Wandering the several streets that comprise this time-capsule town, you'll pass the old newspaper office, miners' boardinghouse, livery stable, and schoolhouse. There are hook-and-ladders so ancient they resemble Roman chariots, and a dentist's office containing fiendish-looking tools. Former Chinese residents are represented by a temple and herb shop, while the nearby apothecary remains stocked with Western-style potions and nostrums. The old justice court serves the legal system no longer. It does, however, serve the public since it is open for touring. Over at the blacksmith shop are tools that bear an unsettling resemblance to those in the dentist's office. Like the four dozen buildings in this outdoor museum, it presents a perfect reconstruction of an imperfect era. Facilities include restrooms, picnic areas, restaurants, groceries, hotels, a museum, and much more. ~ Route 49, Columbia; 209-532-0150, fax 209-532-5064; e-mail calavera@goldrush.com.

Around the next bend in the highway, **Sonora** marks the center of southern Gold Country. The seat of Tuolumne County and one of the largest towns in the Mother Lode, it has been preeminent almost since its founding in 1848. Settled by people from the state of Sonora, Mexico, the town gained an early reputation both for its lawlessness and commercial potential. When rich strikes were discovered here, racist Americans pushed the Mexicans out of the action. They levied a $20-a-month residence tax on "foreigners," which they soon repealed when local merchants complained that the emigration of Mexican miners was hurting business!

Traveling south from Sonora, Route 49 passes through farm country with many cattle grazing and red painted barns set in green pastures on its way to **Jamestown**, which has been ambitiously gentrified. Its restored hotels, attractive restaurants, and antique shops are a prelude to the new, improved Gold Country awaiting you. *High Noon* and *Butch Cassidy and the Sundance Kid* were filmed here.

During the summer months, **Railtown State Historic Park**, the old Sierra Railroad, is open. There's a roundhouse museum with blacksmith shop, a turntable, and historic locomotives. On weekends April through October, you can also ride several miles through the Mother Lode country aboard an 80-year-old locomotive. ~ 5th Avenue and Reservoir Street, Jamestown;

209-984-3953, fax 209-984-4936; www.railtown1897.
org, e-mail foundation@csrmf.org.

In **Chinese Camp**, another falsefront town with a
gilded past, are ruins of the Wells Fargo building, a 19th-
century store, plus an old church and cemetery. Once
home to 5000 Chinese miners, this placid area was the
scene of California's first tong war: about 2000 members
of the Yan Wo and Sam Yap fraternities settled a mining
dispute in 1856 with pikes, tridents, and axes. The present stone and brick post office dates back to 1854. The
St. Francis Xavier Catholic Church was built in 1855.

Route 49 makes a steep descent toward **Don Pedro
Lake**, a long, labyrinthine boating reservoir nestled between pine-covered hills, on its way to **Coulterville**, an
architectural hodgepodge that includes several historic
buildings. The **Northern Mariposa County History Center** sits astride a sturdy stone-and-iron structure, the
former home of Wells Fargo. Open Wednesday to Sunday; closed January. ~ Coulterville; 209-878-3015, fax
209-878-2744.

The region between Jamestown and Mariposa represents the least developed section of the Gold Country.
It's a perfect place to capture a pure sense of the past.

Particularly picturesque is the stretch from Coulterville to Mariposa, where Route 49 weaves
wildly through the Merced River valley. The
sharp slopes and hairpin turns provide grand
vistas of the surrounding mountains.

The mine at the town of **Mariposa** was
discovered in 1849 by the famous scout Kit
Carson and became part of the 45,000-acre
tract owned by his colleague, Colonel John C.
Fremont. The **Mariposa Museum** displays a
collection of artifacts from that era ranging from
children's boots to Indian baskets to mining tools.
Open daily from March through October; shorter winter hours; closed in January. Admission. ~ 5119 Jessie
Street, Mariposa; 209-966-2924.

Along Bullion Street, on a hill overlooking town, the
old jail and **St. Joseph's Catholic Church** still stand. A
study in contrast, the jail is a squat granite building with
a formidable iron door, while the church is tall and
slender with a lofty steeple. Most impressive of these

A MEXICAN GHOST TOWN

North of Mariposa, there's a memorable sidetrip to the ghost town of **Hornitos**. Just pick up Old Toll Road in Mt. Bullion, then catch Hornitos Road; on the way back take Bear Valley Road. All are paved country roads leading through tree-studded hills on this 25-mile roundtrip detour.

A Mexican-style village centered around a plaza, Hornitos was a hideout for the notorious bandito Joaquin Murieta. According to legend, this Robin Hood figure, a semi-mythical hero to the Spanish miners, used a secret tunnel in the fandango hall to escape the law.

The Anglos in this rowdy mining town also claimed a famous citizen. Domingo Ghirardelli, the San Francisco chocolate manufacturer, built one of his earliest stores here in 1859. Several walls still remain, as do many of the town's old buildings. There's also an old jail, measuring little more than the size of a cell but possessing granite walls two feet thick.

The community contains something more than ruins of brick and stone. Because of its removal in time and space, Hornitos reflects the old days more fully than surrounding towns. There are windmills and range fences, grazing cows and crowing roosters. The tiny population goes about its business with an intensity not unlike that of the 15,000 who once lived here. And up on a hill, at a point closer to heaven than the rest of town, the old stone-and-wood church gazes down on the scene.

period structures is the **Mariposa County Courthouse**. The state's oldest court of law, it was built back in 1854 with wooden pegs and square-cut nails. Still in use, the courtroom contains a wood stove, kerosene lanterns, and original wooden benches.

Gold—the mineral that shaped this area's history—is the focus of the **California State Mining and Mineral Museum**. Also on display are California diamonds and benitoite (the state gem), as well as gems and minerals from around the world. Among the historic mining artifacts is a scale model of a quartz mill. Closed Tuesday in winter. Admission. ~ Mariposa County Fairgrounds, south of Mariposa on Route 49; 559-822-2332, fax 559-822-2319.

Route 49 continues for another 30 uneventful miles through the foothills, crossing Fresno Flats to end at a T-intersection with Route 41, which goes west to Merced on Route 99, a major four-laner through the Central Valley. If you wish to continue your explorations of Northern California, the better option is to take Route 120 east from Mariposa toward Yosemite National Park and the beginning of the tour described in Chapter 12.

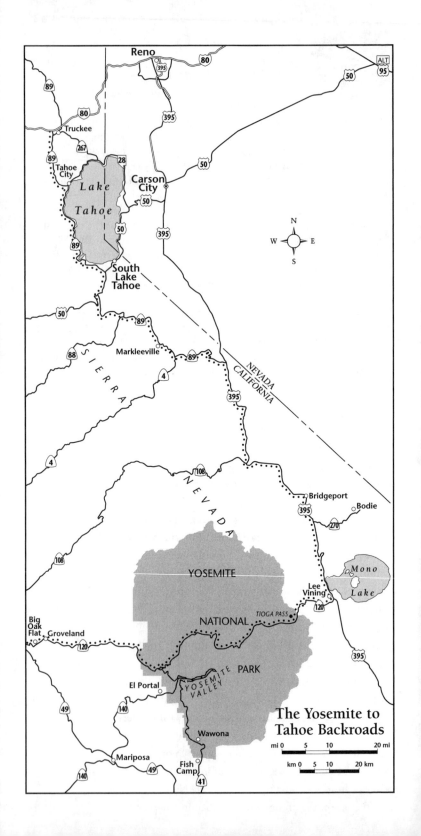

The Yosemite to
Tahoe Backroads

mi 0   5   10   20 mi

km 0   5   10   20 km

12 THE YOSEMITE TO TAHOE BACKROADS

Routes 120, 395, and 89

The mountain roads leading up the east side of the Sierras from Yosemite to Lake Tahoe reveal one of California's strangest and least-known landscapes, where the stark lunar desert of Nevada collides with a mile-high sheer granite wall rising up to two miles into the sky. Route 120, the back road from Yosemite, intersects with Route 395, which in turn links with Route 89 to Lake Tahoe. Along the way are views of bald-domed mountains, lofty and elegant, backdropped by even taller ranges. The road courses just below the ridge of the world, where jagged peaks dominate the sky, with valleys spread below, flat and broad. There are alpine meadows wild with flowers and aspen trees palsied in the wind. The 180-mile drive takes about four hours to drive; add another hour or two if you opt to take a side trip to the superb old-western ghost town of Bodie.

The trickiest part of driving to Yosemite is getting out of the Greater Bay Area. Take Route 580 east from Oakland to Livermore and then Route 205 to the intersection with Route 99. Drive north on Route 99 to the next exit, a distance of about one mile, and proceed eastbound on Route 120 to the park entrance. The total driving distance from Oakland is about 130 miles.

Yosemite National Park is a national institution, one of America's foremost playgrounds, a spectacular park climbing across the Sierra Nevada from 2000 feet elevation to a dizzying 13,000 feet. Summer, holidays, and weekends are particularly crowded in Yosemite Valley. In recent years the place has sometimes assumed the quality of a human zoo, with traffic jams and long lines. There have even been times when the park is so crowded that it's closed to all but those lucky enough to have reservations. But everyone seems intent on crowding into the confines of Yosemite Valley, which covers only 7 of the national park's 1200 square miles. Much of the rest is hardly touched by visitors.

TRAFFIC-FREE YOSEMITE

If possible, it's best to visit Yosemite during the week or in the off-season. Remember, though, that Tioga Pass Road and other scenic routes over the mountains are closed in winter. A particularly nice time to visit is in May (before Memorial Day), when the waterfalls are at their peak due to snow melt and the wildflowers and dogwood are in bloom. Best of all, the summer crowds have not yet descended upon the valley. Also consider walking, bicycling, or using the free shuttle service around the valley; it will save you a headache and help cut down on the traffic flow.

To visit the High Sierra country above the valley, follow Route 120, Tioga Road, in its eastward climb toward the top of the mountain range. This road is closed during snowy months, but in periods of warm weather it leads past splendid alpine regions with meadows, lakes, and stark peaks.

At about 7000 feet, it passes a virgin stand of red fir, then continues to **White Wolf**. The lodge here has cabins, a campground, and a restaurant. Past this enclave a spectacular view of the **Clark Range** is revealed, then the road passes a grove of quaking aspen.

Yosemite National Park

Olmsted Point has a short trail to a granite dome that looks down toward the north side of Half Dome and up to **Tenaya Lake**. This long, slender body of water, set at 8149 feet, is shadowed on either side by bald rockfaces.

Soon **Mt. Conness**, 12,590 feet in elevation, comes into view. Then the highlight of the journey, **Tuolumne Meadows**, with its information center, campground, lodge, store, and restaurant. Statistically speaking, this wonderland constitutes the Sierra's largest subalpine meadow. Located at 8600 feet, its sun-glinted fields are populated with smooth granite boulders and cut by a meandering stream. Conifers border the meadow and are in turn backdropped by bald domes and sharp faces. In summer, mountain wildflowers carpet the hillsides with brilliant shades of red, blue, and yellow, counterpointing the hard gray rocks with gentle forms and soft colors.

EASY LIVING AT
TUOLUMNE MEADOWS

Tuolumne Meadows Lodge, nestled along Route 120 at 8700 feet, has tent cabins available. These are similar to the facilities in the valley, consisting of a bed, complete bedding, sparse furnishings, and, to warm those chilly mountain nights, a wood stove. The experience here is somewhere between hotel living and camping; bathrooms and showers are shared. The nearby lodge contains a dining room and lobby available to tent sleepers. The surprisingly sophisticated cuisine in the lodge dining room features mountain brook trout, Cajun steak, a vegetarian plate, liver, pasta, and prime rib. They also serve hearty breakfasts, but no lunch. Reservations are required for dinner. The entire complex sits in a beautiful meadow bounded by thick forest. Idyllic and easy. Open Memorial Day to early September. ~ Lodging reservations, 5410 East Home Avenue, Fresno, CA 93727; 559-252-4848, fax 559-456-0542; www.yosemitepark.com. BUDGET.

**SLEEPING ON
THE SUMMIT**
Situated at 9600 feet, surrounded by Inyo National
Forest a short distance outside the east gate to Yosemite National Park, is **Tioga
Pass Resort**. With ten log cabins, four motel rooms, a restaurant, and other facilities, this is a perfect jumping-off place for the adventure-minded. The cabins
come complete with kitchens and are rented on a weekly basis. The motel units
are rented nightly. The restaurant serves three meals daily, with a menu ranging
from sandwiches to homemade chili to hearty full-course dinners, not to mention delicious homemade desserts. This resort's proximity to Yosemite makes it extremely popular, so book your reservations early. Summer season runs from mid-
May to mid-October; winter season runs from the week before Christmas through
April. ~ P.O. Box 7, Route 120, Lee Vining; 209-372-4471; www.tiogapassresort.
com. MODERATE TO DELUXE.

Beyond is **Lembert Dome**, a lopsided peak carved
by glaciers. Glittering patches of glacial polish can still
be seen along the dome surface. **Mount Dana** (13,053
feet) and **Mount Gibbs** (12,764 feet) are also part of
this incredible landscape.

Cresting the Sierra Nevada at 9941 feet, Tioga Pass
marks the highest automobile pass in California. Here
the highway—designated the Lee Vining—leaves the
park and enters Inyo National Forest as it begins its descent, passing **Tioga Lake** and **Ellery Lake**, crystalline
alpine gems set at 9523 feet, and twists down the side
of the canyon. Jagged peaks angle upwards so sharply
they seem like fortress walls.

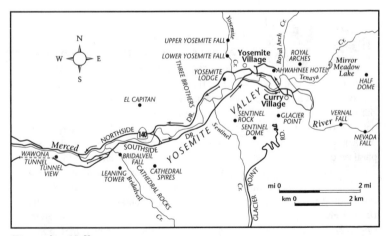

Yosemite Valley

VALLEY OF LIGHT

One of the country's most extraordinary and renowned parks, 748,000-acre **Yosemite National Park** spreads from 2000 to 13,000 feet, climbing from the foothills to the roof of the Sierras. The valley must be experienced; it cannot adequately be described. Once a massive lake fed by the glaciers that created the surrounding cliffs, erosion and stream sediment eventually filled it, creating fields rich in vegetation. Above the valley bed, vertical cliffs extend on either side to the limit of sight. In the far dis-

tance rises **Clouds Rest**, at 9926 feet the highest mountain visible from the valley. In front of that stands **Half Dome**, a monstrous rock that appears to have been cleft in two by the hand of God, leaving a sheer wall 2200 feet straight up. There is **Mirror Meadow Lake**, a mountain jewel named for the peaks reflected in its gleaming waters, and **Royal Arches**, granite shells that have been formed into great arcs by time and glaciation.

Before them looms **Sentinel Rock**, the last remnant of a mammoth block of granite, the rest of which has been cracked and dumped into the valley. It's named for its resemblance to a watchtower, while **Leaning Tower** gains its name from the rock's disconcerting tilt. There are the **Cathedral Spires**, granite shafts rising about 2000 feet above the floor; **Three Brothers**, imposing forms honoring the three sons of Yosemite's greatest Indian chief; and **Yosemite Falls**, among the world's tallest waterfalls, tumbling 2425 feet in three dramatic cascades.

King of kings among these grand geologic formations is **El Capitan**. It might well be the largest exposed monolith on earth, for this hard granite giant measures twice the size of the Rock of Gibraltar. Composed of several types of granite, its sheer cliff rises over 3000 feet from the valley floor. Solitary and unshakable, it seems to peer down upon the human antics occurring far below.

Yosemite Valley is generally a beehive of activity. The busiest spot of all is **Yosemite Village**, a cluster of buildings and shops along the northern wall of the valley. The visitors center keystones the complex. In addition to an information desk, the center hosts a photographic display of the valley and a regionally oriented bookstore. ~ 209-372-0200; www.yosemitepark.com.

Next door is the building housing the **Yosemite Museum** with exhibits illustrating the cultures of the Miwok and Paiute peoples who once inhabited the area. The museum gallery has rotating exhibits on Yosemite Valley. Directly behind the museum spreads a mock village complete with bark dwellings called *umachas* and earth-covered houses

Among the many facilities in the valley are hotels, restaurants, stores, museums, shuttle service, organized nature programs, information centers, picnic areas, restrooms, hiking trails, and stables. Day-use fee, $20 (good for one week). ~ Located along Routes 120, 140, and 41 about 140 miles southeast of San Francisco; 209-372-0200; www.nps.gov/yose. For information on weather, road conditions, and campground status, call 209-372-0200.

Bighorn Watching

Bighorn sheep were reintroduced to the Sierra Nevada in 1986, and the lofty granite cliffs and crags across Lee Vining Canyon from Route 120 are among their preferred habitats. Travelers who stop at any of the roadside wildlife viewing pullouts along the descent from Tioga Pass and survey the canyon walls with binoculars or a long telephoto lens are likely to be rewarded with a look at some of these majestic beasts carefully traversing the treacherous slopes.

Below the road, other cliffs dive into gorges of granite and swirling water. The waterfalls cutting into these rockfaces have worked at the granite for thousands of years, barely chiseling a bed. In places, the highway crosses expanses of crumbling rock where road signs caution about possible rock slides, a warning that is emphasized by numerous small rocks lying in the road and dented asphalt where larger boulders have come crashing down in the past.

by the way...

LAND OF THE FLY PEOPLE

Mono Lake was inhabited for 5000 years by the Kuzedika, a Northern Paiute Indian tribe, who thrived on a high-protein diet of fly pupae and brine shrimp mixed with ground piñon nuts. The name "Mono," which comes from the language of the neighboring Yokut Indians, means "fly eaters."

Elsewhere, below the highway are several excellent campgrounds that have picnic areas and restrooms, though no hookups. There are also lakes and streams for fishing, and roadside trailheads provide hiking access to the national forest backcountry. ~ For Inyo National Forest information, contact the Mono Lake Scenic Area Visitors Center; 760-647-3041.

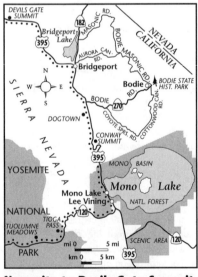

Yosemite to Devils Gate Summit

Route 120 meets Route 395 at Lee Vining near the shore of **Mono Lake**, one of California's strangest and most controversial spots. Located along the western edge of the Great Basin, it's a saline-alkaline body of water, the remnant of a prehistoric inland sea. At first glance it seems eerie and forbidding, an alien place with weird stalagmite-like formations that resemble a moonscape.

Composed of calcite and formed by the confluence of fresh-water springs and salt water, the spire-shaped "tufa" towers of Mono Lake have taken the form of delicate statuary, rising like minarets and rock candy mountains from the surface. They create a provocative landscape of bone-white rock against turquoise water. The reason these underwater fossils are presently above the lake surface is the key to a bitter environmental controversy. For over five decades the distant city of Los Angeles drained water from streams feeding the lake. Together with natural evaporation, that action dropped the lake level about 40 feet and doubled salinity.

BIRDS, BOOKS, AND BROCHURES

Headquarters for the group that has spearheaded the movement to save Mono Lake, the **Mono Lake Committee Information Center and Bookstore** in Lee Vining, is also the most complete source of books on the flora, fauna, and history of the region. Especially recommended is Sue Irwin's *California's Eastern Sierra* (Cachuma Press), a thoroughly researched and beautifully photographed volume covering some of the state's least-known scenic areas. ~ Route 395 at 3rd Street, Lee Vining; 760-647-6595.

Saving the Sea Gulls (and Mono Lake)

Since Mono Lake breeds brine shrimp and brine flies, favored food for sea gulls, it is home to the world's second-largest nesting gull population. In fact, anywhere you go in the Mono Lake area you'll see gulls—incongruously perched atop thorny desert bushes or standing on one foot on granite spires along canyon rims. Grebes and phalaropes also gather in great numbers. Their habitat has been threatened because water diversions drastically lowered the lake. In 1994, the State Water

Board intervened, declaring that water diversion must decrease. As a result, the water level is steadily rising for the first time since 1942. Thirsty Los Angeles will continue to divert a small amount of water but Mono Lake has been mandated to reach a stabilization level in 10 to 20 years. However, the future of this surreal and beautiful lake still hangs in the balance since the Water Board's decision could be appealed.

For a close-up look at these strange stone tufa forests along the lakeshore, take a short side trip south (right) on Route 395 and turn east (left) on the continuation of Route 120 toward Benton, which skirts the volcanic hills of Pumice Valley around the lake's south shore. Five miles down the road, watch for a turnoff to the left marked **Mono Lake South Tufa Reserve**. After paying an admission fee, you can hike a quarter-mile down to the shore on a wheelchair-accessible trail that is paved, although the road into the reserve is not. ~ For information, contact the Mono Basin Scenic Area, Route 395; 760-647-3044, fax 760-647-3046; www.monolake.org, e-mail info@monolake.org.

by the way... **OLDEST LIVING BUSH**

The creosote bush, which grows on the volcanic slopes surrounding the Mono Basin, is believed to be the longest-living plant on earth. Botanists from the University of California at Riverside carbon-dated one of these low, tiny-leaved bushes and determined it to be 11,700 years old, though less than five feet tall—and still growing.

Heading north from the Tioga Road intersection, Route 395 runs through the tiny town of **Lee Vining**, one of those High Sierra villages that seem to consist almost entirely of motels. Travelers passing through during the summer months will find high prices for standard guest rooms; the reason is that these lodgings have a limited window of opportunity to earn their income for the year before deep winter snow closes Route 120 and other roads over the Sierra Nevada, making the Mono Lake area all but inaccessible.

by the way... **IMMORTALITY MISSPELLED**

William Bodey, a gold prospector who staked his claim in the hills east of Dogtown in 1859, froze to death later that year when he was caught in a blizzard while returning from town to his diggings. Nearly 20 years later, the investors who bought Bodey's old claim and developed it into a money-maker named their new mine camp after him. But the sign painter misspelled his name, and the town has been known as Bodie ever since.

Continuing north, Route 395 parallels the Mono Lake shoreline at a discreet distance, passing the Forest Service's **Mono Basin National Forest Scenic Area Visitors Center** and then climbing steeply over the lip of the basin at Conway Summit, 8138 feet above sea level. The road then begins a long, gradual descent, following boulder-strewn defiles, along rumbling rivers laced with whitewater. Here in the rain shadow of the Sierras, vegetation is mainly low, thick, scratchy scrub brush—Great Basin sage, hopsage, rabbitbrush, and creosote bush, sparsely studded in places with piñon and juniper.

Sharp-eyed travelers can spot the remnants of **Dog-town**, one of the first gold mining boomtowns on the east side of the Sierra. It flourished briefly in 1857, and although it never saw large-scale mining operations, it set the stage for the region's biggest gold rush 20 years later. The remains of rock shelters used by the town's miners can still be seen at the roadside parking area.

Eighteen miles north of Lee Vining, a side road turns off to the east (right) to **Bodie State Historic Park**, one of the most fascinating Eastern Sierra sights and well worth the detour. The road is paved for the first ten miles; then the pavement ends for no obvious reason and offers a taste of what "highways" were like during the gold mining heyday as it makes its way across sheep-grazing country. Crossing a broad plateau for the last three unpaved miles, the road affords one of the most awe-inspiring panoramas imaginable of the full length of the Sierra Nevada—a view that in itself is worth the side trip—and in the other direction massive Boundary Peak, which marks the divide between California and Nevada. Strangely enough, Bodie itself has no mountain view at all.

GHOST COUNTY OF THE HIGH SIERRA

Alpine County was packed with gold seekers for just two years in the 1860s, before its only silver vein ran out. Today the county is almost entirely federal land and has fewer residents than any other county in the state—a total of 1200. Included in that total is a small community of American Indians from the Southern band of the Washo Tribe living in Diamond Valley.

Bodie rests like a kind of woodframe time capsule in a high-desert setting. One of the West's finest ghost towns, this mine camp boomed from 1877 to 1888, a period during which it produced the then-staggering sum of $35 million in gold. Once home to 10,000 people, it is now an outdoor museum complete with the houses, taverns, stores, and churches of a bygone era. Mill and ridge tours are available in summer. Because of unmaintained roads, the park is usually accessible only to snowmobilers and skiers during winter. Admission. ~ 760-647-6445, fax 760-647-6486; e-mail bodie @qnet.com.

Over rocky desert ridges and down into valleys redolent with the perfume of sage and piñon, Route 395 makes its unhurried way north through **Toiyabe National Forest**, the biggest national forest in the lower 48 states. Numerous unpaved side roads offer access to canyon lakes along the base of the mountains to the west.

Restaurants are rare and far between along Route 395. There is a homey café en route, however. The folks at **Meadowcliff** serve homemade gravy and biscuits for breakfast, and burgers and chili at lunch, while dinner features country-style cooking like hearty steaks. The food's good, which is mighty fortunate, since this is the only game around. Dinner hours vary in winter; call ahead. ~ 110437 Route 395, Coleville; 530-495-2180, 888-333-8132; www.meadowcliff.com, e-mail stay@meadowcliff.com. BUDGET TO MODERATE.

For maps and information, contact the Bridgeport Ranger District at Route 395, Bridgeport; 760-932-7070; www.fs.fed.us/htnf.

Along the way, Route 395 passes among reddish, rocky hills covered with piñon and through a scattering of forlorn towns, each smaller than the last. **Bridgeport**, a cattle-ranching town on the shore of a reservoir of the same name in a surprisingly green valley, got its start as a lumber and supply center for Bodie and other late-18th-century gold mining towns in the area. Its main sightseeing highlight is the photogenically ornate white **Mono County Courthouse**. The 1880 Italianate building, located on your right as you drive north through the center of town, is the second-oldest continuously used courthouse in California.

Continuing north, the highway crests Devils Gate Summit and then descends gently along the West Walker River, passing between towering cliffs and among tumbled fields of strangely spherical white granite boulders

HISTORIC
HIDEAWAY

The Bridgeport Inn, in an 1877 white-shingle building, reigns over a small-town main-street setting surrounded by snowy peaks. Downstairs there is a parlor with chandelier and granddaddy wood stove. The restored Victorian rooms are appointed with Monterey furniture. The decor is period, simple and elegant. The white-linen dining room features ceiling fans and antique wall fixtures and radiates a congenial atmosphere. The dinner menu, offering prime rib, veal chops, lobster, and catch-of-the-day, is deluxe in price, but breakfasts and lunches here are fairly inexpensive. There's also a cozy Irish pub for evening socializing. The hotel is open from March to the day before Thanksgiving. Be sure to ask for a room within the inn proper. ~ 205 Main Street, Bridgeport; 760-932-7380, fax 760-932-1160; www.thebridgeportinn.com, e-mail reservation@thebridgeportinn.com. MODERATE.

before breaking out into the broad, green pastures of Antelope Valley. The small village of **Walker** at the south end is the site of the valley's school and church. Even smaller, Topaz at the north end of the valley stands on the shore of **Topaz Lake**, a natural lake that straddles the California–Nevada state line.

Less than a mile south of Topaz Lake, turn left onto Route 89. (If you continued north on 395, you'd soon find your relaxing scenic drive at an end as you entered the traffic-snarled highway strip leading into Carson City, Nevada.)

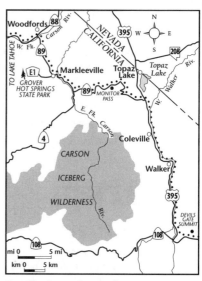

Devils Gate Summit to Markleeville

*R*oute 89 climbs abruptly to the 8314-foot summit of Monitor Pass, affording ever-higher aerial views of Antelope Valley and Topaz Lake before it enters the wooded highlands of Alpine County, the least populous county in California. There is no dramatic transition from the semi-arid ponderosa vegetation of the Sierra's eastern slope to the magnificent mountain forests of the west side. Other varieties of pines gradually begin to appear along the roadside, then shimmering stands of aspen. Soon you'll notice spruce and Douglas fir adding themselves to the mix, and farther on an occasional redwood.

The first sign of civilization along this route, **Markleeville** dates back to 1861, when Jacob Marklee built a toll bridge across the East Fork of the Carson River

The spirit of the Wild West lives on at the **Wolf Creek Restaurant and Cutthroat Bar** in Markleeville. The whitewashed woodframe building was used to house the Alpine Hotel back in the boom days when the town of nearly 3000 was the gateway to the mines of Silver Mountain. Today it's a restaurant and saloon where travelers can stop in for breakfast, lunch, and dinner. Entrées range from New York steak to eggplant parmesan to filet mignon, while the surroundings maintain the feel of a long-gone era. ~ Route 89 at Montgomery Street; 530-694-2150. MODERATE TO DELUXE.

during the silver boom at now-defunct Silver Mountain City. When the mine closed and Silver Mountain City went belly-up, Markleeville became the county seat by default. But Jacob Marklee never got a chance to see it. He had been killed in a gunfight just weeks before.

Set in a mountain meadow and backdropped by 8000-foot peaks, 700-acre **Grover Hot Springs State Park** is a lovely sight. The Toiyabe National Forest and Carson Iceberg Wilderness Area completely surround it; a well-marked dirt road that exits to the south (left) at Markleeville takes you to it; and hiking trails lead from the park to lakes and other points throughout the forest. There is fishing for rainbow and cutthroat trout. The central attractions, however, are the springs. Water from underground springs bubbles up at 148° and is cooled to an inviting 102° to 104° for the park's hot bath. This, together with a swimming pool, is situated in the meadow and open to the public. If you long for an outdoor hot pool in an alpine setting, this is the ticket. Other facilities include picnic areas, restrooms, and showers. Usually closed the last two weeks in September. There are 76 sites (28 winter sites) in two campgrounds within walking distance of the pools. Campgrounds require reservations from about May 15 to Labor Day (800-444-7275); during the rest of the year sites are on a first-come, first-served basis; $15 per night, $12 in winter. Day-use fee, $4. ~ Located off Route 89 at Markleeville; 530-694-2248. ▲ ⫯ ⤧ ⩳ ⩗

HIKING AT THE HOT SPRINGS

Ready to stretch your legs? At **Grover Hot Springs State Park** you'll find a lovely trail that takes you for an easy walk through lush forest to the waterfall that cascades into Hot Springs Creek. It's a mile and a half to the waterfall from the trailhead marked "Charity Valley" outside the state park entrance; or you can shorten the hike by starting at the overflow parking area in the park.

At tiny **Woodfords**, Route 89 meets Route 88 in a T intersection; turn west (left) and continue along the West Fork of the Carson River for about five miles to where the two highways divide again; follow Route 89 as it turns off to the north (right). Soon it starts a nearly straight descent to Lake Tahoe.

There aren't many places where you can waterski from one state to another. Nor can I think of many spots perfect for wilderness hiking during the day and shooting craps at night. And how many lakes can you name that are so clear you can see objects 75 feet below the surface? One of the West's most unique areas, **Lake Tahoe** is a remarkable blend of nature and kitsch.

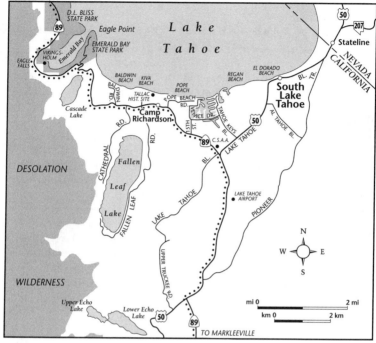

South Lake Tahoe Area

Mark Twain visited the lake over a century ago, long before the gaming palaces, and was overwhelmed. "As it lay there with the shadows of the mountains brilliantly photographed upon its still surface," he remarked in *Roughing It*, "I thought it must surely be the fairest picture the whole earth affords."

Tahoe! The word still carries power. But in recent decades it has become a riddle, an oxymoron. To some it conjures images of dark casinos and fateful gaming tables. To others it evokes thoughts of pristine trackless wilderness and oceanic depths. Never the twain shall meet: Tahoe is an environmental battleground. Developers, wedded to tomorrow's dollar, struggle against environmentalists committed to yesterday's beauty. Every fight the conservationists lose results in more structures along the lake, greater erosion,

LAKE OF MANY NAMES

Explorer John C. Fremont originally called it Mountain Lake, but then changed it to Lake Bonpland in honor of a French botanist. Nine years later, in 1853, the name was changed again to Lake Bigler, honoring the third governor of California, who later fell out of favor during the Civil War because of his secessionist politics. Californians then began calling it Tahoe, the Washoe Indian word for "lake," but the state legislature did not officially change the name until 1946.

LAKE TAHOE'S FOREST PRIMEVAL

If you wonder what lies beyond the trees at the side of the road, don your hiking boots and backpack and head into the roadless backcountry that lies southwest of Lake Tahoe. The **Desolation Wilderness**, extending across 63,475 acres of alpine terrain, is a favorite among outdoor adventurers. In fact, it is the most heavily used federal wilderness area in the United States. With elevations ranging from 6500 to 10,000 feet, the domain encompasses about 130 lakes. Juniper, fir, and pine grow along the streams that tumble through the mountains, but large stretches, stripped by glacial action, are devoid of trees and appear like a moonscape. Because of heavy snowfall, the best time to explore is summer. Other than 15 miles of hiking trails, there are no facilities here. Because of heavy summer use, a reservation fee and quota system has been instituted. A wilderness permit is necessary to enter. Some wilderness permits can be reserved up to 90 days in advance; others are available on a first-come, first-served basis. Camping is hike-in only and requires a permit that costs $5 per person for one night or $10 per person for two or more nights. For reservations call 530-644-6048. ~ Located southwest of Lake Tahoe; accessible from Route 89. Contact the Taylor Creek Wilderness for more information; 530-543-2736.

and another cloud across that glassy water. The resource they seek to protect is a magical place.

The third-deepest lake in North America and tenth-deepest in the world, Lake Tahoe measures an incredible 4589 feet from its surface to its deepest point. Twenty-two miles long and 12 miles wide, with 72 miles of shoreline, it would also be California's largest lake were it not for the fact that part of it is in Nevada. The lake contains over 39,000,000,000,000 gallons of water—enough to cover an area the size of California knee-deep.

FINE FUSION
FOOD

An intimate little Lake Tahoe original, **Evan's American Gourmet Café** is tucked away in a little cottage just past the "Y" on the way to the West Shore. With only 11 tables, the service is attentive, and the ambience, with its soft lighting and cream and burgundy hues, sets the stage for outstanding cuisine. While the menu varies according to the availability of fresh ingredients, dinner here might start with an appetizer such as shiitake crab cakes or seared foie gras with curried ice cream, followed by a main course of venison with balsamic cherries or duck confit with chorizo bread pudding. The homemade desserts are extra-special. Dinner only. ~ 536 Emerald Bay Road; 530-542-1990, fax 530-542-9111; www.evanstahoe.com. DELUXE.

As you gaze out over this huge lake, consider that all its water evaporates before reaching the sea. Although 63 rivers and streams flow into Lake Tahoe, only one—the Truckee River—flows out. It goes only as far as Pyramid Lake, which has no outlet. If the water that evaporates from the surface of Lake Tahoe could somehow be recovered, it would equal the daily water usage of the city of Los Angeles.

Lake Tahoe separates California from Nevada, giving its shoreline a split personality. The Nevada side, referred to as the North Shore, is lined with small towns featuring resort facilities (including some highrises), restaurants, and gaming casinos. In California, South Shore development is localized around two fast-growing main towns—South Lake Tahoe and Tahoe City—separated by about 20 miles of public shoreline and forest. Although the area is administered by Eldorado National Forest, it feels a lot like a na-

TROUT FISHING MADE SIMPLE

Families with small children may wish to try their luck at the **Tahoe Trout Farm**. It's kind of like shooting fish in a barrel; the operators of this private enterprise stock their pond just as fast as you can pull the fish out. It's also kind of like buying fish at the supermarket because you pay by the fish for your catch. Bait and tackle are free. Open Memorial Day through Labor Day. Admission. ~ 1023 Blue Lake Avenue, South Lake Tahoe; 530-541-1491.

A HISTORIC BEACH RESORT

If Lake Tahoe's South Shore were a national park, **Camp Richardson Resort & Marina** would be the park lodge. It's one of a few examples still in operation of the once-exclusive resorts that dominated the lakeshore in the early 1900s. Located on Route 89 just west of South Lake Tahoe, the lakefront resort is situated in piney woods within strolling distance of the beach. This full-facility complex includes access to a marina, lawn sports, and a riding stable. There are also picnic areas, restrooms, and showers. In addition to a spacious lodge, this switch-hitting establishment has cabins for rent as well as more than 250 sites, some with RV hookups.

The lodge is a classic mountain retreat. It offers a cozy lobby with knotty-pine walls, log beams, and a stone fireplace. The rooms are neatly if unimaginatively furnished. The cabins are rustic in appearance but decorated in comfortable fashion. Woodframe in construction, they are set around the resort's wooded acres not far from the lake, with some located right on the water's edge. The cabins include complete kitchen facilities. The **Beacon Bar & Grill** offers lakefront dining. In summer the resort only rents cabins by the week. ~ 530-541-1801; www.camp richardson.com, e-mail info@camprichardson.com. MODERATE TO ULTRA-DELUXE.

STARLIT NIGHTS
BY THE WATER

Camping is permitted at several campgrounds along the southern part of Lake Tahoe. There are 168 sites (no hookups) at **D. L. Bliss State Park**. The sites are $15 to $19 per night from late May to mid-September, with lower fees the rest of the year. ~ Along Route 89, 17 miles south of Tahoe City; 530-525-7232, 800-444-7275 (reservations). **Emerald Bay State Park** boasts 100 tent sites ($15 per night) plus 28 boat-in sites ($10 per night). ~ Along Route 89, 22 miles south of Tahoe City; 530-525-7232, 800-444-7275 (reservations). My favorite campground is **Meeks Bay**, located on a pretty white-sand beach. The 40 tent/RV sites (no hookups) are $16 per night. Open mid-May to mid-October ~ Along Route 89, 15 miles south of Tahoe City; 530-544-5994. There are also **Tahoe National Forest** campgrounds north of the lake along Route 89 between Tahoe City and Truckee. ~ Information: 530-587-3558, fax 530-587-6914.

tional park, with numerous designated points of interest—not to mention world-class scenery.

Route 89 runs into Route 50 at Meyers, a "suburb" on the southern outskirts of **South Lake Tahoe**. Turn northeast (right) and follow the commercial strip of lodges, mini-malls, and building supply stores for about two miles to where Route 89 splits off to the northwest near the town marina. From here, you're within walking distance of the beaches that line the South Shore, even though they're out of sight of the highway. Located within a few miles of South Lake Tahoe are several of the region's loveliest beaches. In town, the pocket park of **Eldorado Beach**, with its patch of sand, commands a sweeping view of the lake. Unfortunately, it's located right on a busy highway, and things can become rather schizophrenic with pristine nature extending out before you and civilization rumbling along behind. Not really a beach, **Regan Beach** is an

Lake Tahoe Area

A Lake Is Born

Unlike nearby lakes of glacial origin, Tahoe was formed by faulting. About 150 million years ago the basin was created when the Carson Range rose to the east while the Sierra Nevada grew to the west, leaving a giant trough between. When volcanoes dammed the end of the basin, rain and snow filled the natural bowl to brimming. Washoe Indians eventually inhabited the lakeshore regions and enjoyed uninterrupted predominance until 1844, when Captain John Fremont and Kit Carson, searching a mountain pass into California, "discovered" the lake. By the 1870s, with the advent of the railroad, Tahoe emerged as a popular resort area.

open picnic area along the waterfront. Nevertheless, it's nicely landscaped with a lawn and shade trees, picnic tables, barbecue grills, sand volleyball courts, and restrooms. Central to South Lake Tahoe on Lakeview Avenue, the park is still off the main thoroughfare.

As you head out of town, the beaches get better. Edged by trees and greenery and backdropped by mountains, the golden swath of sandy beach along Route 89 from **Pope and Kiva beaches** on the edge of South Lake Tahoe to **Baldwin Beach**, near Emerald Bay, is an idyllic site overlooking the entire lake. There is a fee to park at most beach access points.

The extremely beautiful region prosaically known as **Lake Tahoe Basin Management Unit** is concentrated around the South Shore of Lake Tahoe. Its 148,800 acres include some of Tahoe's prettiest beaches, several camp-

CASUAL DINING IN TAHOE CITY

Rosie's Café is one of those laid-back eating spots California is famous for harboring. Just across the street from the lake, the place is bizarrely decorated with old sleds, bicycles, skis, and wall mirrors. It's open all day and into the night, featuring imaginative cuisine. At breakfast there are lots and lots of egg specialties. Lunch carries salads, sandwiches, tostadas, and more. Come dinner, the menu expands to include pasta, vegetarian and stir-fry dishes, roast duckling, steak, and seafood. Tasty and popular. ~ 571 North Lake Boulevard, Tahoe City; 530-583-8504; www.rosiescafe.com, e-mail rosiescafe@aol.com. MODERATE TO DELUXE.

**RUSTIC
LUXURY** ▬▬▬▬▬▬▬▬▬▬▬▬▬▬▬▬

Mountain lodge meets high-class resort at the redwood, multi-gabled **Sunnyside Restaurant and Lodge**. Nestled in pine woods and sitting before its own marina, the lodge has a cozy country lobby with a river-rock fireplace adorned with hunting trophies. Ducks and decoys are everywhere in the 23 lakefront or lakeview accommodations, simply furnished in wicker and wood and featuring individual touches like an old sea chest or armoire. Many have fireplaces and wet bars. ~ 1850 West Lake Boulevard, Tahoe City; 530-583-7200, 800-822-2754, fax 530-583-2551; www.sunnysideresort.com. DELUXE TO ULTRA-DELUXE.

---

grounds, picnic areas, plus ski and horseback riding opportunities; restrooms are found throughout. Day-use fee at several locations. For more information, phone 530-543-2600 or fax 530-573-2693.

From 1880 to 1909, Tallac Resort billed itself as "the grandest resort in the world"—an exclusive hideaway among the pines where wealthy families from San Francisco and Virginia City came to ride horseback, hunt, fish, boat, and stroll along the lakefront promenade. A portion of the promenade can still be seen by the picnic area at **Tallac Historic Site**, but the lodge buildings no longer stand. When the original owner's daughter inherited the resort, she had the buildings removed because of environmental concerns and to reduce taxes. Now this beautiful stretch of shoreline is a lot more egalitarian than it was in its salad days; in fact, it's the only recreation area along the South Shore where you can access the beach without paying a parking fee. ~ Located off Route 89 between Pope Beach and Baldwin Beach.

From Tallac Historic Site, you can stroll east along the shore toward Camp Richardson to see the **Baldwin Estate** (c. 1921), now a privately owned museum with exhibits on the Washoe Indians and other aspects of local history. If you walk west through the woods, a path

**GREAT GATSBY
FESTIVAL**

Tallac Historic Site hosts the annual **Great Gatsby Festival** on the second weekend in August. The two-day event takes you back to 1920s high-society life with a living history program and costumed actors who provide tours. There are vintage vendors, antique cars, food, live music and children's activities. All activities are free or inexpensive except the Sunday afternoon tea and fashion show, which costs $25. Reservations are required. ~ 530-544-7383.

strewn with pine needles leads to **Eagle Point State Park**. Along the way, you'll pass fabled estates including the **Pope House**—the oldest, largest, and most elaborate historic estate on the lake, built in 1884—and the **McGonagle Estate**, a prestigious house designed ironically in the fashion of a log cabin, as well as the **Heller Estate**, commonly called Valhalla, a brown-shingle beauty.

Past Baldwin Beach, Route 89 cuts through dense conifer forests, then passes dramatic outcroppings of granite as it climbs high above water level for a series of grand vistas that take in the length and breadth of the lake, swept by westerly winds and adorned with the sails of careening sloops. Don't bypass the overlook at the inner end of picturesque two-mile-long **Emerald Bay**, a spectacular cove guarded by lofty conifers, the most picturesque site along the entire lake. At the far end, poised between two peninsulas, is a slender opening into the lake. From the vista parking lot, a mile-long foot trail descends the slope to the

A COLD COLD WINTER

Crossing the High Sierra was not always as simple as it is today. During the terrible winter of 1846–47, a party of stalwart pioneers, unable to cross the Sierra because of drifting snow, camped for the winter. Many perished from exposure and hunger, others went insane, and some resorted to cannibalism. Today the **Emigrant Trail Museum** at **Donner Memorial State Park** commemorates their passing. There is also a monument on the grounds. Its base stands 22 feet high—the depth of the snow that winter. Today Route 80, the transcontinental interstate, passes within yards of the Donner party's tragic resting place. Admission. ~ Donner Pass Road, Truckee; 530-582-7892, fax 530-582-7893.

DONNER LAKE

sidetrips Set in a pine-and-fir forest astride three-mile-long Donner Lake, **Donner Memorial State Park** lies north of Lake Tahoe. It was here in the winter of 1846–47 that the ill-starred Donner party, trapped in heavy snow, was confronted with cannibalism or death. Today the accommodations are more commodious. There are campgrounds, a museum, and a resident population of porcupines, beaver, raccoons, and bears (plus perhaps the ghosts of several hungry pioneers). In addition to an information center and museum (open year-round), the park now features picnic areas, restrooms, and showers. Closed August to Memorial Day. Day-use fee, $4. Camping is permitted during the summer in 150 sites; $15 per night. ~ Located just off Route 80, two miles west of Truckee; 530-582-7892, fax 530-582-7893.

best known of all the great Lake Tahoe estates, **Vikingsholm**, a 38-room castle that is not visible from the highway. Open for tours in the summer, this unusual structure was designed along the lines of a medieval Scandinavian castle. It's built of granite and hand-hewn timbers and marked by a series of towers. Admission. ~ 530-525-7277. Anchored offshore, near Vikingsholm, is tiny **Fanette Island**, where a stone teahouse built to similar specifications still sits. Across the road from the Vikingsholm parking lot, a short path leads to a wooden footbridge below **Eagle Falls**, which cascades along granite steps in its tumble from the mountains to the lake. The trail continues beyond the falls into the heart of the Desolation Wilderness.

Emerald Bay State Park and the contiguous **D. L. Bliss State Park** curve along six miles of lakefront. Within their borders lie some of the area's most picturesque sites. The forest that dominates both parks includes Jeffrey and ponderosa pines, incense cedar, quaking aspen, mountain dogwood, and willows. Wildflowers and berries flourish throughout the area. There are picnic areas, restrooms, and showers in both parks. Camping is allowed from late spring to early fall, depending on weather conditions. Day-use fee, $4. ~ 530-525-7232.

One of the Tahoe region's most precious jewels, **Sugar Pine Point State Park** extends along almost two miles of lakefront. Inland it runs nearly four miles. Within that expanse is a forest of Jeffrey and sugar pines. The lakefront is dotted with sandy beaches, and the park possesses several historic structures, among them a pioneer log cabin and an old mansion that's been converted to a museum. There are also hiking trails, a tennis court, picnic areas, restrooms, and showers (available only in

BIKING

When it comes to mountain biking, few places can beat the Sierra Nevada. The **Flume Trail** off Spooner Summit at the junction of Routes 50 and 28 offers challenging rides of 10 to 30 miles. **Angora Lakes Trail** (12 miles) in the Fallen Leaf Lake area is another possibility. Another good bet is **Kirkwood Ski Area** 30 miles south of Lake Tahoe, which has 50 miles of trails. ~ Route 88, Kirkwood; 209-258-6000, 800-967-7500. The resort also provides easy access to hundreds of miles of trails in the **Eldorado National Forest**. The easy **Kirkwood Meadow Loop** (6 miles) is a good way to get acclimated. **Schneider Camp** (7 miles) is an enjoyable ride offering great views of Caples Lake. Remember, it takes a few days to adjust to the high altitude; also plan on drinking plenty of fluids.

You can rent mountain bikes at the **Tahoe Bike Shop**. ~ 2277 Lake Tahoe Boulevard, South Lake Tahoe; 530-544-8060.

summer). Camping is permitted in 175 forested sites; $15 per night. Day-use fee, $4. ~ On Route 89; 530-525-7232, fax 530-525-6730. 🏃 🚴 🏊 🛶

Continuing north along Route 89, you'll soon reach the villages of **Tahoma** and **Homewood**, where bed and breakfasts and large vacation homes look out on a shore lined with marina piers, marking the approach to **Tahoe City**, the main commercial center on the California side of the lake. There are lodges and restaurants, a supermarket, and service stations, as well as big building supply stores and lumberyards—indicating the rapid rate of custom home construction along this part of the lake.

KID PLAY

A Lake Tahoe tradition for more than 30 years, **Borges Family Sleigh Rides** take you gliding over a snowy meadow and through the woods to a spectacular lake viewpoint while the driver entertains with songs, tall tales, and cowboy poetry. Pulled by huge Belgian draft horses, the handmade sleighs come in varying sizes to carry 2 to 20 passengers. ~ Stateline; 775-541-2953, 800-726-7433.

At this point you've seen the best of the Lake Tahoe shoreline. If you wanted to see the rest—another 38 miles of it—you could turn east (right) on Route 28 at Tahoe City and drive to the Nevada side. But for a hospitable sense of the Old West, turn west and truck on up the shallow, lazy, crystal-clear Truckee River, past the turnoff to **Squaw Valley USA**. The site of the 1960 Winter Olympic Games, this ski area is one of California's most famous; it certainly has the largest sign of any Lake Tahoe ski area: a towering steel-grid monument depicting the flags of all nations that participated in the Olympics there.

The 19th-century town of **Truckee** sits astride a mountain pass high in the Sierra. Framed by forested slopes, Truckee is a woodframe town overlooking an old railroad yard and depot. The main street, Commercial Row, is lined with falsefront buildings. Clapboard warehouses and meeting halls with second-story

**A LODGE FIT FOR
OLYMPIANS** ▬▬▬▬▬▬▬▬▬▬▬▬▬▬▬▬▬▬

The **Resort at Squaw Creek** lures guests with an extravagant 405-room hotel that is showcased by a stream and waterfall that plunge 250 feet through the property. Situated a half-mile from Squaw Valley's vaunted ski slopes, the resort is a summer destination as well as winter hideaway. For warm-weather enthusiasts there are two tennis courts, an 18-hole golf course, bike paths, miles of equestrian and hiking trails in the surrounding mountains, and an aquatic center with three pools, a water slide, and a full-service spa. In winter it provides ice skating facilities and easy access to the ski slopes with an on-site chairlift. ~ 400 Squaw Creek Road, Olympic Valley; 530-583-6300, 800-327-3353, fax 530-581-6632; www.squawcreek.com, e-mail info@squawcreek.com. ULTRA-DELUXE.

balconies remain from the town's old lumbering and railroad days. Then as now, Truckee was a gateway. Today it leads to the gambling palaces and ski resorts of Tahoe. Here Route 89 meets Route 80, marking the end of this Yosemite-to-Tahoe tour. The interstate can whisk you to the Bay Area in about three hours.

INDEX

LODGING AND DINING INDEX

PHOTO CREDITS

WRITE TO US

Ulysses 🜍 Press

If in your travels you discover a spot that captures the spirit of San Francisco and Northern California, or if you live in the region and have a favorite place to share, or if you just feel like expressing your views, write to us and we'll pass your note along to the author.

We can't guarantee that the author will add your personal find to the next edition, but if the writer does use the suggestion, we'll acknowledge you in the credits and send you a free copy of the new edition.

ULYSSES PRESS
P.O. Box 3440
Berkeley, CA 94703
E-mail: readermail@ulyssespress.com

HIDDEN GUIDES

Adventure travel or a relaxing vacation?—"Hidden" guidebooks are the only travel books in the business to provide detailed information on both. Aimed at environmentally aware travelers, our motto is "Adventure Travel Plus." These books combine details on unique hotels, restaurants and sightseeing with information on camping, sports and hiking for the outdoor enthusiast.

PARADISE FAMILY GUIDES

Ideal for families traveling with kids of any age—toddlers to teenagers—Paradise Family Guides offer a blend of travel information unlike any other guides to the Hawaiian islands. With vacation ideas and tropical adventures that are sure to satisfy both action-hungry youngsters and re-laxation-seeking parents, these guides meet the specific needs of each and every family member.

Ulysses Press books are available at bookstores everywhere. If any of the following titles are unavailable at your local bookstore, ask the bookseller to order them.

You can also order books directly from
Ulysses Press
P.O. Box 3440, Berkeley, CA 94703
800-377-2542 or 510-601-8301
fax: 510-601-8307
www.ulyssespress.com
e-mail: ulysses@ulyssespress.com

Order Form

HIDDEN GUIDEBOOKS

____ Hidden Arizona, $16.95
____ Hidden Bahamas, $14.95
____ Hidden Baja, $14.95
____ Hidden Belize, $15.95
____ Hidden Big Island of Hawaii, $13.95
____ Hidden Boston & Cape Cod, $14.95
____ Hidden British Columbia, $18.95
____ Hidden Cancún & the Yucatán, $16.95
____ Hidden Carolinas, $17.95
____ Hidden Coast of California, $18.95
____ Hidden Colorado, $15.95
____ Hidden Disneyland, $13.95
____ Hidden Florida, $18.95
____ Hidden Florida Keys & Everglades,
    $12.95
____ Hidden Georgia, $16.95
____ Hidden Guatemala, $16.95
____ Hidden Hawaii, $18.95
____ Hidden Idaho, $14.95

____ Hidden Kauai, $13.95
____ Hidden Maui, $13.95
____ Hidden Montana, $15.95
____ Hidden New England, $18.95
____ Hidden New Mexico, $15.95
____ Hidden Oahu, $13.95
____ Hidden Oregon, $15.95
____ Hidden Pacific Northwest, $18.95
____ Hidden Salt Lake City, $14.95
____ Hidden San Francisco & Northern
    California, $18.95
____ Hidden Southern California, $18.95
____ Hidden Southwest, $19.95
____ Hidden Tahiti, $17.95
____ Hidden Tennessee, $16.95
____ Hidden Utah, $16.95
____ Hidden Walt Disney World, $13.95
____ Hidden Washington, $15.95
____ Hidden Wine Country, $13.95
____ Hidden Wyoming, $15.95

PARADISE FAMILY GUIDES

____ Paradise Family Guides: Kaua'i,
    $16.95
____ Paradise Family Guides: Maui, $16.95

____ Paradise Family Guides: Big Island of
    Hawai'i, $16.95

Mark the book(s) you're ordering and enter the total cost here ⇨ ☐

California residents add 8.25% sales tax here ⇨ ☐

Shipping, check box for preferred method and enter cost here ⇨ ☐

☐ Book Rate   **FREE! FREE! FREE!**

☐ Priority Mail/UPS Ground   cost of postage

☐ UPS Overnight/2-Day Air   cost of postage

Billing, enter total amount due here and check method ☐

☐ Check   ☐ Money Order

☐ VISA/MasterCard_____Exp. Date _____

Name_____Phone _____

Address _____

_____

City _____ State_____ Zip _____

Money-back guarantee on direct orders placed through Ulysses Press.

ABOUT THE AUTHORS

Richard Harris has written or co-written 20 other guidebooks including Ulysses' *Hidden Cancún and the Yucatán*, *Hidden Guatemala*, and the bestselling *Hidden Southwest*. He has also served as contributing editor on guides to Mexico, New Mexico, and other ports of call for John Muir Publications, Fodor's, Birnbaum, and Access guides. He is a director of PENCenter USAWest and president of PEN New Mexico. When not traveling, Richard writes and lives in Santa Fe, New Mexico.

Ray Riegert is the author of seven travel books, including *Hidden San Francisco and Northern California*. His most popular work, *Hidden Hawaii*, won the Lowell Thomas Travel Journalism Award for Best Guidebook. In addition to his role as publisher of Ulysses Press, he has written for such publications as the *San Francisco Chronicle* and *Travel & Leisure*. A member of the Society of American Travel Writers, he lives in the San Francisco Bay area with his wife, Leslie Henriques, and their children Keith and Alice.